D0153096

# The Critical Response to Raymond Chandler

**Recent Titles in**
**Critical Responses in Arts and Letters**

The Critical Response to Ann Beattie
*Jaye Berman Montresor, editor*

The Critical Response to Eugene O'Neill
*John H. Houchin, editor*

The Critical Response to Bram Stoker
*Carol A. Senf, editor*

The Critical Response to John Cheever
*Francis J. Bosha, editor*

The Critical Response to Ann Radcliffe
*Deborah D. Rogers, editor*

The Critical Response to Joan Didion
*Sharon Felton, editor*

The Critical Response to Tillie Olsen
*Kay Hoyle Nelson and Nancy Huse, editors*

The Critical Response to George Eliot
*Karen L. Pangallo, editor*

The Critical Response to Eudora Welty's Fiction
*Laurie Champion, editor*

The Critical Response to Dashiell Hammett
*Christopher Metress, editor*

The Critical Response to H. G. Wells
*William J. Scheick, editor*

The Critical Response to Herman Melville's *Moby Dick*
*Kevin J. Hayes, editor*

The Critical Response to Kurt Vonnegut
*Leonard Mustazza, editor*

# The Critical Response to Raymond Chandler

*Edited by*
J. K. Van Dover

Critical Responses in Arts and Letters, Number 18
*Cameron Northouse, Series Adviser*

**GREENWOOD PRESS**
Westport, Connecticut • London

**Library of Congress Cataloging-in-Publication Data**

The critical response to Raymond Chandler / edited by J. K. Van Dover.
p. cm.—(Critical responses in arts and letters, ISSN 1057–0993 ; no. 18)
Includes bibliographical references and index.
ISBN 0–313–27948–9
1. Chandler, Raymond, 1888–1959—Criticism and interpretation.
2. Detective and mystery stories, American—History and criticism.
I. Van Dover, J. Kenneth. II. Series.
PS3505.H3224Z62 1995
813′.52—dc20 94–42120

British Library Cataloguing in Publication Data is available.



Library of Congress Catalog Card Number: 94–42120
ISBN: 0–313–27948–9
ISSN: 1057–0993

First published in 1995

Greenwood Press, 88 Post Road West, Westport, CT 06881
An imprint of Greenwood Publishing Group, Inc.

Printed in the United States of America

The paper used in this book complies with the Permanent Paper Standard issued by the National Information Standards Organization (Z39.48–1984).

P

**In order to keep this title in print and available to the academic community, this edition was produced using digital reprint technology in a relatively short print run. This would not have been attainable using traditional methods. Although the cover has been changed from its original appearance, the text remains the same and all materials and methods used still conform to the highest book-making standards.**

## Copyright Acknowledgments

The editor and publisher gratefully acknowledge the following for permission to use copyrighted materials:

R. W. Flint, "A Cato of the Cruelties," *Partisan Review* 14 (1947): 328-30. Reprinted by permission of *Partisan Review*.

R. W. Lid, "Philip Marlowe Speaking." *Kenyon Review* 31 (1977): 153-78. Reprinted by permission of the author.

Fredric Jameson, "On Raymond Chandler," *Southern Review* 6:3 (1970): 624-50. Reprinted by permission of the author.

E. M. Beekman, "Raymond Chandler and an American Genre," *Massachusetts Review* 14 (1973): 149-73; pp. 158-68 (footnotes renumbered). Reprinted by permission of the author.

Dove, George, "The Complex Art of Raymond Chandler," *Armchair Detective* 8: (1974-75): 271-4. Reprinted by permission of *The Armchair Detective*, 129 W. 56 St. NY, NY 10019.

Tom S. Reck, "Raymond Chandler's Los Angeles," *Nation* 20 Dec 1975: 661-63. Reprinted by permission of the author.

Peter J. Rabinowitz, "Rats Behind the Wainscoting: Politics, Convention, and Chandler's *The Big Sleep*." Reprinted from *Texas Studies in Language and Literature* 22 (1980): 224-45 by permission of the University of Texas Press.

James Guetti. "Aggressive Reading: Detective Fiction and Realistic Narrative." *Raritan* 2:1 (1982): 133-54; pp. 137-42. Reprinted by permission from *Raritan: A Quarterly Review* Vol. II, No. 1 (Summer

1982). Copyright © 1982 by *Raritan*, 31 Mine Street, New Brunswick, N.J. 08903.

Brian Gallagher. "Howard Hawks's *The Big Sleep*: A Paradigm for the Postwar American Family." *North Dakota Quarterly* 51:3 (1983): 78-91. Reprinted by permission of *North Dakota Quarterly*. Illustrations and references to illustrations have been omitted.

Ernest Fontana, "Chivalry and Modernity in Raymond Chandler's *The Big Sleep*," *Western American Literature* 19:3 (1984): 179-186. Reprinted with the permission of The Western Literature Association, from *Western American Literature* 19 (1984), 179-186. Ernest Fontana, Professor of English, Xavier University, Cincinnati.

Stephen L. Tanner, "The Function of Simile in Raymond Chandler's Novels," *Studies in American Humor* 3:4 (1984-5): 337-346. Reprinted by permission of *Studies in American Humor*.

T.R. Steiner, "The Mind of the Hardboiled: Ross Macdonald and the Roles of Criticism," *South Dakota Review* 24:1 (1986): 29-53; pp. 46-50. Reprinted by permission of *South Dakota Review*.

Johanna M. Smith, "Raymond Chandler and the Business of Literature," *Texas Studies in Language and Literature* 31 (1989): 592-610. Reprinted by permission of the University of Texas Press.

Excerpts from Raymond Chandler's *The Big Sleep, Farewell, My Lovely, The High Window, The Lady in the Lake, The Little Sister, The Long Good-Bye*: U.K. and Commonwealth, reproduced by permission of Hamish Hamilton Ltd.

Excerpts from Raymond Chandler's *The Big Sleep* (copyright 1939 by Raymond Chandler and renewed 1967 by Helga Greene, Executrix of the Estate of Raymond Chandler. Reprinted by permission of Alfred A. Knopf, Inc.), *Farewell, My Lovely* (copyright 1940 by Raymond Chandler and renewed 1968 by the Executrix of the author, Mrs. Helga Greene. Reprinted by permission of Alfred A. Knopf, Inc.), *The High Window* (copyright 1942 by Raymond Chandler and renewed 1970 by Helga Greene, Executrix of the Estate of Raymond Chandler. Reprinted by permission of Alfred A. Knopf, Inc.), *The Lady in the Lake* (copyright 1943 by Raymond Chandler and renewed 1971 by Helga Greene, Executrix of the Estate of Raymond Chandler. Reprinted by permission of Alfred A. Knopf, Inc.), *The Little Sister* (copyright 1949 by Raymond Chandler and renewed 1976 by Mrs. Helga Greene. Reprinted by permission of Alfred A. Knopf Inc.), *The Long Goodbye* (copyright 1953 by Raymond Chandler and renewed 1981 by Mrs. Helga Greene. Reprinted by permission of Alfred A. Knopf Inc.).

# Contents

# Series Foreword

*Critical Responses in Arts and Letters* is designed to present a documentary history of highlights in the critical reception to the body of work of writers and artists and to individual works that are generally considered to be of major importance. The focus of each volume in this series is basically historical. The introductions to each volume are themselves brief histories of the critical response to an author, artist, or individual work has received. This response is then further illustrated by reprinting a strong representation of the major critical reviews and articles which collectively have produced the author's, artist's, or work's critical reputation.

The scope of *Critical Responses in Arts and Letters* knows no chronological or geographical boundaries. Volumes under preparation include studies of individuals from around the world and in both contemporary and historical periods.

Each volume is the work of an individual editor, who surveys the entire body of criticism on a single author, artist, or work. The editor then selects the best material to depict the critical response received by an author or artist over his/her entire career. Documents produced by the author or artist may also be included when the editor finds that they are necessary to a full understanding of the materials at hand. In circumstances where previous, isolated volumes of criticism on a particular individual or work exist, the editor carefully selects material that better reflects the nature and directions of the critical response over time.

In addition to the introduction and the documentary section, the editor of each volume is free to solicit new essays on areas that may not have been adequately dealt with in previous criticism. Also, for volumes on living writers and artists, new interviews may be included, again at the discretion of the volume's editor. The volumes also provide a supplementary bibliography and are fully indexed.

While each volume in *Critical Responses in Arts and Letters* is unique, it is also hoped that in combination they form a useful, documentary history of the critical response to the arts, and one that can be easily and profitably employed by students and scholars.

Cameron Northouse

# Acknowledgments

I am pleased to be able to record a number of debts. A Lilly-Lincoln Grant awarded by the grant committee at Lincoln University provided funds for copying, typing, and postage. Small grants from the Research and Publications Committee were also very helpful. Most of the typing was done by Ms. Kathy Madron. The Media Center at Lincoln University was generous with its Macintosh and its Laserprinter. I made use of the libraries of the University of Delaware, the University of Pittsburgh, and Lincoln University; I was fortunate that these resources were so readily available. Elaine Pennell, the Inter-Library Loan Librarian at Lincoln University was especially helpful.

I am grateful for the encouragement and the assistance provided by Maureen Melino, Coordinating Editor at Greenwood; she was indefatigable in assisting me in the pursuit of copyright permissions. George F. Butler oversaw a careful editing of the text. And I am, of course, grateful for the generous cooperation of the authors and the journals who granted permission to reprint these essays.

It would have been presumptuous to dedicate a volume whose contents consist largely of the work of other scholars, but had I presumed, I would have taken the opportunity to express my gratitude to those institutions and persons responsible for two of the most rewarding years of my professional life. The Fulbright Program permitted me twice to explore detective fiction (and other literature) at two very hospitable German universities. I would have thanked the Council for the International Exchange of Scholars, the German Fulbright-Kommission, the Abteilung für Amerikanistik at the Univerität Tübingen, and the Institut für Literaturwissenschaft (Amerikanistik) at the Universität Stuttgart. Behind these imposing institutions were human faces, including those of Drs. Ulrich Littmann and Reiner Rohr at the Fulbright-Kommission; Zoe Pacquier and Drs. Hans Borchers, Hartmut Grandel, Siegfried Neuweiler, and Eva Warth at Tübingen; Renate Höckh and Drs. Bettina Friedl and Heide Ziegler at Stuttgart. I remember them all with fondness as well as gratitude; I would have thanked them all. Dr. Hans Küng twice welcomed my wife and me to the English seminar which he and Dr. Karl-Josef Kuschel offered at Tübingen. In the midst of theology, they allowed me to talk about detectives. I appreciate their kindness.

Editors, like lexicographers, are, I hope, harmless drudges, but this drudge has been uncommonly fortunate in his family and his friendships, and so, in no particular order, with no pretense to completeness, and with no significance other than to those mentioned, he thanks Sarala, Lara, and Andrew; Bruce and Cindy; Rosie and Brian; Viola and Juan; Mina and Naresh, Arby, Dominique, Dan, and John.

J. K. Van Dover
Newark, Delaware
January 1992, June 1994

# Chronology

1888 23 July, Raymond Chandler was born in Chicago, Illinois. His father, Maurice Benjamin Chandler, was a native of Philadelphia and a descendent of Irish Quakers; he studied engineering, and worked for the railroad. In 1887, in Laramie, Wyoming, he married Florence Dart Thornton, born in Waterford, Ireland.

1895 Following her divorce from Maurice, Florence Chandler took her son to London to live with relatives. Chandler never forgave his father for abandoning the family and he suffered from being treated as a poor relation by his mother's family in England and Ireland.

1900 Chandler entered Dulwich College as a day student. He would always pride himself on his English Public School education.

1904 Chandler graduated from Dulwich.

1905-06 In preparation for taking the Civil Service Examinations, Chandler traveled in France and Germany.

1907 Chandler became a naturalized British citizen to sit for the Examination; scoring highly, he accepted a place as a clerk in the Admiralty. After six months, he resigned.

1908-11 Chandler worked as a literary journalist in London, contributing to the *Academy* and the *Westminster Gazette*. He published 27 poems, seven essays, a handful of reviews, and a number of anonymous paragraphs.

1912 Borrowing £500 from his uncle, Chandler returned to America. He eventually arrived in California and worked at miscellaneous jobs: picking apricots, stringing tennis racquets, bookkeeping.

1917 Chandler enlisted in the Canadian Army. As a platoon commander in France in June 1918, Chandler experienced an artillery barrage which gave him a concussion and killed the other members of his unit. In July he transferred to the Royal Air Force, but the Armistice was signed before he received his commission. He was shipped back to Canada in January 1919 and, following his discharge, returned to Los Angeles.

1919 Chandler, aged 24, fell in love with Pearl (Eugenie Hurlburt) "Cissy" Pascal, the 48 year old wife of his friend Julian Pascal. Cissy and Julian were divorced in 1920, but Chandler and Cissy waited until after his mother died in 1924 to marry.

Chandler began to work in the oil business. Chandler rose to the executive rank (auditor, vice-president, president, director) in a group of related companies (the Dabney Oil Syndicate, the South Basin Oil Company, the Herndon Petroleum Company). Chandler enjoyed early success, but in the late twenties began to drink and to womanize. In 1932 he was fired.

1933 Chandler decided to take up writing as a profession. He spent five months writing the hard-boiled detective story, "Blackmailers Don't Shoot." It was accepted by *Black Mask*, and published in December 1933. Chandler published two stories in 1934; three in 1935; five in 1936; two in 1937; three in 1938; five in 1939; and one in 1941.

1939 Chandler published his first novel, *The Big Sleep*.

1940 Chandler published *Farewell, My Lovely*.

1941 Chandler published *The High Window* an collaborated with Billy Wilder on the screenplay for the film adaptation of James M. Cain's novel, *Double Indemnity*. Chandler signed a contract with Paramount for thirteen weeks at $750 per week. He continued to work for the studio until September 1944.

1943 A twenty-five cent edition of *The Big Sleep* was issued and eventually sold 300,000 copies.

1944 Chandler published *The Lady in the Lake.*

1945 Chandler returned to work for Paramount with a six-month contract worth at least $1,000 per week. He wrote the original screenplay of *The Blue Dahlia.* In July, Paramount permitted him to work at MGM on the screenplay of *The Lady in the Lake*; Chandler was unhappy with the results and had his name removed from the credits. The film was released in 1946.

1946 Chandler moved from Los Angeles to La Jolla, California. *The Big Sleep* was filmed with Humphrey Bogart playing Philip Marlowe (screenplay: William Faulkner and Leigh Brackett; director: Howard Hawks).

1947 Chandler wrote the unproduced screenplay, *Playback.*

1949 Chandler published *The Little Sister.*

1950 Chandler worked on the screenplay of the film adaptation of Patricia Highsmith's novel, *Strangers on a Train.* He engaged in unhappy exchanges with the film's director, Alfred Hitchcock.

1952 Chandler travelled to England with Cissy. Though the trip had awkward moments, Chandler was gratified by his reception as a prominent writer.

1953 Chandler published *The Long Good-bye* (US: 1954)

1953 On 12 December Cissy Chandler died after long illness.

1955 On 22 February, Chandler made a melodramatic suicide attempt, firing a pistol into the ceiling of his bathroom. In April, he travelled again to England. He began important friendships with Natasha and Stephen Spender and with Helga Greene. The latter became his literary agent, a close companion, and, in the end, his heir. In September, he returned to the States, but he soon made another trip to London. He encountered tax problems as a result of these extended visits to England (and as a result of his never having resumed American citizenship. Eventually he successfully sued for the return of his American citizenship.) Chandler continued to make regular trips to England.

1958 Chandler published his last novel, *Playback.*

1959 26 March, Raymond Chandler died of pneumonia in La Jolla. He was buried in San Diego with a small ceremony.

# The Critical Response to Raymond Chandler

# Introduction

*J. K. Van Dover*

I

Though there are those who argue the superior merits of Dashiell Hammett or Ross Macdonald, there is a growing consensus that if the hard-boiled school of detective fiction produced a writer who transcended the limitations of genre and became an important American novelist, it was Raymond Chandler. The genre itself has acquired increasing respectability as a vehicle for serious commentary on American life and values in the twentieth century, but beyond this, Chandler's distinction lies in his dedication to expanding the aesthetic as well as the ethical dimensions of the formulaic tough-guy character and detective story plot. He began his apprenticeship by imitating the pulpiest of the pulps, writing and rewriting a story by Erle Stanley Gardner. Gardner, who became Chandler's closest professional friend in the hard-boiled school, wrote some of the school's simplest, flattest, quickest prose. From this most basic of beginnings, Chandler developed a uniquely sophisticated approach to embodying his vision of the world in a series of detective novels.

Chandler's artistic success as a novelist depended largely upon the aspect of fiction which interested him most: language and style. Plot, traditionally the central concern of detective story writers, and character remain important, but Chandler was probably the first exponent of the genre since it was invented by Edgar Allan Poe to place such an emphasis upon creating a personal style in his narratives. Conan Doyle and Hammett (and others like Sayers and Austin Freeman, etc.) were not accidental stylists, but none of them seems to have been as deliberate as Chandler in his effort to construct a personal voice: an American language with which to capture an American reality.

Although Chandler was a native American, born in Chicago, he came to the American language as half a stranger, having been, as he frequently reminded his correspondents, educated in an English public school. His use of slang and argot, his notorious addiction to clever similes, his employment of devices such as irony, hyperbole, and understatement all derived from a conscious desire to create an American voice that could communicate what Chandler saw as the American reality. He remained slightly alienated from both—from the tough, smart language and from the mean streets of Los Angeles and "Bay City." He did not see himself as fully invested in either: his own idiom was not hard-boiled American (nor was he really a detective); he was a gentleman. The Los Angeles that he lived in (or near) and wrote about was not his real home; London—a remembered London—was. This distance from his medium and his matter is a crucial factor in his development. Neither the language of his novels nor their subject matter was natural or spontaneous. It is not so surprising, then, that Chandler could work comfortably within the artificial formulas of the detective story.

The second distinctive element of Chandler's art of the novel lay in his sense of place. Southern California during Chandler's tenure was characterized by a muscular decadence. Los Angeles expanded enormously in population and area during this period; its accumulation of transplanted citizens and its atmosphere of uncontrolled growth might signify the realization of the American Dream of material success or of the American Nightmare of crime and chaos. Oil and entertainment provided conspicuous sources of more or less legitimate wealth, and the sunny climate was celebrated. But there was also corruption on a large scale; political graft and organized crime were highly visible. Hollywood became the national Babylon, the origin of idols and abominations; and occult religious sects found receptive audiences. Chandler found this region a fertile scene for his detective's investigations. Philip Marlowe's territory gave refuge to extremes of some of the characteristic tendencies of twentieth century America, and Chandler's novels were thus able to explore important issues within the limits imposed by the genre.

These qualities of Chandler's fiction—his sense of style and of place—justify treating Chandler as a major American novelist of the twentieth century. Other qualities—the formulaic plots and characters, the lapses into sentimentality and melodrama, the repetitiveness—may be less creditable (and, as well, there may be moral and political objections to his treatments of women, minorities, homosexuals). But he certainly achieved his goal of breaching the custom of regarding a detective story structure as a presumptive obstacle to the creation of significant fictions, and when his case is finally disposed of by literary historians, it will surely be filed under "Novelists, American," not "Novelists, Crime and Mystery."

## II

The evolution of the critical response to Chandler's work has been remarkable in its steadiness and its degree. Beginning with reviews of his first novel, *The Big Sleep*, in 1939, he was recognized as a significant new voice in the popular subgenre of the hard-boiled detective story. By the late 1940s he was being acknowledged as a master, even *the* master of that subgenre, and some critics were arguing that the subgenre was not so minor. Toward the end of his career he had the satisfaction of having his genre novels reviewed as novels: he had not abandoned his formulas, but he had forced the admission that they could serve ends of a deliberate artist. In the decades since his death in 1959, academic scholars have increasingly discovered that Chandler's work rewards study, and, perhaps more importantly, other novelists in America and elsewhere have come to recognize Chandler's achievement and its implications for their own art of fiction. Books, articles, and dissertations have begun to explore his stories and novels from a variety of perspectives. Raymond Chandler's name now appears frequently on official maps of American literature—off the Hemingway-Faulkner highway, but not so far off.

A comparison can be drawn with the critical reception of other writers who worked in Chandler's genre and were of Chandler's generation. Dashiell Hammett, Chandler's predecessor and precedent, Dorothy Sayers, and Agatha Christie have each, for quite different reasons, also been the objects of several book-length scholarly studies. Three of the Hammett books—nearly half the total—are biographies, and this reflects the degree to which the interest in Hammett lies in the man as much as in the work, the man as an innovative writer, but also as the thin man who stood firm against pressures to conform in mid-century America. Sayers is valued as much as a literary, social, and religious thinker as she is for her detective fiction. Furthermore, the discussion of her Peter Wimsey stories frequently operates on the pleasant, but at best pseudo-critical pretense that the stories are true narratives (in the manner of the Baker Street Irregulars' treatment of the Sherlock Holmes stories). Even more often, the Christie scholarship consists of these noncritical commentaries: *companions*, *who's who*'s, and *lives and times* of her principal detectives, Poirot and Marple. No one seems yet to have played the game of pretending Philip Marlowe was a real person (though Chandler himself occasionally indulged the pretense playfully in his letters). Chandler published only a few essays in his career as an American writer; "The Simple Art of Murder" is a landmark, but it stands alone. The detective novels and stories are his primary literary legacy. And Chandler's life, as laid out in Frank MacShane's excellent 1976 biography, offers little to attract unusual admiration or interest, except to those critics who find his marriage to a woman eighteen years his senior problematic. Chandler's novels have not had to compete with his heroism for attention.

As a result, the discussion of Chandler's work has avoided some of the preoccupations which have characterized the criticism of other detective and mystery novels. His fiction has been treated as fiction, and it has been treated from a broad range of critical perspectives.

Formalists, Marxists, linguists, regionalists, and others have analyzed it. Chandler has been read as a social critic, as a romanticist, as a film writer, as a western author, as an urban author, and inevitably and above all, as a stylist. He has even been read as an important American novelist. His rise to this eminence in the 1980s and 1990s began in 1939 with a few brief notices of *The Big Sleep*. *The Critical Response to Raymond Chandler* attempts to chart this progress.

## III

*The Saturday Review of Literature*'s short "Summing Up" and "Verdict" on *The Big Sleep* neatly encapsulate the themes of the first decade of responses to Chandler's fiction: "Lot of nastily addled ten-minute eggs rampaging in tough but high-gloss lingo from super-heated start to fantastic finish" (Summing Up); "Hammettic" (Verdict).[1] The three main components of this typical response are 1. Chandler is a disciple of the hard-boiled school ("Hammettic"); 2. Chandler has a distinctive vernacular style ("high-gloss lingo"); and 3. Chandler often deals with sordid subject matter ("nastily addled").

Although Dashiell Hammett did not invent the hard-boiled genre—that credit is usually assigned to Carroll John Daly—Hammett was the one to establish it in the 1920s as a new American paradigm in detective fiction. His Continental Op stories and, more importantly, his five novels published between 1929 and 1934 were seen by readers and by critics as having established a revolutionary new type of detective, scene, and ethos in a genre which had been dominated by the Sherlock Holmes and his multitude of imitators. Philo Vance, S.S. Van Dine's cerebral and implausible New York City puzzle-solver, was the most popular American detective at the time. Hammett, as Chandler himself in a famous passage acknowledged, "took murder out of the Venetian vase and dropped it into the alley." He "gave murder back to the kind of people that commit it for reasons, not just to provide a corpse; and with the means at hand, not hand-wrought dueling pistols, curare and tropical fish."[2]

Chandler's debt to Hammett was, as he knew, great. Chandler himself had not been a detective; he had little direct knowledge of the alley into which Hammett dropped the corpse. Hammett's success made his proletarian detectives and their mean streets available to Chandler when, having lost his career as an executive in the oil business, Chandler studied the pulps with the deliberate intention of crafting a new livelihood for himself. The "Hammettic" paradigm was already the pulp standard, especially in the most famous of the pulp magazines, Captain Shaw's *Black Mask*, where Chandler published his own first story in 1934. Most other reviews of Chandler's first novel mentioned either Hammett or *Black Mask* as a quick way of labelling its character (cf. *The New Republic*, *The New Yorker*, *Time*, *The Spectator*).

Chandler could have no objection to being affiliated with Hammett, though from the first it was his intention to go beyond Hammett. He could find gratifying *The Saturday Review's* comments relating to his style: the "high-gloss lingo," "super-heated start" and "fantastic finish." This recognition of *The Big Sleep's* superior quality, at least within its genre, was also widely shared. *The New Republic's* review attributed "some of the day's best commercial prose" to *Black Mask*, and called *The Big Sleep* "something a good deal more than a who-done-it."[3] English reviews, though confused by the prose—the *The Spectator* finding "charming dialogue" where the *TLS* found only "the obscurest American slang"[4]—praised its "tightly-knit," "fast-moving" action and "many thrilling episodes."

But if he could accept the pigeon-hole and enjoy the praise, Chandler could, and did, object to the implication of *The Saturday Review's* phrase, "Lots of nastily addled ten-minute eggs." The "nastiness" of his novel seemed to strike many reviewers in 1939: "Pretty terrifying story of degeneracy" (*New Yorker*), "a mess of murderers, thugs and psychopaths" (*Time*), a "full strength [blend] of sadism, eroticism and alcoholism" (*The New Statesman*).[5] But the review which most emphasized this "nasty" aspect of *The Big Sleep*, and the one which Chandler most resented, appeared in *The New York Times*. Isaac Anderson began, "Most of the characters in this story are tough, many of them are nasty and some of them are both," and concluded: "The language used in this book is often vile—at times so filthy that the publishers have been compelled to resort to the dash . . . . As a study in depravity, the story is excellent, with Marlowe standing out as almost the only fundamentally decent person in it."[6] A week after Anderson's review appeared, Chandler wrote to his publisher, Alfred Knopf: "I have only seen four notices, but two of them seemed more occupied with the depravity and unpleasantness of the book than with anything else. In fact the notice from the *New York Times* . . . deflated me pretty thoroughly. I do not want to write depraved books."[7]

Although Anderson emphasized the dark elements in Chandler's next novel, *Farewell, My Lovely* (1940), even he admitted the "grisly skill" with which the "several kinds of dreadfulness" were handled.[8] And the general trend in the reception of this and the next two novels, *High Window* (1943) and *The Lady in the Lake* (1944), followed the lines of the first two themes struck in the reviews of *The Big Sleep*: Chandler's affiliation with the "tough-guy" or "hard-boiled" school was noted, usually with an implied or explicit commendation of the school; and Chandler's excellence within that commendable school was reasserted. The depravity charge disappeared. Anderson went out of his way in his review of *The High Window* to observe that Marlowe is "hard-boiled enough to be convincing without being disgustingly tough."[9] And his review of *The Lady in the Lake* proclaimed Chandler a "master" of his type of fiction.

This early recognition of Chandler's mastery (of, to be sure, a "type" of fiction) is feature of many of the brief reviews accorded his work. Chandler is described as a "neat craftsman" (*New Republic*) who produces "excellent" (*Time*) or "aces high" (*Saturday Review*) writing; his detective "stands head and shoulders above most of the rough-and-ready private dicks in fiction," and his novel (*The Lady in the Lake*) is "Tough, beautifully organized, and with a great deal more meat on its bones than the usual story of this type" (*New Yorker*) and "An astringent, hard-bitten, expertly constructed and convincingly characterized story of the just-tough-enough school" (*Time*). The English reviewers continued to be enthusiastic; even the *Guardian* critic, who was clearly not impressed with the tough-guy school (its "general standards," he declares, "resemble those of the jackal and the ape"), cited *Farewell, My Lovely* as "a favourable specimen," though he too had difficulty with the American language as Chandler recreated it: he found the writing "often picturesque and vivid, though often, too, incomprehensible to the mere Englishman" (*Manchester Guardian*).[10]

By the mid-1940s, then, Chandler's four Philip Marlowe novels had made a widely favorable impression upon mystery-and-crime reviewers. But his novels continued to be assigned one-paragraph reviews in columns such as "Criminals At Large" or "Mystery Stories" or "Mystery and Crime." There he was acclaimed a master; elsewhere, he was invisible. The next stage in the critical response was his emergence from the mystery columns into larger arena of literary debate. The first step in this emergence came, ironically, as a result of Edmund Wilson's notorious polemic against the pretense to literary merit by any detective stories.

In "Why Do People Read Detective Stories," published in *The New Yorker* on 14 October 1944 (and reprinted with its two follow-up articles in *Classics and Commercials*, 1950), Wilson declared his complete disappointment in the genre, subjecting Rex Stout, Agatha Christie, and Dashiell Hammett to dismissive treatments. One of the replies to Wilson's essay came from the prominent critic Bernard DeVoto. In December 1944, DeVoto used his column in *Harper's*, "The Easy Chair," to defend the genre, and as an item in his defense, he raised the name of Raymond Chandler: "If distinguished prose as such is what Mr. Wilson wants, let him try Mr. Raymond Chandler. In fact, let him try Mr. Chandler on any ground, for he is one of the best mystery writers now practicing, has carried the Hammett subspecies to a distinction its originator never attained, and in a recent movie greatly improved on Mr. Cain's dialogue."[11] DeVoto repeats the emphases of the first reviews of *The Big Sleep*—Chandler's brilliant style, Chandler's debt to Hammett—but he does so in a major feature of a major literary journal. He does refer to a new element in Chandler's career that was to become a major concern of later academic studies: his work in Hollywood. *Double Indemnity* had been released in April 1944, and DeVoto credits Chandler (and, although DeVoto omits the credit, Billy Wilder) with improving upon the original. (In light of John Dickson Carr's later attack on Chandler's style, it is interesting that DeVoto next singles out Carr for *his* "excellent prose.")

In January 1945, Wilson published his response to his critics (in addition to "the umbrageous Bernard De Voto," he cites Jacques Barzun, Joseph Wood Krutch, Somerset Maugham, and Chandler himself). "Who Cares Who Killed Roger Ackroyd?" offers Wilson's views on six detective story whose virtues the critics claimed he had overlooked: Dorothy Sayers, Margery Allingham, Ngaio Marsh, John Dickson Carr/Carter Dickson, and Raymond Chandler. Wilson finds the three women to be worthless—"dull," "tedious," "unreadable" respectively, and Carr, by contrast, to be at least relatively enjoyable. But Chandler is marked as an exception: "His *Farewell, My Lovely* is the only one of these books that I have read all of and read with enjoyment." To retain the purity of his anti-detective bias, Wilson then perversely denies that Chandler belongs to the Hammett school. Rather, he situates him in the Graham Greene/Alfred Hitchcock line: "It is not simply a question here of a puzzle which has been put together but of a hidden conspiracy that is continually turning up in the most varied and unlikely forms. To write such a novel successfully you must be able to invent character and incident and to generate atmosphere, and all this Mr. Chandler can do, though he is a long way below Graham Greene."[12] He follows this slightly equivocal praise with an expression of disappointment that the formula-imposed resolution of the novel's mysteries lacked interest or plausibility. But Wilson begins the tradition of marking Chandler as The Great Exception—the detective story writer whose detective stories are—almost, anyway—literature.

The next important step in the making of The Great Exception came in *The New York Times Book Review*, the *Review* whose charge of depravity in 1939 had so offended Chandler. On 17 June 1945 the *Review* published D.C. Russell's four column review of Chandler's first four novels. Russell, the son of AE, was an acquaintance of Chandler's, and he seized the opportunity to argue at length that Chandler's work did not at all belong in a "Criminals At Large" category. Unlike Wilson, he did not deny Chandler's hard-boiled affiliation. Rather, he offered a defense of the genre: "A class of fiction that is a new literary form, that has steadily thrived in spite of casual treatment, that is read by increasing numbers of people, among whom are many of great intelligence, should be worth more than a mere ticketing as light entertainment."[13]

His advocacy of Chandler in particular is based primarily upon his admiration of Chandler's style, "his most expert use of the English language: "There is not a page in Chandler's novels that is written carelessly, that is not studded with a prodigal invention of phrases and analogy.... Chandler indeed can be unreservedly recommended not only to those who like good mystery fiction but also to those who like good novels." Chandler's novels may be mysteries, they may be tough, but they are, Russell affirms, potentially as good as novels about "love or farm life or the Negro." They are, if they were properly marketed by publishers and properly reviewed by journals, potentially best-sellers.

Russell's comments confirm that Chandler's work had risen to a new level of respectability (though his emphasis upon "best-selling" as a measure of mainstream acceptance evades aesthetic judgments about the legitimacy of genre fiction). Chandler helped his cause by publishing a pair of notable essays in the quite respectable *Atlantic Monthly* ("The Simple Art of Murder," December 1944, and "Writers in Hollywood," November 1945). The second of these provided the starting point for R.W. Flint's 1947 essay on Chandler, "A Cato of the Cruelties," which appeared in the leftist intellectual journal, *The Partisan Review* . Flint was, to be sure, slumming the field of popular culture, and his interest lay as much in the 1947 film of *Lady in the Lake* as it did in the novels. But however condescending, his account of Marlowe as "the American middle-class Existentialist" demands that readers take the figure seriously: "He is forever rolling the stone uphill—a little too sentimental and self-pitying for a true Stoic, but an existentialist nonetheless. Whatever the alternatives, Marlowe acts and acts alone: his life is all decision—a blind plowing through the wildest ambiguities always into the heart of insecurity and danger." Flint actually preferred the film Marlowe to the novel Marlowe, but he did offer a serious interpretation of the moral significance of Philip Marlowe's encounter with his world—"that miasmic, Dantesque background of California roadways, police stations, office buildings, and fake interiors in which Chandler specializes."[14]

Chandler received further endorsements as The Great Exception from two important Englishmen in the late 1940s. W.H. Auden's essay, "The Guilty Vicarage," included in his 1948 collection, *The Dyer's Hand*, is probably the most famous analysis of the appeal of the detective story. Auden's topic is the classical British mystery, with its corpses in the library and its butlers who didn't do it, which he sees as a fable of the Great Good Place defiled by murder but restored by the detective. He interrupts his discussion to exempt Chandler from being judged by the peculiar standards of the genre: "Mr. Raymond Chandler has written that he intends to take the body out of the vicarage garden and give murder back to those who are good at it. . . . Actually, whatever he may say, I think Mr. Chandler is interested in writing, not detective stories, but serious studies of a criminal milieu, the Great Wrong Place, and his powerful but extremely depressing books should be read and judged, not as escape literature, but as works of art."[15]

Auden's valuable imprimatur has been invoked by many of the scholars who began to examine Chandler's novels as "works of art." Chandler himself was ambivalent about it. ""I'm just a fellow who jacked up a few pulp novelettes into book form. How could I possibly care a button about the detective story as a form? . . . along comes this fellow Auden and tells me I am interested in writing serious studies of a criminal milieu. So now I look at everything I put down and say to myself, Remember, old boy, this has to be a serious study of a criminal milieu."[16] In fact, the critical respectability was making Chandler self-conscious; he was having difficulties finishing *The Little Sister*, and he even contemplated abandoning Marlowe.

Further intimidating praise came from the novelist and playwright, J.B. Priestly, who included in his new feature, "Letters from Two Islands" in *The New Statesman and Nation* an unsolicited encomium prompted by reading a proof copy of *The Little Sister*. Priestly professed himself fascinated with "the unusual and pleasing spectacle of a man trying to turn a cheap, popular formula into something much better." He finds that Chandler illuminates the hard-boiled world ("corpses, whisky for breakfast, luscious nymphomaniacs") with "a genuine if sour wit and much oblique social criticism." "To read him is like cutting into an over-ripe melon and discovering that it has a rare astringent flavour. He reduces the bright Californian scene to an empty despair, dead bottles and a heap of cigarette butts under the meaningless neon lights, much more adroitly than Aldous Huxley and the rest can do."[17] Chandler would later meet Priestley at his home in La Jolla and in London.

*The Little Sister* was published in 1949. Despite his promotion as The Great Exception, Chandler found his novel still generally reviewed in a column on mysteries. He might receive two or three paragraphs instead of one, and the reviews were consistently favorable, but he was still a mystery novel writer. *The New Statesman* assigned him only ten lines in its "Red Herrings" column; the reviewer, Ralph Partridge, actually referred to Priestley's "favourable preview" of the novel, but the genre seemed to retain its claim to Chandler. A significant breakthrough, however, came at *Time*, which gave *The Little Sister* a full six-paragraph review, with a photograph of the author. It opened with "To be caught with a Raymond Chandler whodunit in hand is a fate no highbrow reader need dread." And though it ended on a negative note, deploring Chandler's persistence in a limiting genre ("Shamus Marlowe is in real danger of becoming an old retainer, Chandler of becoming a talented hack"), it did treat Chandler as a novelist.[18]

Not all of the attention his work was receiving pleased Chandler. In 1949 he received "a strange little brochure" ("evidently privately printed") from one "G. Legman." In a letter to James Sandoe, he described it as "substantially a bitter and possibly envious attacks on all kinds of murder mystery, crime books, realistic sexy writing cum murder," and he referred to a "nasty" letter from Legman which apparently called Chandler "a homosexualist."[19] In 1963, Legman published his interpretation of Marlowe's homosexual proclivity in *Love and Death*: "Chandler's Marlowe is clearly homosexual—a butterfly, as the Chinese say, dreaming he is a man."[20] Legman cited as evidence Marlowe's apparent abstinence from sexual intercourse, his "anti-female necrophilia," and his affinity for certain attractive men. Others have repeated the charge; it is probably not coincidental that Marlowe's non-abstinence is graphically proven—twice—in *The Long Goodbye*, the novel published directly following Chandler's receipt of Legman's "little brochure."

One sign of the rise of Chandler's popularity can be seen in the reissuance of his early short stories in a series of collections beginning in 1946. Their bibliography is often confusing, as books with the same names sometimes have different contents (the differences between American and British editions add to the confusion). The most complete collection, *The Simple Art of Murder*, was issued in 1950 by Houghton Mifflin; it omitted only Chandler's first short story, "Blackmailer's Don't Shoot," and the eight stories which Chandler had "cannibalized" to produce *The Big Sleep*, *Farewell, My Lovely*, and *The Lady in the Lake* and which he refused permission to republish. The title-piece of the book was the polemical essay in defense of the hard-boiled style which Chandler had published in *The Atlantic* in 1944. It was this collection, and especially its title essay, that led to a major attack on Chandler's rising reputation.

*The New York Times Book Review* invited John Dickson Carr to write a long review of *The Simple Art of Murder* (24 September 1950), the second time that the *Review* had permitted a Chandler work to escape the "New Mystery Stories" column. The first occasion had permitted D.C. Russell to argue that Chandler was good enough not be confined to that category; the second allowed Carr to argue that Chandler could not be rated competent even by the standards of that category. Carr, an American who had become a major practitioner of the British tradition of the detective story, devoted most of his full-page review, "With Colt and Luger," to a contemptuous dismissal of Chandler's defense of his style in his collection's title essay. Carr concludes his discussion with the advice, "If, to some restraint, he could add the fatigue of construction and clues . . . then one day he may write a good novel." Turning to the stories at hand, he concedes that the collection contains at least three stories worth reading (Carr preferred above all Chandler's parodic detective story, "Pearls Are a Nuisance"). His final observation returns to an attack on Chandler's style: "Mr. Chandler will do even better when he discovers that you cannot create an American language merely by butchering the English language."[21]

Carr was no envious second-rater; he sincerely regarded Chandler's fiction (and, especially, Chandler's defense of that fiction) as a sinister diversion from the legitimate line that descended from Sherlock Holmes—the line of "the formal English detective story." But whatever its motive, his disparagement was perverse and vain. It outraged Chandler, who saw in it the conspiracy of Eastern snobs to denigrate his work.[22] It also outraged other readers, and the *Book Review* devoted its "Letters to the Editor" page on 5 November to a continuation of the debate. The letters in defense of Chandler did not alter Carr's mind. He merely reiterated the central items in his indictment of Chandler's craft: its "muddy writing and bad construction."

The first charge, an obtuse objection to Chandler's style, is easily dismissed. The blimpish locutions of Carr's own detectives only emphasize Chandler's art and originality; even Philip Marlowe's "janes" and "frails" are preferable to Dr. Fell's "wenches." But Carr had a point with regard to Chandler's plots. In his original review Carr blamed the fault on Chandler's laziness—his aversion to "the fatigue of construction and clues." Though opinion has been far from unanimous, many reviewers and critics have cited the weakness of his plots as a major fault in Chandler's fiction. It was a flaw he himself recognized ("Most writers think up a plot with an intriguing situation and then fit the characters to it. With me a plot, if you could call it that, is an organic thing. It grows and often overgrows"[23]). Carr's own art of the detective novel depended upon the calculated distribution of clues and misdirections; he made the locked room formula, requiring the most careful narrative construction, his specialty. And he was not alone in thinking that this sort of construction was a necessary virtue—even a defining characteristic—of the mystery genre. His condescending advice assumed that Chandler's aim was also to produce the ideal mystery puzzle. Taking this still common assumption seriously, Carr attempted to demonstrate that Chandler and his school had failed radically in their effort to resituate the puzzle on the mean streets urban America. That this was not exactly their ambition eluded him.

Carr's invective did not deter the rise of Chandler's reputation, though his work continued to be judged in its generic context. Chandler was most gratified by the embrace of the British. Somerset Maugham singled Chandler out for highest praise in his essay "The Decline and Fall of the Detective Story" (1952). Though he misspelled Marlowe's name (an error which irritated Chandler, who had been corresponding with Maugham), Maugham praised Chandler for having succeeded "in making Marlow a vivid human being." Invidious comparisons between Chandler and Hammett have become a staple of detective story criticism. Maugham's early exercise concluded to Chandler's advantage: "Raymond Chandler maintains an unswerving line. His pace is swifter. He deals with a more varied assortment of persons. He has a greater sense of probability and his motivation is more probable. Both write a nervous, colloquial English racy of the American soil. Raymond Chandler's dialogue seems to me better than Hammett's. He has an admirable aptitude for the typical product of the quick American mind, the wisecrack, and his sardonic humour has an engaging spontaneity."[24] Maugham ended his essay by suggesting that Chandler might even prove to be unsurpassable. Though he disagreed with Maugham's conclusion that the form was exhausted, Chandler was flattered by the treatment.

*The Long Goodbye* (1954), Chandler's longest and in some respects most ambitious novel, did not receive the special notice it might have been accorded. It was still assigned to the familiar "Mystery and Crime" columns. *The New Yorker* dismissed it as "hardly seems worth all the bother"[25]—but most reviewers at least praised it as offering more of what Chandler was good at. The British journal, *The Fortnightly*, did give Luke Parsons six pages to review Chandler's career to date. Parsons commented upon the ethos of the novels, and raised the vexed question of their "realism." In his conclusion, he made a significant effort to place Chandler in the literary gamut: "he comes half-way between the prolific time-killers like Erle Stanley Gardner and serious novelists such as John Steinbeck and Ernest Hemingway."[26]

The reviews of Chandler's last novel, *Playback* (1958) were, if anything, generous. Composed in difficult circumstances, *Playback* is the only publication of Chandler's mature career (1934-1958) that can be called an embarrassment. Reviewers were content to note its strengths and to observe that Chandler's weakest effort was superior to best of most others.

A movement to reappraise Chandler's career began after his death. In 1960, George P. Elliott published an important essay, "Country Full of Blondes," in *The Nation*. He drew particular attention to Chandler's skill at creating an version of Southern California in his fiction, a version that was, Elliott wrote, "so congenial and so strong that it affected his readers' versions. Chandler's fictions are one of the reasons Southern California now is seen the way it is."[27] Elliott placed Chandler in a class with Frank Norris and James Fenimore Cooper and argued that literary historians ought to examine his merits more seriously. The publication of *Raymond Chandler Speaking* (1962), a collection of Chandler's letters and essays (with a story and a novel fragment) offered an opportunity for the examination to begin. Several journals published substantial essays devoted to discussions of the meaning and the significance of Chandler's career. Richard Schickel, in *Commentary*, argued that Chandler "was at least the equal of a middle rank 'serious' novelist—perhaps the equal, on occasion, of a first-rate one."[28] Wilson Pollock was a bit more superficial in his two page review in *The New Republic*, but J. MacLaren-Ross composed a long, thoughtful comparison of the accomplishments Chandler and Hammett in *The London Magazine*.[29]

## IV

The remainder of the 1960s saw other discussions of Chandler's work in intellectual journals, but it still remained largely ignored by scholars. Two early indications that the academy was turning its attention toward writers like Chandler did appear in the decade. Philip Durham's fine booklength study of Chandler's work, *Down*

*These Mean Streets A Man Must Go*, published by a university press, made an impressive argument for treating Chandler as a serious American novelist. And Matthew J. Bruccoli's first bibliography of Chandler's work, *Raymond Chandler: A Checklist*, began to sort out the publication history of the novels and the stories. Herbert Ruhm's 1968 essay, "Raymond Chandler: From Bloomsbury to the Jungle—and Beyond," also deserves mention as an important early scholarly approach to Chandler.

In the 1970s, Chandler criticism came of age. Scholars began to publish studies of his work in journals like *Kenyon Review*, *Kansas Quarterly*, *Film Heritage*, *Massachusetts Review*, and *Western American Literature* as well as in genre journals such as *Armchair Detective* and *Clues*. Three important landmarks marked the decade. The Marxist critic, Fredric Jameson, published an influential essay, "On Raymond Chandler," in *Southern Review* in 1970. Frank MacShane's excellent biography, *The Life of Raymond Chandler* (1976) provided a standard life of the author. Miriam Gross collected fifteen critical and biographical essays on Chandler for *The World of Raymond Chandler* (1977). The biography and the collection of essays occasioned favorable retrospective considerations of Chandler's achievement in the *New Yorker*, *Nation*, *New Republic*, and the *New York Times Book Review*.

The main themes of Chandler criticism were thus laid out in the 1970s; the 1980s saw an even greater number of scholars working to extend and refine these themes. Chandler studies had become a legitimate academic enterprise. A major factor in the legitimizing of Chandler studies was the legitimizing of the academic study of mystery and detective fiction in general. Post-modernist writers, mandarin literary theorists, and mere college professors all contributed to the argument that this low-brow genre was a meaningful cultural and literary phenomenon, one justifying sober commentary. The standard taxonomies divided the genre into at least two parts—the classical, British form and the hard-boiled, American form—and Chandler, along with Hammett (and, often, Ross Macdonald), was taken as one of the pre-eminent craftsmen of the second form. As a result, his work was discussed in nearly all of the several book-length inquiries into the genre that have appeared since 1970. Moreover, the hard-boiled American form, in part because it has obvious ties to a mainstream in high-brow American literature (the Hemingway stream) and because it seems to reflect the element of violence which is commonly attributed to the American character, has received special attention from critics interested in the conjunction of hard-boiledness and Americanness. Chandler's novels offer ideal texts for such studies.

In addition to these broader examinations of Chandler's art and ideology, some half dozen particular aspects of his achievement seem to have preoccupied scholars. The single most popular is not strictly literary: the topic of Chandler and film has drawn a substantial body of criticism (see, for example, Ferncase, Gallagher, Luhr, Maxfield, Nolan 1969, Pendo, Ponder, Shatzin, Spiegel, Telotte). Film Noir has been a major object of cinema scholarship, and Chandler's work in Hollywood lies centrally in the Noir tradition. His film career offers several facets. The films of his novels, especially *The Big Sleep* and *The Lady in the Lake* (both 1946), have attracted attention. His own screenplays, especially his original script of *The Blue Dahlia* (1946) and his adaptation of James M. Cain's *Double Indemnity* (1944) have also been frequently discussed. Chandler described his own experiences in Hollywood (and his less than favorable judgment on its encouragement of art) in a pair of essays, "Writers in Hollywood" (*Atlantic*, November 1945) and "Oscar Night in Hollywood" (*Atlantic*, March 1948). These experiences were to some degree reflected in the Hollywood episodes of *The Little Sister*. Those who knew him during his period of working in Hollywood have recorded their reminiscences about his sometimes erratic and extreme behavior.

Another major preoccupation of his critics has been Chandler's ambivalent relation to the southern Californian natural and social environment, an environment which attracted and repelled him, emotionally and intellectually. It can be argued that Chandler was *the* chronicler of Los Angeles during a crucial stage in its development, a stage in which it became in some important respects a representative American city. As a private investigator, Philip Marlowe seems ideally situated as an observer of all levels of the city's life. His investigations carry him everywhere, and his moral voice, with its ironies and its integrity, provides a judgmental perspective on the panorama of corruption and competition (and sometimes of love and sacrifice) that the novels portray. Marlowe's engagement with his world has been studied by a number of scholars interested in this interaction between the detective and his particular urban environment (see Babener, Fine, Reck, Schwoch, Skenazy 1984, Warner, Wasserberg).

Chandler's style is certainly the principal basis for his claim to consideration as a major novelist. Most commentaries on his work recognize this claim with at least a nod. Several offer more detailed discussions, citing striking examples of his genius for description and for sharp similes (see Lott and Tanner). James Guetti has made an interesting argument regarding the function of the hard-boiled staple, the "wisecrack," as a means of controlling experience. There is one highly technical linguistic analysis (Crombie). But considering the importance of the topic, the examination of the way Chandler's special voice works effectively to convey a particular story and a particular moral environment has only begun.

Chandler called his practice of joining two or more short stories to produce a novel "cannibalism." There have been some very useful discussions of this process (Durham 1964, Mills), but here too there is surely more to be said about the gains and the losses it involves. A first-rate novelist constructed three good novels from eight previously published short stories, combining and connecting characters and plots as well as expanding descriptions and dialogue. Chandler's technique offers an extraordinary opportunity for analyzing the creative process in all these aspects. Nor have the individualstories been adequately discussed on their own merits. Jerry Spier and William Marling make interesting observations on the short stories in their surveys of Chandler's work, but there is surely more to be said about the evolution of Chandler's artistic technique and moral vision. That there has been little appreciation of Chandler's early, English ventures into belles lettres is perhaps more understandable.

Critics have often discussed Chandler in relation to another author for purposes of comparison or of indicating influence (almost always Chandler's influence on a follower; other than his debt to Hammett, the sources of his own inspiration have not been much studied). Entire articles have been devoted to discussing Chandler and his connections with Americans such as Ross Macdonald (Steiner) and Robert B. Parker (Greiner), Europeans such as Georges Simenon (Parsons) and Nicholas Freeling (Winston), and even with the Uruguayan novelist, Hiber Conteris (Hart, Paul).

Scholars have often focussed their studies on one or two of the novels, and drawn their conclusions from these. Thorough examinations of single works have, however, been relatively rare. Three novels have received most individual attention: *The Big Sleep* (Fontana, Rabinowitz, Sharratt), *Farewell, My Lovely* (Knight 1980, Wells), and *The Long Good-bye* (Finch 1972, Kaye, Tate). There is certainly more to be said about these novels as autonomous works of fiction, and the middle novels—*The High Window, Lady in the Lake,* and *The Little Sister* —also need to be examined on their individual merits. Even *Playback* deserves further study; the nature of Chandler's failure should be as revealing as the nature of his success.

*The Critical Response to Raymond Chandler* includes essays representing each of these principal approaches (and others as well). Other essays, often of comparable quality, have for reasons of space been excluded, but readers are referred to the bibliography. The advantage of a collection such as this one lies its making accessible essays from a wide variety of often relatively inaccessible journals. It was, therefore, decided not to include excerpts from books which, presumably, will be as accessible as this book is. Several of the best discussions of Chandler's work are part of larger, book-length inquiries. The function of this collection is to provide a snapshot of the current state of Chandler studies. Scholarly interpretations of the hard-boiled genre in general and of Chandler's work in particular have been proliferating. It is perhaps time to consolidate the main lines of recent inquiry and to define the important problems that require further investigation. By gathering divergent views, *The Critical Response to Raymond Chandler* attempts to contribute to the process of establishing the scope and the significance of Chandler's literary achievement.

---

1 *Saturday Review of Literature* 11 February 1939: 23.

2 Raymond Chandler, "The Simple Art of Murder," in *The Simple Art of Murder* (NY: Ballantine, 1977: 16.

3 *The New Republic* 15 February 1939: 56.

4 *The Spectator* 31 March 1939: 558; *Times Literary Supplement* 11 March 1939: 152.

5 *The New Yorker* 11 February 1939: 84; *Time* 6 March 1939: 63; *The New Statesman and Nation* 10 June 1939: 910.

6 *New York Times Book Review* 12 February 1939: 20.

7 *Selected Letters of Raymond Chandler* (NY: Columbia UP, 1981): 4.

8 *New York Times Book Review* 17 November 1940: 29.

9 *New York Times Book Review* 16 August 1942: 17.

10 *The New Republic* 7 October 1940: 482; *Time* 7 September 1942: 116; *Saturday Review of Literature* 6 November 1943: 29; *The New Yorker* 6 November 1943: 92; *Time* 6 December 1943: 104; *Manchester Guardian* 10 December 1940: 7.

11 *Harper's* December 1944: 36.

12 *Classics and Commercials* (NY: Farrar Strauss, 1950): 262-63.

13 *New York Times Book Review* 17 June 1945: 7.

14 *Partisan Review* 14(1947): 328-30.

15 *The Dyer's Hand* (New York: Vintage, 1948).

16 *Selected Letters of Raymond Chandler* (NY: Columbia UP, 1981): 114-15.

17 *The New Statesman and Nation* 9 April 1949: 349,

18 "Murder at the Old Stand," *Time* 3 October 1949: 82-83.

19 *Selected Letters*, 118.

20 *Love and Death* (NY: Hacker Art Books, 1963): 70.

21 *New York Times Book Review* 24 September 1950: 36.

22 See his letter to Dale Warren, 4 October 1950, in *Selected Letters of Raymond Chandler* (NY: Columbia UP, 1981): 226-27.

23 Letter to James Sandoe, 23 September 1948, in *Selected Letters of Raymond Chandler* (NY: Columbia UP, 1981): 129.

24 "The Decline and Fall of the Detective Story," in *The Vagrant Mood* (London: Heinemann, 1952): 119.

25 *The New Yorker* 27 March 1954: 36.

26 "On the Novels of Raymond Chandler," *The Fortnightly* May 1954: 351.

27 "Country Full of Blondes," *Nation* 23 Apr : 160.

28 "Raymond Chandler, Private Eye," *Commentary* Feb 1963: 161.

---

[29] "Man With a Toy Gun," *New Republic* 7 May 1962: 21-22; "Chandler and Hammett," *London Magazine* March 1964: 70-79.

# Chandler and the Reviewers: American and English Observations on a P.I.'s Progress, 1939–1964

*J. K. Van Dover*

The critical reception of Chandler's novels offers little in the way of controversial argument or oversight. The endorsements of D.C. Russell in *The New York Times Book Review* in 1945 and by J.B. Priestley in *The New Statesman* in 1949 and the indictment of John Dickson Carr in *The New York Times Book Review* in 1950 are perhaps the outstanding moments. For the rest, his novels were reviewed regularly with respect and regularly in columns assigned to mystery and detective fiction. Chandler was regularly acknowledged to be excellent at his chosen craft, but mystery and detective fiction columns are rarely the venues for extended analyses of the particular qualities of excellence. Chandler's virtues were quickly reduced to shorthand allusions—"tough," "fast-moving," "excellent dialogue." The simplest category was "hard-boiled," a term which encompassed ill-defined aesthetic and moral dimensions and which might be applied to performances ranging from the best-selling crudities of Carroll John Daly and Mickey Spillane through James M. Cain, John O'Hara and John Steinbeck to the highbrow triumphs of Dos Passos and Hemingway. The nuances of Hemingway's tough guys and tough world could be explored and praised or damned in pages of commentary; the nuances of Chandler's guys and Chandler's world were invisible in the single paragraphs allotted to him.

And Dashiell Hammett's meteoric career, concentrated in the burst of five novels published between 1929 and 1934, was bound to overshadow his followers. If Hammett's work was the necessary basis for Chandler's craft, it was also the inevitable obstacle to its recognition. Hammett's priority (and, to be sure, his achievement) guaranteed that Chandler's innovations would be seen as superficial derivatives. Chandler would always play Olds to Hammett's Ford (or Benz to Hammett's Mercedes?). Even in surveys of the hard-boiled genre, "Hammett" was the usual citation; eventually "Hammett and

Chandler" became the standard (and then "Hammett/Chandler/Macdonald"). Not until the 1970s, more than a decade after Chandler's death, did the literary surgeons begin to sever the cord that bound Chandler to Hammett and to probe his individual merits.

And so, for the most part, contemporary reviewers on both sides of the Atlantic quickly recognized Chandler as a master of an important subgenre of detective fiction, and only as that. A tendency to overestimate his final novel even balanced an underestimation of his first. Except for some early charges of depravity and some late charges of careless plotting, Chandler had little to complain of in the reception of his novels. And with these exceptions, Chandler's objections were less to the estimations than to the estimators: he always resented the editorial prejudice that inevitably assigned his books to genre reviewers. "Criminals At Large" was, he thought with some justice, a literary ghetto in which the highest praise was rendered faint and damning. He was defiantly proud of his commitment to the detective story and of his achievement in transforming it to serve his artistic vision, but ironically, public recognition of that achievement evidently depended upon denying its basis. He would never be praised for making the detective novel a legitimate vehicle for serious fiction, and he would not abandon his vehicle.

Late in his life, Chandler did think he was at last properly appreciated by a critical establishment. He was greatly gratified by his reception in English literary circles in the 1950s, finding an artistic validation that he had missed in America. But a reader of reviews may be puzzled by his pleasure. Considerations of his last two novels in the *Manchester Guardian*, the *New Statesman*, or *Times Literary Supplement* were still subsumed under collective genre reviews such as "Detection and Thrillers" or "Keeping up with the Bonds." The English ghetto might be more sophisticated than the American—it probably was; but it seems hardly less limiting. Chandler's enjoyment was doubtless derived from the uncondescending intellectual atmosphere which he discovered in London, and which conveyed itself through personal connections and occasional essays (such as those by Maugham and Auden) rather than through review columns.

What follows is a chronological synopsis of the important reviews of the books Chandler published in his lifetime. Its purpose is to reflect the relatively uncontroversial view of Chandler's work through his twenty-year career as a novelist.

## The Big Sleep
1939

The most important review of *The Big Sleep* was the paragraph from "New Mystery Stories" which Isaac Anderson devoted to the debut of the new hard-boiled writer (*New York Times Book Review* 12 February 1939: 20). Anderson began, "Most of the characters in this story are tough, many of them are nasty and some of them are both." And after three sentences of plot summary, he concluded with charge that it was an excellent "study in depravity," a charge which upset Chandler.

Anderson did not mention Hammett; most other reviews did:

> This Chandler, like Dashiell Hammett, is a graduate (*cum laude*) of Black Mask; and it goes without saying that his first novel is something a good deal more than a who-done-it. If you have any feeling for subtle workmanship, don't give it the go-by.
> ("New Books: A Reader's List" *The New Republic* 15 February 1939: 56)

> Pretty terrifying story of degeneracy in southern California by an author who makes Dashiell Hammett seem as innocuous as Winnie-the-Pooh.
> ("Mysteries" *The New Yorker* 11 February 1939: 84)

> Lot of nastily addled ten-minute eggs rampaging in tough but high-gloss lingo from super-heated start to fantastic finish. Hammettic.
> ("Sergeant Cuff" "Summing Up" and "Verdict" *Saturday Review of Literature* 11 February 1939: 23)

> Detective Marlowe is plunged into a mess of murderers, thugs and psychopaths who make the characters of Dashiell Hammett and James Cain look like something out of Godey's Lady's Book.
> ("February Mysteries" *Time* 6 March 1939: 63)

The English reviewers were less apt to cite Hammett. The *TLS* reviewer noted Chandler's "affinities" with Peter Cheney. While apparently disapproving of Chandler's use of "the obscurest American slang, " he concluded, "There are many thrilling episodes among professional criminals and the story goes with a swing" ("Detective Stories" *Times Literary Supplement* 11 March 1939: 152). The *TLS* gave Chandler the last ten lines of a column covering five mystery writers; Nicholas Blake, in *The Spectator*, granted him seven in a long review of twelve genre writers, and he did make the Hammett connection:

> *The Big Sleep*, as its title suggests, is American and very, very tough after the *Thin Man* fashion. Almost everyone in the book, except the detective, is either a crook or wonderfully decadent, and the author spares us no blushes to point out just how decadent they are. . . The action is tightly knit and fast-moving, however, and there is some charming dialogue.
> ("The Big Shots" *The Spectator* 31 March 1939: 558)

Although he confessed himself addicted to American tough thrillers, Ralph Partridge devoted only a few lines of his twelve-novel review in *The New Statesman and Nation* to a joint commentary on *The Big Sleep* and *The Frightened Women* by George Harmon Coxe, assuring his readers that

> these two are full strength blends of sadism, eroticism and alcoholism. If you like to pretend you read the stuff for any reason but sordid mental intoxication, these ingredients are crystallised round a central thread of detection. But if you take your medicine straight, you'll never notice it.
> ("Death with a Difference" *The New Statesman and Nation* 10 June 1939: 910)

## Farewell, My Lovely
1940

Chandler's reputation was already consolidating by the appearance of his second novel. *The New Republic* gave it three sentences: the first praised *The Big Sleep* ("a fast, tough detective story with excellent dialogue and a screwy plot"); the second noted the improvements in the second:

> This new one is faster and tougher and the plot is better too. Mr. Chandler is a neat craftsman and writes like a breeze.
> ("New Books: A Reader's List" *The New Republic* 7 October 1940: 482)

Sergeant Cuff, in the *Saturday Review of Literature*, also noted Chandler's command of pace—"Swift and savage"—and commented on Marlowe's embodiment of the hard-boiled virtue of resilience—"practically indestructible sleuth" (12 October 1940: 38).

*The New Yorker*, never enthusiastic about Chandler, rated the novel "better than average," but did not find it better plotted and paced, declaring it "loose-jointed in spots" ("Mystery and Crime" 5 October 1940: 68). Isaac Anderson in the *New York Times Book Review* picked up on this flaw as well:

> Like many "swift-moving" tales, it is sometimes confusing in its rapid succession of incidents which may or may not have an integral connection with the plot.
> ("New Mystery Stories," *New York Times Book Review* 17 November 1940: 29)

On any book review page other than "New Mystery Stories" this matter of loose plot construction would have been relatively unimportant; in the columns in which Chandler was reviewed it remained a preoccupation.

Anderson also reiterated, in milder form, his moral objections to Chandler's vision: "This is a tough one: superlatively tough, alcoholic, and for all its wisecracks, ugly rather than humorous." "Ugly" is surely preferable to "depraved," and Anderson does proceed to praise the art with which Chandler drew his ugly picture of American life: "the appeal of 'Farewell, My Lovely' is in the toughness, which is extremely well done." And he concludes:

> The story's ever-present theme is police corruption, seen in a murky variety. And several kinds of dreadfulness are handled with a grisly skill.

The three paragraphs Anderson allotted to Chandler are no more than those allotted to the other seven mystery writers he covered (of whom only Erle Stanley Gardner and perhaps John Rhode seem to have left any impression even within the history of the genre).

The English view hardly differed from the American. Nicholas Blake, in the few lines he assigned to *Farewell, My Lovely*, identifies it as a "tough, sexy, American thriller" and praises the dialogue and the pace:

> The dialogue crackles, the killer kills, the girls are good value, the action covers a great deal of ground and hard knocks at terrific speed.
> ("The Big Shots" *The Spectator* 22 November 1940: 558)

The *Manchester Guardian's* paragraph expressed some doubt about the morals and manners of Chandler's characters.

> Some readers, however, may find a sort of fearful joy in an introduction to a world in which no one seems to have much idea of self-respect, where whisky can be a man's sole sustenance, where the really nice young ladies remark, "I would like to be kissed, damn you!" where, in fact, the general standards resemble those of the jackal and the ape.
> ("Mystery Stories" *Manchester Guardian* 10 December 1940: 7)

Still, the reviewer observes, "Mr. Chandler does try to give some semblance of humanity even to his most brutal characters" (perhaps conjuring visions of humane jackals and apes). He pronounces *Farewell, My Lovely* a "favourable speciman of its class." And contradicting some of the Americans, he finds that "the plot is clever and well constructed."

## The High Window
1942

*The High Window* broke no new ground in the eyes of reviewers. Most remained favorable:

> Private Investigator Marlowe is in fine form and the author has given him a superior bunch of screwballs to work out on. The witty dialogue and the eccentric personnel recommend this lively number.
> ("New Books: A Reader's List," *The New Republic* 7 September 1942: 294)

> Excellent writing, fantastic characters and shrewd detecting place it among the best.
> ("Murder in August" *Time* 7 September 1942: 116)

And *The New Yorker* remained neutral:

> For those who like their mysteries hard-boiled.
> ("Mystery and Crime" *The New Yorker* 22 August 1942: 48)

Isaac Anderson continued to be troubled by Chandler's plotting, faulting an over-reliance on luck and coincidence. But he concludes positively:

> Raymond Chandler has given us a detective who is hard-boiled enough to be convincing without being disgustingly tough, and that is not mean achievement.
> ("New Mystery Stories," *New York Times Book Review* 16 August 1942: 17)

## The Lady in the Lake
1943

Chandler was now clearly acknowledged as one of the biggest frogs in his small pond:

> This is a fine example of the type of fiction of which Raymond Chandler is a master.
> (Isaac Anderson. "Crime Corner," *New York Times Book Review* 31 October 1943: 10)

> About as tough as they come, plus an airtight plot, interesting characters, copious action, and aces-high writing.
> Extra good.

> (Sergeant Cuff, "Summing Up" and "Verdict," *Saturday Review of Literature* 6 November 1943: 29.)

> An astringent, hard-bitten, expertly constructed and convincingly characterized story of the just-tough-enough school.
> ("Mysteries in November" *Time* 6 December 1943: 104.)

> This one is easier to guess than any of the author's previous books, but it's an A-one job.
> ("New Books: A Reader's List," *The New Republic* 29 November 1943: 758)

And *The New Yorker* at last came around:

> Philip Marlowe . . . stands head and shoulders above most of the rough-and-ready private dicks in fiction. . . . Tough, beautifully organized, and with a great deal more meat on its bones than the usual story of this type.
> ("Mystery and Crime" *The New Yorker* 6 November 1943: 92)

## Red Wind
1946

The first collections of Chandler's pulp short stories had been published in 1944 as volumes in the "Murder Mystery Monthly" series. *Red Wind* was the first to be published straightforwardly and be reviewed. Isaac Anderson's notice in the *New York Times Book Review* recalled the Hammett precedent and again emphasized Chandler's hard-boiled-ness:

> Not since the advent of Dashiell Hammett have we encountered a tougher crew of men and women, and it is arguable whether Hammett ever has packed more violence into a single book than is pictured here or has done it more skillfully.
> ("Criminals at Large," *New York Times Book Review* 5 May 1946: 40)

## Spanish Blood
1946

Anderson continued to emphasize Chandler's toughness: most of the stories "may be just a bit too gory for some tastes." When he wrote for the pulps, Chandler "was even tougher than he is now." Anderson singles out for praise the one story in which "there is no killing, perhaps because the two men who figure in it are too rugged to succumb to treatment that would have landed ordinary humans on slabs in the morgue. This story is called 'Pearls Are a Nuisance,' and it is the most entertaining story in the lot." ("Reports on Criminals at Large," *New York Times Book Review* 8 September 1946: 10)

("Pearls Are a Nuisance," Chandler's one attempt to parody the genre he mastered, may serve as a sort of test case. Critics unsympathetic to Chandler's art of fiction seem to prefer it. John Dickson Carr also gave it special praise when he reviewed the 1950 collection, *The Simple Art of Murder.*)

The *Saturday Review of Literature*, by contrast, preferred the title story, but it too acknowledged the "gore" which it found, apparently with less distaste than did Anderson, throughout the collection (*Saturday Review of Literature* 10 August 1946: 32). *The New Yorker* maintained its superior pose:

> Mugg-weather stuff, and if you happen to be a suggestible type, you may raise quite a thirst, since the consumption of spirits in this tale is second only to the mortality.
> ("Mystery and Crime," *The New Yorker* 7 September 1946: 95)

## The Little Sister
1949

The *Little Sister* appeared after a seven year hiatus during which Chandler served his time in Hollywood. It marked the end of a stage in Chandler's development as a novelist. The five novels of the thirties and the forties represented his attempts to exploit the conventions of the hard-boiled form; in his sixth Marlowe novel, *The Long Goodbye* (1954) he would make an ambitious effort to go beyond the form. (The seventh and last novel, *Playback*, would mark a retreat.) *The Little Sister* thus ended the first phase of Chandler's career as a novelist.

It also marked a stage in his critical reception. In America, it was given a full notice in *Time* and Harvey Breit offered an extended comment in the *Atlantic*. There was a changing of the guard at the *New York Times Book Review*, as Anthony Boucher replaced Isaac Anderson as the crime and mystery reviewer. And, most importantly for Chandler, the English establishment seemed to acknowledge his achievement through the unsolicited endorsement of a genuine Man of Letters, J.B. Priestley.

*Time's* review, illustrated with a photograph of the author, ran for six paragraphs. It opens with a defense of Chandler's legitimacy: "To be caught with a Raymond Chandler whodunit in hand is a fate no highbrow reader need dread" ("Murder at the Old Stand," *Time* 3 October 1949: 82-83). It admits that since 1939, Chandler had produced four novels which exceeded the usual level of the genre.

> They had everything a good detective story needs: ingenuity, suspense, pace, credibility. But they had a lot more. Their

> private-eye hero, Philip Marlowe, was just tough enough, just sentimental enough to move like a born natural through the neon-nylon wilderness of a Los Angeles world that the movies never made until Chandler showed them how. Chandler's tense situations mushroomed naturally with almost no trace of fabrication. Best of all, he wrote fresh, crackling prose and it was peppered with minted similes: a face "that fell apart like a bride's piecrust," "old men with faces like lost battles."

The *Time* review praises Chandler's "taut, sound thriller from which plot-and-motive addicts will have their fun" and notes his "exact and vigorous storytelling," but it twice makes the point that more—"something more like a full-blown novel"—is now expected of Raymond Chandler. He must prove himself in non-genre fiction or risk becoming, in the final words of the review, "a gifted hack." Chandler was especially offended by the phrase.

*The Atlantic* had been publishing Chandler's essays on "The Simple Art of Murder" (1944), "Writers in Hollywood" (1945), and "Oscar Night in Hollywood" (1948), but Harvey Breit's three-paragraph response to *The Little Sister* was, at best, diffident.

> Mr. Chandler offers more than the usual whodunit manipulator. Along with solutions, he displays a highly colorful prose, and air of quiet poise, and a number of the best-looking women in America.
>
> ("Reader's Choice," *The Atlantic* October 1949: 81-82)

Breit confesses to belonging to the Edmund Wilson persuasion.

> Mr. Chandler's virtues, from Mr. Wilson's "post of observation," are merely diversions, thrown in to entertain and amuse. They are embellishments; they are not intrinsic elements that transform the genre. Mr. Chandler is skillful, but his characters are still puppets, and Mr. Chandler is still a puppeteer.

This is actually somewhat less generous than Wilson, who did admit that Chandler had the artistic gift for telling stories and that he, unlike all other mystery writers, was "able to invent character and incident and to generate atmosphere," if at a level lower than Graham Greene. Breit also repeats Wilson's connection of Chandler with Hammett, but where Wilson's whole point was that in the matter of fictional art, Chandler did *not* belong to Hammett's school, Breit complacently announces that Chandler "is immensely indebted to Hammett and the whole genre." He closes his review with the recommendation that a good thriller like *The Little Sister* might serve as an "anesthetic" to someone compelled to undergo an operation in a primitive area. For a writer who sought to create a new *esthetic* in a conventional genre, the advice was especially offensive.

Chandler never liked Anthony Boucher, the mystery writer and influential reviewer; he classed him with John Dickson Carr as men who were prejudiced against his kind of fiction and who should, therefore, excuse themselves from reviewing it. In his first review of a Chandler novel, Boucher begins with high praise for Chandler's career to date: he is "the legitimate successor to Dashiell Hammett.

> His new novel, "The little Sister," has been awaited with as much eagerness as Hammett's ten-year-promised novel—especially by those critics and readers who have felt that Hammett and Chandler are significant exponents not merely of the detective story but of the American novel.
>
> (Anthony Boucher. "Chandler, Revalued," *New York Times Book Review* 25 September 1949: 24)

But. . .

> It is partly, of course, this heightened expectation which make "The Little Sister" seem unsatisfactory. But partly, too dissatisfaction comes from the revelation of an abyss of emptiness.

Boucher allows in passing a kind word for Chandler's prose—"still vigorous, clean, distinctive." Then, with some irony in a review entitled "Chandler, Revalued," he raises the issue of Chandler's depraved vision, an issue which Isaac Anderson had raised in the *New York Times Book Review* in 1939, but then allowed to lapse.

> But the great distinction dividing this from all other detective stories is its scathing hatred of the human race. The characters, aside from the little sister, are reasonably well-painted cardboard, brought to life only by the sheer force of their viciousness. An honorable motive, a decent impulse would be as out of place in these pages as a coarse word in the mouth of an Eberhart heroine.

Boucher concludes with a disparagement of Chandler's famous claim that the hard-boiled writers "rescued murder from the vicar's garden and gave it back to the people who are really good at it." Boucher claims that the actresses and gangsters of *The Little Sister* "provide simply the spectacle of a prose writer of high attainments wasting his talents in a pretentious attempt to make bricks without straw—or much clay, either."

The American reviews thus tended to praise what Chandler had done and to deplore that he was still doing it. The English, though they continued to consign him to columns like "Red Herrings," at least did not hesitate to approve the consistency of his excellence. Robert Kee shows both an enthusiasm for what Chandler does, and the inkling of an awareness that it may not, after all, be so unimportant.

> With a whoop of delight we notice that nestling in the middle of our parcel all this time has bee a new Raymond Chandler. We suspend our function as a reviewer and carry him of to a deck-chair to read him in three hours dead. . . Remembering sadly that in a fiction review we are meant to be concerned with "important" literature, we decide to exclude Chandler. But it is difficult to suppress a subversive thought that any man who can so effectively compel one to read his book, even though it is only about an improbable hard-boiled Hollywood where sleeping men sprout ice-picks from the backs of their necks, must have a real literary merit.
> ("Fiction," *The Spectator* 22 July 1949: 122)

The *TLS's* paragraph makes the same moral point as Boucher, but without the puritanical disapproval.

> Toughness is the outstanding characteristic of Philip Marlowe, Mr. Raymond Chandler's private investigator. . . Mr. Chandler handles an involved plot with accomplished dexterity, and his narrative moves briskly along, taking in its stride a bevy of skillfully sketched characters, who are practically without virtues of any kind and who dwell in a half-world of whisky and wisecracks, cynicism and sensuality, film-making and violence.
> ("Running and Walking," *Times Literary Supplement* 19 August 1949: 533)

And Ralph Partridge's brief notice in *The New Statesman* echoes this English tendency toward favorable, but short comments.

> Mr. J.B. Priestley gave a favourable preview to *The Little Sister* in *The New Statesman* earlier this year. The astringent flavour that Mr. Priestley relishes is not quite as uncommon as he supposes among tough Californian thriller-writers. But Raymond Chandler is certainly far ahead of the others in the sophisticated wisecracks with which he punctuates this Hollywood saga of crime, drink, and sex.
> ("Red Herrings," *The New Statesman and Nation* 23 July 1949: 108)

Partridge's reference is to the important paragraph which Priestley had buried near the end of a long, discursive new feature entitled "Letters from Two Islands" which the *New Statesman* had introduced a few months earlier. Between a paragraph on his aversion to international conferences and one on Sydney Smith's recipe for "A Winter Salad," Priestley raises the name of a hard-boiled mystery writer.

> By the way, do you ever read Raymond Chandler? I have just devoured a proof of his last story. He fascinates me, chiefly, I think, because he offers me the unusual and pleasing spectacle of a man trying to turn a cheap, popular formula into something much better. He does it, too. He accepts the familiar pattern of the contemporary thriller (American in origin but now largely and badly imitated here, where it really does not belong), the world of corpses, whiskey for breakfast, and luscious nymphomaniacs, but it illuminates it with a genuine if sour wit and much oblique social criticism. To read him is like cutting into an over-ripe melon and discovering that it has a rare astringent flavour. He reduces the bright Californian scene to an empty despair, dead bottles and a heap of cigarettes under the meaningless neon lights, much more adroitly than Aldous Huxley and the rest can do; and suggests, to my mind, almost better than anybody else the failure of life that is somehow short of a dimension, with everybody either wistfully wondering what is wrong or taking savage shortcuts to nowhere. Not knowing him (for he is since my time as a California visitor), I cannot say if he is conscious of what he is doing, which makes his work all the more fascinating. Try him, and then the hope with me is that he will not soon be lost to us behind a long Hollywood contract; although in this last story he pours acid by the bucket into the studios and agencies.
> ("Letters From Two Islands," *The New Statesman and Nation* 9 April 1949: 350)

Priestley's recognition of Chandler's achievement marked a major advance in his reputation.

## The Simple Art of Murder
1950

*The Simple Art of Murder* collected twelve of Chandler's pulp stories and an essay. It occasioned the only significant critical controversy his work ever inspired in the reviews.

Instead of assigning the collection to Anthony Boucher's "Criminals At Large," the *Times Book Review* gave John Dickson Carr, a master of one of the two major traditions in detective fiction, a full page to consider the merits of the chief exponent of the other major tradition. Carr devotes the first half of his fifteen page review to a rebuttal of the polemical essay, "The Simple Art of Murder." Dismissing it as a "piece of naïveté," Carr ridicules Chandler's assertion that "murder must become realistic." He scores points on the question of what exactly constitutes realism: are the streets and accents of Los Angeles inherently more realistic than those of Surbiton or Bognor Regis?

Carr then proceeds to his major indictment: Chandler's cavalier attitude toward the puzzle element in mystery fiction.

> "The fellow who can write you a vivid and colorful prose," says Mr. Chandler, "simply can't be bothered with the coolie labor of breaking down unbreakable alibis." In plain words, this hypothetical fellow won't work. He can't be bothered to learn craftsmanship, as Poe did and Stevenson did. Aside from the hypothetical, Mr. Chandler has emphasized his own dislike for plot-construction. The realistic method, he says, has freed him from "an exhausting concatenation of insignificant clues,"—raised eyebrows department—and he can now let the characters work out the story for themselves.
> ("With Colt and Luger," *New York Times Book Review* 24 September 1950: 36)

And Carr now can fault what had been hitherto been seen as a virtue: Chandler's face-paced narration.

> Here we see the main weakness in Mr. Chandler's novels. From the first page he goes whooping along at high speed, magnificently if somewhat confusedly, until he reaches the last chapter. There he takes one sweet spill into a net. He thrashes wildly, but he can't get out; he can't explain why his characters acted as they did, and he can't even talk intelligibly. This presumably, is realism.

Carr's charge, just from his perspective, is that Chandler's art is defective in the essential requirement of detective fiction. Carr admits, if with some ambivalence, Chandler's virtues as a stylist ("His similes either succeed brilliantly or fall flat. He can write a scene with an almost suffocating vividness and sense of danger—if he does not add three words too many and make it funny."), but until Chandler adds "the fatigue of construction and clues" to his art, he will not write "a good novel." Carr's point, however, only makes sense when that last phrase is revised to "a good detective novel. Interestingly, Carr exempts Hammett from this criticism; *he* never disdained clues.

Finally Carr considers the stories at hand. "Many are good and two are first-class." The two he prefers are "Pickup on Noon Street" ("a fine study in terror") and, best of all, the burlesque, "Pearls are a Nuisance." He concludes with a phrase of praise ("an admirable collection") and sentence of denigration ("Mr. Chandler will do even better when he discovers that you cannot crate an American language merely by butchering the English language").

Carr's review elicited three refutations from readers in the 5 November issue of the *Times Book Review*. He was unmoved.

> Am I prejudiced? Of course I am: against muddy writing and bad construction. Am I envious? Somehow I think not: few

> architects would envy a house designed by a fellow architect who could not be bothered to put in the doors and the windows.
>
> ("A Reply," *New York Times Book Review* 5 November 1950: 34)

Other reviewers found less to object to in the collection. Charles Rolo reported in *The Atlantic*:

> This 500 pages' worth of Chandler is a choice package of sexy redheads and mean killers, fast gunplay, corpses whichever way you look, and a vernacular which puckers the senses like an electric shock.
>
> ("Reader's Choice," *The Atlantic* November 1950: 102)

And *The New Yorker*, which had found *The Little Sister* "well put together" (1 October 1949: 88), saw "an unavoidable monotony" in the collection, but admitted that Chandler's admirers would take pleasure from the adventures of Marlowe and "several other private detectives, just as tough and chivalrous" ("Mystery and Crime" *The New Yorker* 30 September 1950: 107).

## The Long Goodbye
1954

*The Long Goodbye* posed a challenge to the reviewers. It followed the apparent break-through of *The Little Sister*, and it clearly offered itself as an ambitious attempt to include something new and important within the detective story form. Scholars have, in the decades following, debated its success; many rate it Chandler's best. Contemporary reviewers liked it. Charles Rolo, in *The Atlantic*, likened *The Long Goodbye* to cavier and Chandler's "run-of-the-mill" competition to "salmon's eggs." He cited Somerset Maugham for support, and noted,

> Philip Marlowe has just showed up again in *The Long Goodbye* . . . a little older and more prone to bitter repartee, but still as tough as they come and as rudely chivalrous behind his mask of cynicism. . . .
>
> *The Long Goodbye* has not quite the same sparkle and bounce as Chandler's early novels, not quite the same profusion of similes that pucker the senses like an electric shock. But the somewhat quieter plotting makes for a more thoughtful tone, a deeper cut. I think that Mr. Chandler's fans get their money's worth.
>
> (Charles Rolo, "Reader's Choice," *The Atlantic* May 1954: 82-83)

> Usual excellent job by classic performer; perhaps his best. An old master.
>
> ("Sergeant Cuff," "Summing Up" and "Verdict," *Saturday Review of Literature* 24 April 1954: 37)

*Time* reviewed *The Long Goodbye* jointly with Ian Fleming's first novel, *Casino Royale*, and had kind words for both.

> Good writing is a mystery to most mystery writers. But the border line between a good mystery and a good novel is occasionally crossed, and two new yarns get well over the border.
>
> ("Murder Is Their Business," *Time* 29 March 1954" 98)

This border line was a crucial one for Chandler, but *Time* failed to define it. It contrasts the "rather mellow and gentlemanly" Marlowe with Mickey Spillane's "neo-Neanderthal" Mike Hammer, offers a few comments on plot and style ("Chandler still brings some of his sentences to a halt with the too-arresting simile or metaphor"), and concludes: "Chandler's world has a rasping authenticity, from its lingo to its lingerie."

Anthony Boucher recalled his disappointment with *The Little Sister*, but now declares himself "more than assuage[d]" by *The Long Goodbye*. Part of his relief may be due to his observation that Chandler has shifted his focus from the world of professional criminals to that of the upper middle class. Boucher concludes with a gratifying tribute.

> On the whole, despite occasional outbursts of violence, it's a moody, brooding book, in with Marlowe is less a detective than a disturbed man of 42 on a quest for some evidence of truth and humanity. The dialogue is as vividly overheard as ever, the plot is clearly constructed and surprisingly resolved, and the book is rich in many sharp glimpses of minor characters and scenes. Perhaps the longest private-eye novel ever written (over 125,000 words!), it is also one of the best—and may well attract readers who normally shun even the leaders in the field.
>
> ("Criminals at Large," *New York Times Book Review* 25 April 1954: 27)

The dissenting voice in this chorus of praise for the old master came from the imperceptive *New Yorker*, whose lukewarm endorsements now turned chill.

> In this long book (316 pages), Mr. Chandler has practically abandoned anything resembling a coherent plot to devote himself to an exhaustive study of manners and morals in California, the status of both of which appears to be grotesque. . . . The author's mannerisms have seldom been more pro-

> nounced; the story, which has to do with nymphomania in exalted circles as much as anything else, hardly seems worth all the bother.
> ("Mystery and Crime," *The New Yorker* 27 March 1954: 35)

The English reviews continued their habit of offering discerning praise in generic reviews. Ralph Partridge considered *The Long Goodbye* in a column covering eight mystery writers.

> Mr. Chandler's style by now can be regarded as fixed: he has published no new work for the last four years, but *The Long Good-Bye* shows that nothing has happened in the interim to modify his evangelical outlook on life. Here comes Philip Marlowe again, crusading along the Californian coast against venal cops, corrupt politicians, ugly gangsters, and self-indulgent women, in fact the entire mammon of unrighteousness. . . . And all the reward Marlowe ever receives for his services is an occasional drink, an occasional woman, a succession of physical injuries, and an addition to his embittered memories. He is a very remarkable creation: the perpetually crucified redeemer of all our modern sins. In *The Long Good-Bye* there is one jarring note of sentimentality; but Mr. Chandler's language has lost none of its impetus, the rhythm of his prose is superb, and the intensity of feeling he packs into his pages makes every other thriller-writer look utterly silly and superficial.
> ("Detection and Thrillers," *The New Statesman and Nation* 9 January 1954: 47-48)

The *TLS* discussed *The Long Goodbye* in conjunction with two other novels (by Georgette Heyer and Ian Stuart Black). It allotted Chandler more than half the review, but still could not justify awarding it separate treatment. The judgment is highly favorable.

> Mr. Chandler's new novel is cast in much the same shape as its predecessors. Philip Marlowe, the private detective, tells the story, the scene is set in southern California and the familiar police officers, gangsters and lovely ladies make their usual impressive appearances. People continue to be horribly rude to each other and the style is still enlivened with brief and pungent similes. Still superficially disillusioned, Marlowe is as altruistic as ever . . . . Once more he finds himself pitting his wits, his toughness and his rueful integrity against the old conspiracy of wealth and authority; police, racketeers, lawyers and rich folk try to silence and confuse him, but he solves his problem, and though justice is not seen to be done he has stood up for the truth and triumphed.
>
> In early middle age now, Marlowe tends to reflect more frequently on the predicament of society, and his vision is sombre and violent as he thinks of the incessant evil and suffering

> of the big city. Wealth, as always, fascinates him, and he measures its dire effects on those who are possessed by it. . . . Marlowe is a connoisseur of men and women, a serious and involved student of moral fibre, in his own laconic and elliptical fashion, and there are one or two studies of weakness in the present book which should command respect.
>
> ("Mild and Bitter" *Times Literary Supplement* 1 January 1954: 5)

The only qualification that the reviewer adds concerns the improbabilities which Chandler's story-telling sometimes conceals. He concludes that "the illusion is still strong and the old mixture of realism and convention has lost little of its potency."

## Trouble Is My Business
1957

Anthony Boucher announced the republication of "four classic Raymond Chandler novelettes," and described them as representing "the school of hard-boiled detection at its best" ("Criminals At Large," *New York Times Book Review* 8 September 1957: 10).

## Playback
1958

*Playback* was Chandler's final novel. It has been almost universally regarded as his weakest. The contemporary reviews were, if anything, rather kind. Most softened their disappointment with references to Chandler's past glories.

> I missed . . . in *Playback* the climate of malevolence and danger, the exotic characterizations, the driving pace and imaginative mayhem that made Chandler's earlier books masterpieces of that kind. And the language . . . isn't as electrifying as it used to be. But even though Chandler is nowhere near the top of his form, *Playback* is certainly several cuts above the run-of-the-mill thriller.
>
> (Charles Rolo, "Reader's Choice," *The Atlantic* November 1958: 176-77)

> Raymond Chandler is by now in the uncomfortable position of an acknowledged Old Master who writes very little, so that each book he does produce is bound to be subjected to unusually close scrutiny. And these circumstances are, I fear, unfortunate for *Playback*. . . .
>
> This is Mr. Chandler's seventh, shortest and slightest novel . . . . It's all smooth, competent, enjoyable and undistinguished. A

dozen of Chandler's imitators can do as well, and two or three consistently do better. If Chandler produced books at the rate of Erle Stanley Gardner, this would seem satisfactory enough; but after a wait of four and a half years it's a mousy labor from such a mountain.

(Anthony Boucher, "Criminals at Large," *New York Times Book Review* 16 November 1958: 53)

The English reviewers again placed Chandler in his genre and then remarked on his superiority to it. Simon Raven was perhaps excessively generous.

> *Playback* is worthy Chandler—beds, bullets, and Spartan jokes: beds strictly for loving, bullets strictly for killing, and Spartan jokes to beguile the very few sterile minutes in which neither tumescence nor entombment is immediately in prospect.
>
> ("Moravia Deserta," *The Spectator* 11 July 1958: 67)

Ralph Partridge was equally kind.

> Mr. Chandler's plots may drift up one picaresque side-alley after another, like a dog looking for a lamp-post (in *Playback* his detective even forgets what he is supposed to be detecting); but that stately stride of his cuts down the sub-Chandlers tagging behind him before they ever turn into the straight: his style is stupendous and shows no sign of flagging. *Playback* should be greeted as just another variation on the theme of Marlowe's manliness.
>
> (Ralph Partridge, "Detection and Thrillers" *The New Statesman and Nation* 30 August 1958: 254)

The *TLS* reported that Chandler was no longer "playing in the big leagues" (as he had in *The Big Sleep* and *Farewell, My Lovely*). But *Playback* offered some excellent minor league action.

> Marlowe's perceptions are still acute. His thinking is intuitive, his honesty impeccable as ever. But he is more concerned with the sheer technique of his trade—eavesdropping with a stethoscope, using a tire-lever to break a gunman's wrist. His cynicism no longer has the flavour of piercing regret, and middle age has made him capable of corny sentiment. . . .
>
> Californian life still offers its macabre ironies. . . . Marlowe has kept his mannerisms, but he has moved with the times. The tension and symbolism of the great early Chandlers may not be so much in evidence in *Playback*, but still this is a good book.
>
> ("Death Comes As the End," *Times Literary Supplement* 11 July 1958: 395)

The fullest discussion of the novel came from W.L. Webb in the *Manchester Guardian*. Webb rebuts John Dickson Carr's denigration of Chandler's "realism": "Chandler's brilliantly suggestive reporting of the seedy side of California made Marlowe's corner of the world far more real than the conventional Oxbridge and Barsetshire settings." He almost reverses Edmund Wilson's judgment that Chandler was to be credited with a talent just below that of Graham Greene. Webb declares

> In his hey-day the only English thriller-writer who could touch his [Chandler's] level was Graham Greene; and Chandler, being a full-time, professional entertainer and a mite less artistically ambitious, was always easier to read.
> ("Keeping up with the Bonds," *Manchester Guardian* 11 July 1958: 6)

Chandler has been, Webb affirms, "the undisputed, much imitated and inimitable head of his profession."

But like the American reviewers, Webb has to admit that the latest novel is disappointing. "I have to report, with deep regret, that the new Chandler, *Playback* . . . shows symptoms of a series decline." The plot is, even for Chandler, careless and rambling; there are no memorable minor characters, and, "sadder still," *Playback* is marred by "a disproportionately large shot of casual sex"; Marlowe is in danger of becoming "a dirty old man." Webb attributes the introduction of gratuitous sex to the competition posed by the Bond novels; whatever its source, the alteration in Marlowe's sexual habits in *Playback* has drawn continued attention from critics.

## Killer in the Rain
1964

This final collection of stories reprinted those which Chandler refused permission to reprint in his lifetime. They are the "cannibalized" stories which he had used to construct three of his novels (*The Big Sleep*, *Farewell, My Lovely*, and *Lady in the Lake*). Anthony Boucher commended the posthumous decision to publish them because, he said, they "are not merely fascinating footnotes to the study of professional creativity; they are in themselves excellent and occasionally even (though I can feel Chandler's argumentative ghost beside me as I write) better than the later product—tighter and more simple in construction, and more direct in prose, relatively free from the occasionally strained phrase-making of the novels" ("Criminals At Large," *New York Times Book Review* 20 September 1964: 28).

# A Cato of the Cruelties

## *R. W. Flint*

Raymond Chandler has, in the past, written for the *Atlantic* on the ethics of Hollywood, just as the late Wendell Wilkie once wrote on ethics in general for *The American Scholar*. There has been enough respectability in the wares of these two successful specialists in the American ethos to suit the upper-middlebrow market, and enough authenticity in their attitudes to cover the objections of litterateurs.

Philip Marlowe, private dick, is our myth, the closest thing to flesh and blood that Hollywood has recently seen fit to apotheosize. Who, then, is this Marlowe and what is his mighty line? To be solemn first, Philip Marlowe is as much of the existentialist hero as modern America has stomach for. We've become used to the French version, but the term, like pragmatism, means a *way* of philosophizing rather than a body of doctrine. It's a fruitful term, and we should try to salvage it from the purely cultic interpretation that is threatening, though fear more than anything else, to discredit its legitimate use. Marlowe is the American middle-class Existentialist, the People's Existentialist, you might say, insofar as his function cuts across class lines. The marks of his integrity are a searing doubt as to the motives of his fellow countrymen—popularized by Bogart with literary antecedents in Lardner and many others—and a profound awareness of fate. But the red badge that sets him apart is an almost Biblical faith in the value of decision. He is forever rolling the stone uphill—a little too sentimental and self-pitying for a true Stoic, but an existentialist nonetheless. Whatever the alternatives, Marlowe acts and acts alone: his life is all decision—a blind inevitable moral energy plowing through the wildest ambiguities always into the heart of insecurity and danger.

Marlowe's world is the laissez-faire liberal world turned inside-out—a jungle of predatory creatures making amusing patterns out of their guilt and boredom, and desperately lonely. On the surface, nothing happens for obvious reasons. If external amiability isn't faked, it's at least better to assume so until told otherwise. Under-

"A Cato of the Cruelties," *Partisan Review* 14 (1947): 328-30.

neath this casual cruelty—the convention set by Cain, Hammett, et al.—move the tides of human destiny and decision, as crude as the surface is intricate and ambiguous.

The Marlowe epics screen better than they read, and I suspect it's because Chandler strains too much in the books to be arty, although he is often brilliantly successful in patches. His conventions admirably suit the movies where the camera, if it's alert, establishes the proper sense of desolation—that miasmic, Dantesque background of California roadways, police stations, office buildings, and fake interiors in which Chandler specializes.

We have come a long way from Holmes to here. The plot is complex and we are still thrown a few clues from time to time, but suspense grows now out of a human rather than a literary situation; it is continuous rather than cumulative, like life in a Camus novel or in modern "crisis" theology. Our hero is no longer the wizard, the mental giant, the latter-day Paracelsus: he is not even the intellectual master of the situation. Where Holmes needed all the glamor he could muster to make Victorian respectability seem worth an elaborate defense, Marlowe lives by the light of his sentimental but genuine humanity: he's the fall-guy, *der reine Narr*, Parisfal-Cassandra whom nobody believes because he has no aces up his sleeve.

In another of his functions, that of father-confessor, he departs radically from the fiction detective tradition. His goodness is obvious enough to become a catalyst in a corrupt society—the great strength that is intended to compensate for his lack of subtlety and the conventional insouciance. Everyone confesses his basic sickness as well as his immediate troubles to Marlowe. In the current Chandler film, *Lady in the Lake*, for example, the weak capitalist, in Marlowe's healing presence, is strong enough to throw over his vicious secretary and confess his loneliness; the crooked cop can't look at Marlowe without a self-revealing yen to "work him over": the old people confess their utter exhaustion and fear; the slick playboy knocks Marlowe cold for telling the truth, but is soon recompensed by being shot full of holes in his shower by a former sin; and finally, we have the vicious secretary herself, still the superb, capable American Girl who we have come to know so well from the tradition that starts, perhaps, in Henry James and enters the crime milieu in Nora of *The Thin Man*, but is omnipresent in such creatures as the wooden young lady in *All the King's Men*, and Isabel Bolton's final hypostatization as the "European" paragon of *Do I Wake or Sleep*. The Girl is Marlowe's greatest challenge and his greatest conquest; to her, like Hamlet to his mother, Marlowe "must be cruel, only to be kind"—the therapy of harshness which Marx also prescribes for our bourgeois ills.

A comparison of Marlowe's state of mind and that of the follower of Marx would be suggestive. Both have the attitude of a Jewish prophet toward a bad world: both are proximately tough to counter a degenerate laissez-faire that has learned to use sham-morality brilliantly, but both are ultimately tender and apocalyptic. I don't claim to find any political sophistication in Chandler: I merely suggest the implications of his theory of man, which he would doubtless deny. Leftism in general, insofar as it has popular attributes in America, seems to have settled temporarily on the *PM* level of pervasive general "concerns" mixed with a folksy, sexy assertion of man's finiteness and dependence on nature. It's a mixture too usually dismissed by the exacerbated intellectual who, however, welcomes the image of Marlowe as a sign of "vitality" in the movies.

# Philip Marlowe Speaking

*R. W. Lid*

"You know something, Marlowe? I could get to like you. You're a bit of a bastard—like me."—*The Long Goodbye*

Raymond Chandler wrote about Los Angeles during its period of kooky architecture. Chateaus and villa and castles, all redolent of other lands, dominated the lush hillsides of Beverly Hills and Bel Air. Down below, in Hollywood, could be found the gingerbread counterpart to this not quite real world of the very rich and the very exclusive—restaurants, drive-ins, commercial buildings, even conservative establishments like banks which took on the shapes of stuffed animals and items of headdress, or of recognizable physical objects, or bore broad resemblance to sugar-frosted palaces of desert sheiks. The casual observer of this sun-drenched land, faced with the imagination gone rampant, might wonder if perhaps it would all suddenly disappear in a cataclysm, or somehow turn back into a pumpkin; but Raymond Chandler was an intimate of the scene, and he mapped its contours, including the grandeur of its physical landscape, backed by mountains and edged by the Pacific Ocean, with an eye for detail equalled only by Ernest Hemingway. Chandler was extraordinary cultural historian, and, while time and circumstance have somewhat lessened the immediacy of his Los Angeles of the'30s and'40s, they have not rendered it obsolete.

It was the period when Fred Allen cracked that Southern California was a fine place to live—if you were an orange. Los Angeles was by and large a cultural desert situated in an oasis. Religious faddists and health cultists were common, and dreams of all kinds seemingly came true: the obscure car-hop in a drive-in might, next week, be a starlet posing for publicity stills at Warner Bros. Or so legend had it. Hollywood itself was the land of perpetual youth, of

"Philip Marlowe Speaking." *Kenyon Review* 31 (1977): 153-78.

ever-hopefuls, and also of wistful, aging Ponce de Leons. To be an "extra" was to be precisely that, a supernumerary waiting for a bit role in life from the casting office. Chandler's fiction overwhelmingly captures the sense of missed opportunity, the lost chance, the closed door. At some remove from the events of his fiction, he obviously felt these things himself, including a sense of personal wreckage.

It was Chandler's seriousness which set him, like Dashiell Hammett, apart from the *Black Mask* school of hard-boiled writers out of which they emerged. The extraordinary colloquial quality of Chandler's prose was an aspect of this seriousness; it made available the expression of his vision. Chandler's sun-bleached landscape, for all the Hollywood glitter, is in part a fallen paradise, a Garden of Eden after the serpent has done his work.

As Chandler so often reminds us, his demiparadise is a land of drifters, grafters, and minor hoodlums; of lone women on the make or on the downhill; of sad drunks and mean drunks, and just drunks: people with better days behind them. In this world cops, as often as not, are crooked, politicians corrupt, and businessmen walk the narrow line between legitimate and illegitimate enterprise. "There ain't no clean way to make a hundred million bucks," says Bernie Ohls, a tough and honest cop, to Philip Marlowe, Chandler's private detective, in *The Long Goodbye*. Some 60 pages later, in the same novel, Chandler's private detective says to Ohls: "We're a big rough rich wild people and crime is the price we pay for it, and organized crime is the price we pay for organization. We'll have it with us a long time. Organized crime is just the dirty side of the sharp dollar." In both instances the voice speaking is the thinly disguised voice of the author. It is almost as if Chandler, making his own goodbye in his last serious novel, wanted to state directly what the plots of his earlier novels had failed fully to convey. For it was part of Chandler's originality that he saw the American psyche as criminally obsessed with the dollar, and perhaps without being fully aware of it, society itself as criminal. In the end Chandler's romantic sensibility recoiled from the vision of evil which his art insisted upon.

Something of the same sense of a lost paradise which haunts the last page of *The Great Gatsby* pervades Chandler's Pacific Eden. I have in mind Nick Carraway's evocation of "the fresh, green breast of the new world" and his vision of its trees, which "had once pandered in whispers to the last and greatest of all human dreams." Chandler similarly poses through the juxtaposition of landscape and people the imaginative possibilities of the American continent, and also suggests some reasons for the failure to realize them. But unlike Fitzgerald in *Gatsby*, Chandler in his fiction was mainly concerned with the aftermath of the dream, the fallen state of the world after the dream has not merely become tawdry and tarnished but exists only as a debased passion.

Chandler's Marlowe drives north, out of Los Angeles, on the inland route some forty miles. It's a bad night for him. He is in a sardonic mood, commenting on the scene before him. He eats dinner in a restaurant. ("Bad but quick. Feed'em and throw'em out. Lots of business. We can't bother with you sitting over your second cup of coffee, mister. You're using money space.") Then he stops in a bar for a brandy and comes out to drive home. ("I stepped out into the night air that nobody had yet found out how to option. But a lot of people were probably trying. They'd get around to it.") He turns toward the ocean and the coastal route back to Los Angeles.

> The big eight-wheelers and sixteen-wheelers were streaming north, all hung over with orange lights. On the right the great fat solid Pacific trudging into shore like a scrubwoman going home. No moon, no fuss, hardly a sound of surf. No smell. None of the harsh wild smell of the sea. A California ocean. California, the department-store state. The most of everything and best of nothing. Here we go again. You're not human tonight, Marlowe.
>
> Malibu. More movie stars. More pink and blue bathtubs. More tufted beds. More Chanel No. 5. More Lincoln Continentals and Cadillacs. More wind-blown hair and sunglasses and attitudes and pseudo-refined voices and waterfront morals. Now, wait a minute. Lots of nice people work in pictures. You've got the wrong attitude, Marlowe. You're not human tonight.
>
> I smelled Los Angeles before I got to it. It smelled stale and old like a living room that had been closed too long. But the colored lights fooled you. The lights were wonderful. There ought to be a monument to the man who invented neon lights. Fifteen stories high, solid marble. There's a boy who really made something out of nothing.
>
> (*The Little Sister*)

Landscape in Chandler directly reflects the half-insubstantial quality of American life—the sense of people exploiting things to make their lives real and meaningful: to be better people than they are. But the ground bass is always there. It is themselves they have exploited in their search for the equivalents of class and station, position, genealogy, tradition.

Chandler was a master at portraying the schizoid aspects of American culture and the ways in which the base and ideal and their manifestations are so closely intertwined as to be inseparable, if not indistinguishable. The lives of his characters reveal this split in motive and intention and conduct, just as the patterns of his novels reveal the cohesiveness of American life which underlies and makes a whole of this self-perpetuating opposition.

Marlowe crosses and crisscrosses the landscape of greater Los Angeles, which provides almost infinite variety of background, moving from terrain to terrain, locale to locale, setting to setting. Chandler bears down so heavily on landscape in his novels that physical property almost takes on a value and meaning of its own; one is reminded of the motion pictures and the way in which the camera invests physical props with significance by panning back and forth over them, by lingering with them. But, while the vastly different places Chandler's Marlowe visits, and the people he encounters, are seemingly held together by a thread of meaning solely of Marlowe's making, a pattern gradually emerges, a meaningful arrangement and sequence of events; and behind the pattern lies, broadly speaking, the pattern of American society as Chandler sees it: mobile, fluid, a reticulated crisscrossing of people through time and circumstance. One begins to see why, in Chandler's fiction, the world of Los Angeles' Bunker Hill, with its decayed buildings and decaying people, is just a stone's throw away from the deep lawns and private driveways and stately mansions of Santa Monica: why, in other words, all segments of society are inextricably linked in Chandler's sun-filled but nightmarish landscape.

In *Farewell, My Lovely,* Marlowe tried to help the police find Moose Malloy, an ex-con who had negligently killed a man in Marlowe's presence. Malloy was bent on finding "little Velma," once a singer in a dance hall which changed hands and clientele some eight years earlier. Because Velma may lead to Malloy, Marlowe looks for clues to her whereabouts. He begins by locating the deceased dance hall owner's wife, Jessie Florian:

> 1644 West 54th Place was a dried-out brown house with a dried-out brown lawn in front of it. There was a large bare patch around a tough-looking palm tree. On the porch stood one lonely wooden rocker, and the afternoon breeze made the unpruned shoots of last year's poinsettias tap-tap against the cracked stucco wall. A line of stiff yellowish half-washed clothes jittered on a rusty wire in the side yard.

The woman he meets inside will be just as burnt out, an alcoholic with a face gray and puffy, dressed in "a shapeless flannel bathrobe many moons past color and design." Eventually, Marlowe will connect Mrs. Florian with Lindsay Marriott, who later the same day hires him to act as a bodyguard in a transaction involving the buying back of a stolen jade necklace. The worlds of the drunken Jessie Florian and Marriott, who lives off rich women, are vastly different. He lives in a house overlooking the Pacific, with carpeting in the living room so thick it almost tickles Marlowe's ankles when he goes to see him. "It was the kind of room where people sit with their feet in their laps and sip absinthe through lumps of sugar." Jessie Florian and Marriott become linked when Marlowe learns that Marriott not only put up the money to refinance Mrs. Florian's home but also sends her monthly check, supposedly because she was once a servant in his family. They also become linked in death. First Marriott, then Mrs. Florian, is murdered. But only near the end of the novel does Marlowe connect them both to Velma.

In the course of *Farewell, My Lovely*, Marlowe is led by events to Aster Drive, where there are "great silent estates, with twelve-foot walls and wrought iron gates and ornamental hedges; and inside, if you could get inside, a special brand of sunshine, very quiet, put up in noise-proof containers just for the upper classes." Here, without realizing it at first, he finds Moose Malloy's "little Velma" in the person of Helen Grayle, the wife of a millionaire. Marlowe has gone to Aster Drive because Mrs. Grayle possessed the jade necklace which Marriott was supposedly redeeming when he was killed. Hence Marlowe's discovery of the identify of Velma is far from direct, almost accidental in one sense, and involved people who seemingly have no relation to each other until Marlowe, digging into the past and beneath the surface of events, demonstrates those relations.

In his best novels Chandler gave a high gloss of reality to these intricate alignments of people and events. In most he kept the artificiality of the form at bay. In one or two he lost control, for reasons too various to concern us here. But, in general, it could be fairly said that Chandler extended the form by making available to writers who came after him a more complex understanding of the fabric of society and a more serious and sensitive view of its dynamics. This is no small achievement in itself.

Along with Hammett, Chandler gave the detective story back its inherent realism. But he also added a personal dimension to the form—and here Marlowe played a less traditional role than the one described above, in which his function was to search out and make visible the links between people and events and reveal the developing pattern of significance.

Chandler once said that "Marlowe just grew out of the pulps. He was no one person." In the sense in which he meant it, his statement is true enough. Marlowe (who was to have been called Mallory, perhaps in Chandler's mind a link with the author of *Morte D' Arthur*; the name involvement would be in keeping with Chandler's intense literary sense) had his antecedents in the various heroes of Chandler's *Black Mask* stories. Significantly enough, he appeared under his own name at just the time Chandler turned from shorter fiction to the novel. In part Marlowe seems to have made possible this shift to the longer form, as he did the emergence of a highly personal voice, one that seemed to speak directly to readers everywhere in the authentic rhythms of American speech. Precisely how Marlowe made these developments possible for his British-educated author is a somewhat complex matter, as is the whole question of Chandler's relationship with his narrator-hero and its meaning for his art.

Like some other famous detective-heroes, including Poe's Dupin and Conan Doyle's Sherlock Holmes, Marlowe is to a certain extent an obvious projection of his author. Chandler gave Marlowe his own wit. He gave him an education which allowed Marlowe to make use of Chandler's own, which was classical and literary. He imbued him with his own romanticism. "I'm a romantic," Marlowe says. "I hear voices crying in the night and I go see what's the matter. You don't make a dime that way. You got sense, you shut your windows and turn up more sound on the TV set." Marlowe's self-derision is intended by his author to redound to his credit, and to the belie the sentimentalism in his voice. There is also irony here, at least for the author, in the fact that as a private detective Marlowe has no status, no authority, no assured place in society. Like his author, Marlowe as detective is an idealist hiding behind cynicism and wise talk, and, while he never fully articulates his reason for remaining a private detective, his actions suggest some, as his author intended. Basically they are old-fashioned reasons, for Marlowe in certain ways is, like his author, an old-fashioned sort of person. He is Chandler's knight, righting the balance in a wronged and fallen universe. He corrects injustices, stands up for the underdog, speaks out for the little guy. As Chandler put it in "The Simple Art of Murder," "Down these mean streets a man must go who is not himself mean, who is neither tarnished nor afraid. . . . He is the hero; he is everything." Marlowe as a projection of Chandler's romantic ego satisfied some imaginative need of his sedentary author directly to intervene in the violence of the world, to propitiate and ameliorate those brute aspects of life which his hurt sensibility found it difficult to accept. But, as Chandler's knight said in *The Big Sleep*, looking down at a wrong move he had made in a chess game, "knights had no meaning in this game. It wasn't a game for knights."

Marlowe is the wholly honest man, a saint in a world of sinners. For all his wisecracking and whiskey drinking, he has a rather narrow and somewhat puritanical code. He is loyal to his clients, hard-working, more interested in justice than in his fee, impervious to bribery, or a roughing-up by police or hoodlums. He takes the threats against his life as they come. He is impossible to impress; he sees through sham and hypocrisy. He is also a bit too good to be true—and Chandler understood this limitation, particularly in his later years, when his relationship with his hero underwent a subtle transformation. But this is the Marlowe we remember from Chandler's fiction. We are apt to overlook the other Marlowe, a sadder, wiser Marlowe, a lonelier man than his earlier self, who lived alone and seemed to like it.

This other Marlowe is not a new figure on the scene. He represents a deepening of those aspects of his author's personality which were held in check by dint of will and by the very art which Marlowe made possible. The appearance of this disenchanted

Marlowe late in Chandler's writing career suggests that from the first Marlowe's presence in Chandler's fiction involved a more serious displacement of personality than his identity as mere fictional alter ego would imply.

No matter how closely Chandler on occasion identified with his hero in fiction, there are ways of telling them apart, and these have significance for Chandler's art. Marlowe was a native Californian, Chandler wasn't. In fact Chandler was a native American solely in the legal sense. He was born in Chicago in 1888. But then, while he was a child, his mother returned to England, and he grew up there, attending an established public school. It was not until 1912 that he arrived in California. He brought with him, as he put it, a beautiful wardrobe and a public school accent.

But while Chandler's wasn't a native American voice, Philip Marlowe's invented voice is. Commenting on the significance for his art of his British childhood in a letter published in the posthumous collection, *Raymond Chandler Speaking*, he said: "I had to learn American just like a foreign language. To learn it I had to study and analyze it. As a result, when I use slang, colloquialisms, snide talk or any kind of off-beat language I do it deliberately." In Chandler's hands the American language became racy and direct, occasionally colorful, always fast-paced. It was the language of the wisecrack and the sharp comeback. It had thought content without being muscle-bound by the formulas of language. It leveled people, took the stuffing out of them. It acted as a liberating force and gave Marlowe freedom of action to cross class and social barriers. Ultimately it was a means of dealing with the democratic experience, with American classlessness and rootlessness. The American language was Marlowe's invisible armor.

It is remarkable that Chandler's studied American-ness produced an authentic American voice; yet something like this happened. Confronted with his own feelings of deracination, with the sense of being caught between cultures, Chandler saw the potentialities of the American language from the multiple perspective of both outsider and insider. Elsewhere in his letters he reminds us of his alien-ness. As a young man he lived briefly in Paris. There he met a good many Americans. "Most of them seemed to have a lot of bounce and liveliness and to be thoroughly enjoying themselves in situations where the average Englishman of the same class would be stuffy or completely bored. But I wasn't one of them. I didn't even speak their language. I was, in effect, a man without a country." Chandler's sense of rootlessness followed him through his entire life. Perhaps it accounts for the way he made the loneliness of life in big city America one of his major themes. So insistent was this overmastering feeling that it hung on right through *The Long Goodbye*, in which Chandler tried to lay the ghost of his British self.

Chandler's alien voice can be heard quite clearly in the volume *Raymond Chandler Speaking*, particularly in his letters to his English publisher, Hamish Hamilton, and to Charles W. Morton, an editor for the *Atlantic Monthly*. Often he sounds like an exile from John Bull's island. He raises the old school tie, he adopts a somewhat patrician attitude toward writing, insisting on his amateur status. ("The English writer is a gentleman first and a writer second," he remarked in his "Notes on English and American Style," pointing to what he considered to be one of the defects of English style.) It is almost incredible to find him writing, in 1949: "I'm still an amateur, still, psychologically speaking, perfectly capable of chucking writing altogether and taking up the study of law or comparative philology." At this point in his career Chandler, who was sixty years old, had published his major fiction: *The Big Sleep* (1939), *Farewell, My Lovely* (1940), *The High Window* (1942), and *Lady in the Lake* (1943); in 1949 he published *The Little Sister*, which suggested a falling-off of his talent. Only *The Long Goodbye* remained to be written. (*Playback*, published after *The Long Goodbye*, had already been written as a screenplay in 1947. It was never produced and Chandler later turned it into a book. Properly speaking, it is not part of the Chandler canon.)

It is hard at times to estimate the sincerity of the Chandler of the letters, for one thing because, without being a poseur, he is obviously posing to a certain extent. This Chandler is bent on justifying his career and propagating his reputation. And underneath, much of the time, he is feeling sorry for himself. He unjustly arraigns other writers. He makes mock modest comparisons between his achievements and those of others, denying that he is in their class as a writer but implying all the while that he is every bit their equal or better. He is seemingly humble while really prideful, his ironic sense of self dominating his feeling: "What greater prestige can a man like me (not too greatly gifted, but very understanding) have than to have taken a cheap, shoddy, and utterly lost kind of writing, and have made of it something that intellectuals claw each other about?" He is also neglecting Hammett, whose earlier achievement might be described in precisely the same terms.

He will knock the intellectuals, while being one himself. He harbors petty grievances. He sees himself in most situations as wronged. He is contentious. He indulges himself by answering letters from readers in which he argues in detail the personal habits of Marlowe, momentarily turning him into a real person. There is a certain self-laceration here, because he knows the reader is interested in Marlowe, not Chandler. And all the while, it strikes one, Chandler is strangely disaffected with Marlowe; or perhaps he is merely aware that in Marlowe he created a man more admirable than himself, forgetful that without Raymond Chandler there would be no Marlowe. In any case, he envisions Cary Grant as the movie actor who could best portray Marlowe as he conceives of him—a transplanted Englishman with inherently nice manners. One can't help but feel that Marlowe would be amused by this identification; but, I think, he would also find it revealing of his author, and in keeping with his character.

The Raymond Chandler of these letters, which were written mainly during his sixties, is a man under considerable personal and psychological stress. He is preoccupied with himself in ways that are somewhat touching, and also pathetic. He shows a certain helplessness. He suffers mild paranoia. And he reveals, without intending to, something of the transformation of character, the rearrangement of personal experience, which went on in the creation of his fiction, as well as the role Marlowe played in this transmutation.

Essentially Marlowe released in Chandler a vein of self-criticism and self-knowledge. He tapped the secret resources, the reserves of his author's personality, those hidden forces which drove him to fiction, and made them available to the fiction writer as they weren't to the letter writer. All of Chandler's hostile emotions, his loneliness, his self-pity, which he never fully mastered, were transformed in fictional creations which not only bore a striking resemblance to the real world but revealed memorable truths about the world.

Marlowe gave Chandler someone to talk to, as well as speak through, so that the speaking voice we hear in Chandler's fiction is not an alien voice but that of a man purified in the fire of the human inferno.

In his book on Chandler, *Down These Mean Streets a Man Must Go*, Philip Durham accurately enough describes Chandler's art in terms of the "objective" tradition in fiction, though he unnecessarily limits the perspective of the author to the eyes of his first-person narrator:

> Theoretically, at least, the author tells us nothing; the only person in the novel from whom we can learn anything is Marlowe. If we receive knowledge of any other character it is only if and when Marlowe wants us to have it. What we know about Los Angeles is what Marlowe tells us or allows others to tell us. The detached author is not on the stage, and we are not even sure he is in the wings. The burden is always on the author never to let us know how he feels, never to give us any "dear reader" asides, and never to tell us how his characters feel; the characters must tell us everything we know about them by their own actions and expressions.

Durham's lengthy statement belabors the obvious point about the restrictions of point of view, while ignoring the equally obvious through more subtle point that all objectivity in fiction depends on a carefully preserved authorial attitude. The author is hidden from view—but he is also just around the corner; his felt presence in his work is not limited. It is dangerously misleading, in Chandler's case, to say that "we are not even sure" the detached author is "in the wings. The burden is always on the author never to let us know how he feels. . . ."

Chandler's novels are all written in the first person, with Marlowe as narrator; but Marlowe's voice, as I have tried to suggest, is not the only voice we hear in Chandler's fiction. Behind Marlowe stands the author, and sometimes we are aware of his subtle intrusion upon the seemingly objective account events as offered us by his narrator-detective. An instance in point is chapter thirty-one of *Farewell, My Lovely*. The scene is a Los Angeles homicide bureau where Marlowe has gone to make a statement concerning the murder of Jessie Florian. Marlowe has only recently become aware of her connection with Lindsay Marriott, and this and other matters surrounding their deaths from the substance of the conversation between Marlowe and the homicide detective.

The chapter opens in the following manner, with the voice seemingly belonging to Marlowe, who at first sight merely appears to be setting the scene for the interview to follow between himself and Randall:

> A shiny black bag with a pink head and pink spots on it crawled slowly along the polished top of Randall's desk and waved a couple of feelers around, as if testing the breeze for a takeoff. It wobbled a little as it crawled, like an old woman carrying too many parcels. A nameless dick sat at another desk and kept talking into an old-fashioned hushaphone mouthpiece, so that his voice sounded like someone whispering in a tunnel. He talked with his eyes half closed, a big scarred hand on the desk in front of him holding a burning cigarette between the knuckles of the first and second fingers.

By the end of this paragraph, if not before, the reader is aware that more is going on here than the mere description of a homicide office at police headquarters. For one thing, the matter of the paragraph—the pink and black bug making its way across Randall's desk, the detective sitting at the other desk—has been arranged less as a sequence of fact that as two juxtaposed images (reinforced by parallel grammatical structures) which, taken together, provide commentary not only on the law in our society but also on the individual, particularly the individual before the law. This is more obvious than it may at first appear, for midway through the passage occurs the arresting image by which the insignificant bug in its progress across the desk is compared to an old woman carrying too many parcels—surely a reminder of the old woman, Jessie Florian, insignificant in the run of things, a peripheral figure even in the events which lead to her death. Jessie Florian had been wobbly not merely in her drunkenness but in the intent and purpose of her greed.

In his second paragraph, Chandler's art reinforces while it generalizes the suggestiveness of his Kafkaesque image:

> The bug reached the end of Randall's desk and marched straight off into the air. It fell on its back on the floor, waived a few thin worn legs in the air feebly and then played dead. Nobody cared, so it began waving the legs again and finally struggled over on its face. It trundled off into a corner, towards nothing, going nowhere.

At this point Chandler's bug has taken on a broad symbolic overtones. It will continue its journey to nowhere through the pages of the chapter, to be rescued, significantly, by Marlowe, but only after it has served to suggest a dimension of meaning which it is impossible for Marlowe to relate directly.

Meanwhile, the nameless detective will abruptly leave the room at one point, his presence no longer required when Randall, a personalized representative of the law as opposed to this generalized figure, takes his place. The effect Chandler achieves in the first paragraph with the description of the nameless detective is, I think, harder to explain than that of the black bug with the pink head and pink spots. The detail is in part traditional, the category of image equally traditional. The "big scarred hand" of the detective, for example, conveys not only the idea of physical bigness but also of brute strength and physical violence, realities associated in the mind of the public with the police in general. The detective's repose and even the burning cigarette are suggestive of the patience and tired watchfulness of the law. But beyond this there is the detective's namelessness, his voice, which sounds like someone whispering in a tunnel (and hence is equally "nameless," unidentifiable, generalized), and his half-closed eyes—all in all the picture of an inscrutable figure which personifies the law as Chandler see it.

In the first two paragraphs of chapter thirty-one we have been listening, largely without awareness, to the voice of the author. Chandler's art has been such that he has been speaking to us through Marlowe with relative directness undetermined by the needs of plot and character. As the chapter progresses the author is heard even more directly. After Randall has entered the room and Marlowe signed the prepared statement, the two men go on to discuss various aspects of the murders. Included in the discussion is Randall's slightly disguised threat that Marlowe should get out of the case and let the police handle things. ("We got friendly this morning. Let's stay that way. Go home and lie down and have a good rest.") Near the end of the chapter the talk turn to the Marriott-Florian relationship:

> "I have a theory about that," he [Randall] said. . . . "I think Jessie Florian was Marriott's lucky piece. As long as he took care of her, nothing would happen to him."
>
> I turned my head and looked for the pink-headed bug. He had tried two corners of the room now and was moving off disconsolately towards a third. I went over and picked him up in my handkerchief and carried him back to the desk.
>
> "Look," I said. "This room is eighteen floors above ground. And this little bug climbs all the way up here just to make a friend. Me. *My* lucky piece." I folded the bug carefully into my pocket. Randall was pie-eyed. His mouth moved but nothing came out of it.
>
> "I wonder whose lucky piece Marriott was," I said.
>
> "Not yours, pal." His mouth was acid—cold acid.
>
> "Perhaps not yours either." My voice was just a voice. I went out of the room and shut the door.
>
> I rode the express elevator down to the Spring Street entrance and walked out on the front porch of City Hall and down some steps and over to the flower beds. I put the pink bug down carefully behind a bush.
>
> I wondered, in the taxi going home, how long it would take him to make the homicide bureau again.

In Marlowe's voice—which is "just a voice"—we hear his recognition of not only the helplessness he feels and its source, which he acknowledges, but also his awareness of the aloneness of the individual in the big city. And beyond Marlowe's voice we hear the voice of the author. That is, we realize that something is being said beyond what the dialogue appears to be saying—and this something, I think, we take to be a statement by the author about American society. Chandler is commenting on the sheer puniness of the individual in America, his weakness before both the forces of corruption and the machinery of the law, which is not merely beyond his control but is seemingly beyond anyone's control, dispensing justice, and sometimes injustice, in the light of partial and imperfect truth. Society is the corrupter of the individual, the predator.

In Chandler's eyes, the breakdown in authority, which is part and parcel of the democratic process, is justification for Marlowe's attitude and temper of mind where the police are concerned:

> "Until you guys [the police] own your own souls, you don't own mine. Until you guys can be trusted every time and always, in all times and conditions, to seek the truth out and find it and let the chips fall where they may—until that time comes, I have a right to listen to my conscience, and protect my

> client the best way I can. Until I'm sure you won't do him more harm than you'll do the truth good. Or until I'm hauled before somebody that can make me talk."
>
> (*The High Window*)

Marlowe intervenes, intercedes; Marlowe runs afoul of the law: this partial pattern reappears in novel after novel. But Marlowe's combativeness, his slow-burning but explosive personality, is ultimately unable to cope with the hostility of the law and the oppressiveness of society in general. Perhaps this failure in part accounts for the habitual fatigue and weariness in Marlowe's voice, for the somber, almost dolorous ground tone against which he makes his wisecracks and smart retorts. In Chandler's fiction, much of the time Marlowe is a modern Sisyphus, a man forever pushing an unbearable burden uphill. In the end Marlowe, with his author, retreats to sentimentality as an antidote, a palliative to the brutalizing effects of society.

This turn toward sentimentality can be seen in chapter thirty-one of *Farewell, My Lovely,* where in the end Marlowe's pink bug is revealed as a sentimental symbol whose adventures fail to reveal any serious meaning. For all the Kafkaesque overtones, what is missing is something comparable to the terror and horror of the *Metamorphosis*. Kafka's bug, we are reminded, was *a real person*; Chandler's is merely a pink bug.

Chandler's uneasiness about the persistent sentimentality of this scene makes itself obvious. The author attempts to glide over any scrutiny of Marlowe's emotions by focusing on the reactions of the homicide detective, Randall. When, at one point, Marlowe says that the hug is his lucky piece and puts it carefully in his pocket, Randall becomes "pie-eyed." His mouth moved but nothing came out of it." The effect of such exaggerated language is to reduce Randall from the status of a real person to that of a stock character. He momentarily becomes the familiar dumb cop of the "B" grade movies.

In the last chapter of *Farewell, My Lovely*, Marlowe's pink bug again makes its appearance. Randall and Marlowe are discussing the suicide of Helen Grayle ("little Velma"), who, discovered in another city, shot herself rather than return to stand trial for the murders of Marriott and Moose Malloy. Randall finds her death unnecessary. With a clever lawyer, which her elderly millionaire husband could have easily supplied, she would never have been convicted of either murder. Marlowe, however, has an explanation for her conduct and suicide:

> ". . .Who would that trial hurt most? Who would be least able to bear it? And win, lose or draw, who would pay the biggest price for the show? An old man who had loved [not] wisely, but too well."
>
> Randall said sharply: "That's just sentimental."

> "Sure. It sounded like that when I said it. Probably all a mistake anyway. So long. Did my pink bug ever get back up here?"
>
> He didn't know what I was talking about.

Both the allusion to Shakespeare's *Othello* and the mention of the pink bug are intended to undercut Randall's "That's just sentimental," as is Marlowe's "It sounded like that when I said it." None of this attempt to make sentimentality a principle of structure seems to me fully satisfying, as well as it is done. For one thing, because structure is moral and causal. To manipulate structure as Chandler does at the end of *Farewell, My Lovely* by fantasying an explanation of events is to turn off the vision which has controlled the book's meaning. In the end one has to speak not merely of Chandler's sentimentalism but of a more serious failure in his art: the dishonesty of a vision which failed to follow its own light at crucial points.

This lack of honesty infects, at various levels, both plot and character in Chandler's work. One sign of the moral juggling I am speaking of is reflected in the derivation of his novels—in the way he "cannibalized" his published stories for his novels, borrowing pieces and bits as they suited his purposes. There is nothing inherently wrong in a writer reusing the materials of his earlier fiction, but in Chandler what the reweaving of fragments ultimately suggests is an unsureness about the moral values he is attaching to people and events. Then, too, Marlowe on occasion invests in some of the figures he encounters a moral worth which nothing in either situation or character allows for. In *The Big Sleep* he speaks of Harry Jones, a small-time grifter who is trying to sell him some information, as "A small man in a big man world. There was something I like about him." Marlowe's vagueness here is particularly revealing, for there is nothing very likable about Harry Jones at this point except perhaps a certain stick-to-it-iveness. In the next chapter he will show a certain loyalty by refusing to reveal to Lash Canino the whereabouts of the woman Gladys, with whom he is in partnership. But his painful death by cyanide at Canino's hands in this chapter is gratuitous. It seems motivated as much by Chandler's desire to make the gangster worse than he is as to make Harry Jones better than he is.

Chandler's failure to sustain a morally dispassionate view of his characters can be seen throughout *The Little Sister*, in some ways the least successful of his novels. The sequence of events rather implausibly hinges on the movie star Mavis Weld wanting to take the blame for the murder of her gangster-lover by her "little sister" from Manhattan, Kansas. The trouble is that Chandler shows us nothing in the character of the movie star which would let us assume she would act this way. And the half-sister, Orfamay Quest, is an exceptionally unpleasant person, smug, hypocritical, a small-town puritan whose ethic has gone sour and become evil. Chandler uses Orfamay (and Manhattan, Kansas) to vent his anger against those aspects of middle-class American life which he finds offensive. In the end, "the little sister" is portrayed as a person worse than she would be in real life, just as Mavis Weld is seen as a better person than she would be. The moral confusion of *The Little Sister,* reflects the confusion in plot in the novel. Marlowe, for example, takes the law into his own hands and rearranges the evidence at the scene of murder. His action apparently stems from his conviction that Mavis Weld is innocent—though he never informs us of this, and he has little reason for believing it.

I am not here quarreling with Marlowe's role in Chandler's fiction nor with his author's conception of his hero, though both are open to question, but with Chandler's denial of his own vision, basically with his desire to improve upon and to soften the harsh quality of life which his own works reveal.

Over the years readers of Chandler's novels, as well as commentators on his art, have been struck by the heavy vein of gratuitous emotion in the Marlowe of *The Long Goodbye,* Chandler's last novel of importance, published in 1954. It was first pointed out by Chandler's agent, Bernice Baumgarten, when she received the manuscript of the novel in May 1952. She apparently made a number of specific objections to the book as it stood, and Chandler replied in part: "I knew the character of Marlowe had changed and I thought it had to because the hardboiled stuff was too much of a pose after all this time. But I did not realize that it had become Christlike, and sentimental, and that he ought to be deriding his own emotions. . . ." To his English publisher, who had apparently written Chandler to encourage and sympathize with him in the work at hand, he wrote: "Most of the points Bernice criticized in detail would have been changed automatically in revision and a great many that she did not criticize. . . . Be of good cheer. I don't mind Marlowe being a sentimentalist, because he always has been. His toughness has always been more or less a surface bluff. . . ." Seemingly the mask between author and hero had worn paper-thin. Marlowe's toughness, as we have maintained all along, had always been in part a mechanism of defense for his author.

The sentimentalism of Marlowe in *The Long Goodbye* has been variously attributed, sometimes to Chandler's age (he was now sixty-four), sometimes to the fact that his wife Cissy, who was eighteen years his senior, was seriously ill during the writing. Chandler was exceptionally close to his wife, who had been an invalid for many years, and he was clumsily to attempt suicide after her death in 1954. Both Chandler's age and his wife's illness undoubtedly contributed to the emotional tone of the book, but more relevant for his art is the discovery that, upon scrutiny, *The Long Goodbye* turns out to be a profoundly autobiographical novel in which the author on an imaginative level explores his own past and those aspects of his personality which continued to engage him. Ultimately the emotion that Marlowe expends in *The Long Goodbye* is for his author and the butt-end of his days.

In retrospect, even the minor figure of the writer in *The Long Goodbye* bears a broad resemblance to Raymond Chandler. Roger Wade is the author of a dozen best-selling historical novels; Chandler was the author of a half-dozen highly successful detective novels. Also, Chandler wanted to be a historical novelist but was talked out of it by his publisher. Wade drinks excessively, he has trouble finishing the book he is working on. He thinks little of himself and his talent. "You're looking at a small time operator in a small time business. . . . All writers are punks and I am one of the punkest." In discussing with Marlowe the possible reasons for Wade's drinking, his wife offers the suggestions that perhaps she's the cause. "Men fall out of love with their wives." Marlowe replies: "I'd say it's more likely he has fallen out of love with the kind of stuff he writes." In terms of the plot of *The Long Goodbye*, both Mrs. Wade and Marlowe are partly right.

The parallels to Chandler's life give one pause. His drinking was well-known: he had recently had trouble bringing to a conclusion *The Little Sister*, and he had a marked capacity for professional self-abasement which derived from much the same source as Wade's: he wrote in a popular form. In the United States, unlike England, detective fiction has never been taken seriously by the critics. This irony was not lost on Chandler, as his letters make clear. The limited respect paid detective fiction undoubtedly contributed to his defensiveness about his art and also to the neglect, real or imaginary, which he intensely felt from time to time. One also has to remember that Chandler was far better educated than the mass of his readers; he had daily to face the fact that it *was* the tough talk, the violence, the glamor of crime that captured and held them. Most would never have a glimmering of the range of knowledge he displayed in his books or the art with which he wrote them.

It would of course be a dubious procedure to read Roger Wade's statements in *The Long Goodbye* as having a point-by-point application to Chandler personally, though it seems likely that on some level Chandler was working out the ambivalence he felt toward his own achievement as a writer in way impossible to relate in his correspondence. In *The Long Goodbye* Roger Wade's wife and his publisher want to hire Marlowe to guard him from drinking and doing himself bodily harm so he can finish the book he is working on. Marlowe wants to refuse but never fully does so. He rescues Wade from the ranch of a doctor in Sepulveda Canyon who is drying him out, and he intervenes on other occasions. It is almost as if Marlowe were Roger Wade's guardian angel, and also as if, on another level, one part of Raymond Chandler were keeping watch over another. Not surprisingly, in terms of events in the novel Wade's compulsive drinking is only in a limited way connected with his writing: all the talk about writing is in point of fact irrelevant—except that it vitally concerns Raymond Chandler.

In the end Marlowe cannot save Roger Wade from suicide, or, rather, from being murdered, for his wife kills him and makes it appear in suicide; but this event occurs only when the plot of Chandler's long novel demands his death—when, in effect, Chandler's new alter ego has said all that he wants him to say. By then, the essential parallel between Chandler's doubles has been directly sounded. At one point in the novel, the writer says to the detective: "You know something, Marlowe? I could get to like you. You're a bit of a bastard—like me." When, much later in the novel, Marlowe informs Wade's publisher, Harold Spencer, of his death, the words he uses echo this conversation: "Roger Wade is dead, Spencer. He was a bit of a bastard and maybe a genius too. That's over my head. He was an egotistical drunk and hated his own guts." Where in all this maze of romantically conceived self-criticism Raymond Chandler really stood is perhaps impossible to tell, and ultimately it is unimportant, for it is clear that Chandler was harder on himself than anyone else ever was—or will be.

What appears to have happened by the time Chandler wrote *The Long Goodbye* is that the paradox of his personality had largely resolved into new components. Chandler was no longer overly much interested in Marlowe as a projection of his own personality. Marlowe still went down mean streets in the service of his author, but now he was bent less on being the hero than on exploring the other selves of Raymond Chandler.

The main character in *The Long Goodbye* is Terry Lennox, an American with a British accent and British mannerisms, ("I lived there. I wasn't born there," he says of himself, much as Chandler speaks of himself in one of his published letters.) Lennox is in a number of ways a curious figure in the novel. He appears only in the opening pages and again at the end, yet his ghostly presence dominates the book, in part because of Marlowe's strong but irrational attachment to him. A minor but curious matter in the novel is that Terry Lennox's real name is Paul Marston; his initials are the same as Philip Marlowe's.

Marlowe first encounters Terry Lennox in the parking lot of a Sunset Strip nightclub. Lennox has drunkenly fallen out of a Rolls Royce. The woman with him (his ex-wife, the daughter of a millionaire) drives off in the Rolls, leaving him stranded. Marlowe fells sorry enough for Lennox to see him safely home to his Westwood apartment. "I'm supposed to be tough but there was something about the guy that got me. I didn't know what it was unless it was the white hair and the scarred face and the clear voice and politeness. Maybe that was enough." The prematurely white hair and the scarred face are both the result of Lennox's experience in the British Commandos during World War II. The clear voice and the politeness are aspects of his English-ness. Seemingly what Marlowe is in part admiring in Lennox is his British reticence, the stiff upper-lip, the code of the gentleman. For Lennox is in severe financial trouble here at the beginning of the book, and he is unable to bring himself to ask anyone for help—specifically, his ex-wife, or the two men whose lives he saved in the Commandos. The one, Mendy Menendez, is a Los Angeles gangster; the other, Randy Staff, is the operator of a Las Vegas gambling casino. Both feel under obligation to him.

Marlowe has no reason to see Lennox again, but by chance encounters him one day around Thanksgiving staggering along a row of shops on Hollywood Boulevard, disheveled and drunk. The police are about to pick him up as a vagrant but Marlowe gets to him first and takes him away in a taxi cab. He sobers him up and gives him $100; with that, Lennox sets off for Las Vegas and a job with Randy Starr. The next Marlowe hears of Terry Lennox is in the newspaper: he has remarried his ex-wife, Sylvia Potter, in Las Vegas at Christmas. And then, seemingly because Marlowe has been kind to him, Lennox begins occasionally to drop into his office late in the afternoon and take him off for a drink in a quiet bar. (Lennox now has his drinking under control.) The bar visits, including the gimlets they drink, become a ritual between the two. But finally Marlowe walks out on Lennox in disgust. Lennox has revealed the weak and unpleasant side of his personality. He married, and apparently remarried, Sylvia Potter for her money. His wife, he says, is a nymphomaniac; he regards himself as a highly paid pimp. Lennox carries on in this vein until Marlowe, disgusted, gets up to leave. "You talk too damn much," he says, "and it's too damn much about you."

A month later Marlowe is awakened at 5:00 in the morning by Lennox, gun in hand. He has apparently killed his wife—but Marlowe will not let him talk about it because Lennox wants him to drive him across the border to Tijuana, where he can catch a plane and disappear into the interior of Mexico. Knowingly to help Lennox escape the law would be to become an accessory to a crime. Yet Marlowe is prepared to violate the spirit, if not the letter, of the law; and this is only the first of several extraordinary actions Marlowe performs for this man whom he barely knows but feels strongly attached to. Upon his return from Tijuana, Marlowe is mercilessly grilled by the police about the disappearance of Terry Lennox; he is also subjected to a good deal of physical abuse—yet he refuses to talk, to reveal anything that will help the police find Lennox. Then Lennox is discovered dead in a Mexican village, an apparent suicide. Marlowe, who has had a letter from Lennox, does not think he has killed himself and insists on pursuing the matter, defying Sylvia Lennox's father, the millionaire publisher Harlan Potter, who wants the whole matter closed. Marlowe also does not think Lennox killed his wife. And, in the end, it turns out that Marlowe is right—she was killed by Eileen Wade, who had been Paul Marston's wife in England during the war. In a suicide note, she writes:

> I have no regrets for Paul whom you have heard called Terry Lennox. He was the empty shell of the man I loved and married. He meant nothing to me. . . . He should have died young in

> the snow of Norway, my lover that I gave to death. He came back a friend of gamblers, the husband of a rich whore, a spoiled and ruined man, and probably some kind of crook in his past life. Time makes everything mean and shabby and wrinkled.

Eileen Wade was her own private fantasies, idealized and romantic, about the life she shared in wartime England with Paul Marston.

In the course of events in *The Long Goodbye* Marlowe is wrong about one thing; Marston-Lennox is not dead, as everyone believes. His death was faked to free him from involvement with the police. At the end of the novel Lennox reappears in Marlowe's office, hair dyed, with a face altered by plastic surgery, and a Mexican accent. But Marlowe sees through the disguise, and, as they talk, he once more becomes disenchanted with Terry Lennox, who can mix with hoodlums as easily as with honest men, who, though a nice guy, has no morals at all. "You're a moral defeatist," Marlowe says to him. "I think maybe the war did it and again I think maybe you were born that way." Lennox has his own version of what changed him, as he reveals several pages later:

> "I was in the Commandos, bud. They don't take you if you're just a piece of fluff. I got badly hurt and it wasn't any fun with those Nazi doctors. It did something to me."

"I know all that," Marlowe replies. "You're a sweet guy in a lot of ways. I'm not judging you. I never did. It's just that you're not here any more. You're long gone." Marlowe sentimentally returns to Lennox a $5000 bill which Lennox, just as sentimentally, had sent him from Mexico; and then he says goodbye forever to his bogus Englishman.

It is likely that somewhere in Chandler's past, perhaps in the time spent in the Canadian army in World War I, lie some milder but similar experiences to those Terry Lennox suffered in the Commandos. Seemingly he associated with people who were without moral fiber, who made him feel morally stained, much as Lennox makes Marlowe feel crummy, and he carried the scars of these experiences with him, much as Lennox did. It is unlikely that we will ever know what those experiences were, and, again, it is unnecessary to, as long as we realize that Chandler is burying some ghost of his former self in *The Long Goodbye*.

The ghostly British figure Marlowe takes his long farewell of had been a long time emerging in Chandler's fiction, though, rather surprisingly, he was announced as early as his first novel, *The Big Sleep*. I say "announced" because he is murdered before the novel begins and hence we never meet him, though a good deal of the novel is indirectly given over to searching for him. Ironically enough, everyone assumes Marlowe is searching for him, though he really isn't. But let me draw the parallels between the two novels which will make this development clear.

At the core of both *The Big Sleep* and *The Long Goodbye* lie precisely the same situation and some of the same characters, though the alignment of characters and their involvement in the plots of each novel are different. In each novel there is a millionaire with two daughters. One daughter is married to the figure who is in effect missing in the novel, Terry Lennox in *The Long Goodbye*, Rusty Regan in *The Big Sleep*. (It is just possible that "the big sleep" is the sleep of the men Chandler wanted to be.) In each case the men are British in background (Regan was an Irishman; Chandler, incidentally, was of Irish decent). In each case these men are liked by the millionaire in question, in part for having the basic masculine traits; they are good men, decent, kindly. Rusty Regan gave General Sternwood a kind of companionship in his old age which he found in no one else. Terry Lennox, as we have suggested, had about him many admirable things. Both men, incidentally, had been involved in fighting; Reagan was in the Irish Rebellion.

In each novel one of the daughters is a nymphomaniac. In *The Big Sleep*, it is Carmen Sternwood, the unmarried daughter; at the end of the novel we learn that she insanely killed Regan. She also tried to murder Marlowe because, like Regan, he rejected her advances. At one point in the novel she takes off her clothes and climbs into Marlowe's bed, only to be thrown out of his apartment by him practically before she can get her clothes back on. In *The Long Goodbye*, the second daughter, Linda Loring, brings her suitcase and spends the night with Marlowe, who willingly accepts her. The sexual conduct of Marlowe here, it seems to me, represents less a shift in his moral code, as some critics are quick to suggest, than a deepening realism in his portrayal by his author. Throughout the earlier books Marlowe vacillated between the epicene and the hardboiled.

The realignment of figures in *The Long Goodbye* is somewhat more complex than I have suggested here, but the significant point is that in this second and complementary version Chandler has come as close as he ever was to come to tapping those personal resources which motivated his art; he has come so close, in fact, that he all but takes his leave of the characters who fill his imaginative landscape.

But that farewell is only partly taken. There is, after all, a significance to Terry Lennox's reappearance which is extraneous to the novel; Chandler could not kill that part of himself, though he could do more than temporize with it, as he had done earlier. Marlowe's direct confrontation with his British counterpart involves a psychological reconciliation of some complexity for their creator.

It is obvious in his letters that Chandler's Americanization of self was never a fully accomplished fact. He was to some extent always a lonely stranger in the land of his birth. Even something which seems so typically American as Marlowe's love-hate relationship with the cops, which is carried on more or less elaborately from book to book, most probably goes back in part to the world of the British schoolboy. Chandler's authority fixation no doubt has other sources, including the seeming domination of his life by women. He lived with his mother until she died, then married a woman much older than himself. But what is most troubling and sometimes terrifying in the work of Raymond Chandler, who created an authentic American voice which still speaks to millions of readers, is that there hangs on about the world he created something of the inconsistency of nightmare. Perhaps for this reason he wrote what in the end must be considered screen versions of life, substituting the prismatic glamor of Hollywood and the West Coast for a closer look at those facts of life which in his awareness he found unbearable.

# On Raymond Chandler

*Fredric Jameson*

## I

> A long time ago when I was writing for the pulps I put into a story a line like "He got out of the car and walked across the sun-drenched sidewalk until the shadow of the awning over the entrance fell across his face like the touch of cool water." They took it out when they published the story. Their readers didn't appreciate this sort of thing—just held up the action. I set out to prove them wrong. My theory was that the readers just *thought* they cared about nothing but the action; that really, although they didn't know it, the thing they cared about, and that I cared about, was the creation of emotion through dialogue and description.

That the detective story represented something more to Raymond Chandler than a mere commercial product, furnished for popular entertainment purposes, can be judged from the fact that he came to it late in life, with a long and successful business career behind him. He published his first and best novel, *The Big Sleep,* in 1939, when he was fifty years old, and had studied the form for almost a decade. The short stories he had written over that period are for the most part sketches for the novels, episodes that he will later take over verbatim as chapters in the longer form; and he developed his technique by imitating and re-working models pro-

"On Raymond Chandler," *Southern Review* 6:3 (1970): 624-50.

duced by other detective story writers: a deliberate, self-conscious apprenticeship at a time of life when most writers have already found themselves.

Two aspects of his earlier experience seem to account for the personal tone of his books. As an executive of the oil industry, he lived in Los Angeles for some fifteen years before the depression put him out of business, enough time to sense what was unique about the city's atmosphere, in a position to see what power was and what forms it took. And as a born American, he spent his school years, from the age of eight, in England, and had an English Public School Education.

For Chandler thought of himself primarily as a stylist, and it was his distance from the American language that gave him the chance to use it as he did. In that respect his situation was not unlike that of Nabokov: the writer of an adopted language is already a kind of stylist by force of circumstance. Language can never again be unselfconscious for him; words can never again be unproblematical. The naïve and unreflecting attitude towards literary expression is henceforth proscribed, and he feels in his language a kind of material density and resistance: even those clichés and commonplaces which for the native speaker are not really words at all, but instant communication, take on outlandish resonance in his mouth, are used between quotation marks, as you would delicately expose some interesting speciman: his sentences are collages of heterogeneous materials, of odd linguistic scraps, figures of speech, colloquialisms, place names and local sayings, all laboriously pasted together in an illusion of continuous discourse. In this, the lived situation of the writer of a borrowed language is already emblematic of the situation of the modern writer in general, in that words have become objects for him. The detective story, as a form without ideological content, without any overt political or social or philosophical point, permits such pure stylistic experimentation.

But it offers other advantages as well, and it is no accident that the chief practitioners of art-for-art's sake in the recent novel, Nabokov and Robbe-Grillet, almost always organize their works around a murder: think of *Le Voyeur* and *La Maison de Rendezvous*; think of *Lolita* and *Pale Fire*. These writers and their artistic contemporaries represent a kind of second wave of the modernist and formalistic impulse which produced the great modernism of the first two decades of the twentieth century. But in the earlier works, modernism was a reaction against narration, against plot: here the empty, decorative event of the murder serves as a way of organizing essentially plotless material into an illusion of movement, into the formally satisfying arabesques of a puzzle unfolding. Yet the real content of these books is an almost scenic one: the motels and college towns of the American landscape, the island of *Le Voyeur*, the drab provincial cities of *Les Gommes* or of *Dans le labyrinth*.

In much the same way, a case can be made for Chandler as a painter of American life: not as a builder of those large-scale models of the American experience which great literature offers, but rather in fragmentary pictures of setting and place, fragmentary perceptions which are by some formal paradox somehow inaccessible to serious literature.

Take for example some insignificant daily experience, such as the chance encounter of two people in the lobby of an apartment building. I find my neighbor unlocking his mailbox; I have never seen him before, we glance at each other briefly, his back is turned as he struggles with the larger magazines inside. Such an instant expresses in its fragmentary quality a profound truth about American life, in its perception of the stained carpets, the sandfilled spittoons, the poorly shutting glass doors: all testifying to the shabby anonymity which is the meeting place between the luxurious private lives that stand side by side like closed monads, behind the doors to the private apartments: a dreariness of waiting rooms and public bus stations, of the neglected places of collective living that fill up the interstices between the privileged compartments of middle-class living. Such a perception, it seems to me, is in its very structure dependent on chance and anonymity, on the vague glance in passing, as from the windows of a bus, when the mind is intent on some more immediate preoccupation: its very essence is to be inessential. For this reason it eludes the registering apparatus of great literature: make of it some Joycean epiphany and the reader is obliged to take this moment as the center of his world, as something directly infused with symbolic meaning; and at once the most fragile and precious quality of the perception is irrevocably damaged, its slightness is lost, it can no longer be half-glimpsed, half-disregarded.

Yet put such an experience in the framework of the detective story and everything changes: I learn that the man I saw does not even live in my building, that he was in reality opening the murdered woman's mailbox, not his own; and suddenly my attention flows back onto the neglected perception and sees it in renewed, heightened form without damaging its structure. Indeed, it is as if there are certain moments in life which are accessible only at a price of a certain lack of intellectual focus: like objects at the edge of my field of vision which disappear when I turn to stare at them head-on. Proust felt this keenly. His whole aesthetic is based on some absolute antagonism between spontaneity and self-consciousness. For Proust we can only be sure we have lived, we have perceived, after the fact of the experience itself; for him the deliberate project to meet experience face to face in the present is always doomed to failure. In a minor way the unique temporal structure of the best detective story is a pretext, a mere organizational framework, for such isolated perception.

It is in this light that the well-known distinction between the atmosphere of English and American detective stories is to be understood. Gertrude Stein, in her *Lectures in America,* sees the essential feature of English literature to be the tireless description of "daily life," of lived routine and continuity, in which possessions are daily counted up and evaluated, in which the basic structure is one of cycle and repetition. American life, American content, on the other hand, is a formless one, always to be re-invented, an uncharted wilderness in which a few decisive, explosive, irrevocable instants and stand out in relief. Hence the murder in the placid English village or in the fog-bound London club is read as the sign of a scandalous interruption in a peaceful continuity; whereas the gangland violence of the American big city is felt as a secret destiny, a kind of nemesis lurking beneath the surface of hastily acquired fortunes, anarchic city growth and impermanent private lives. Yet in both, the moment of violence, apparently central, is nothing but a diversion: the real function of the murder in the quiet village to be felt more strongly; and the principal effect of the violence of the American detective story is to allow it to be experienced backwards, in pure thought, without risks, as a contemplative spectacle which gives, not so much the illusion of life as the illusion that life has already been lived, that we have already had contact with the archaic sources of that Experience of which Americans have always made a fetish.

## II

> We looked at each other with the clear innocent eyes of a couple of used car salesman.

European literature is metaphysical or formalistic, because it takes the nature of the society, of the nation, for granted and works out beyond it. American literature never seems to get beyond the definition of its starting point: any picture of America is bound to be wrapped up in a question and a presupposition about the nature of American reality. European literature can choose its subject matter and the width of its lens; American literature feels obliged to put everything in, knowing that exclusion is also part of the process of definition, and that it can be called to account as much for what it does.

The last great period of American literature, which ran more or less from one world war to the other, explored and defined America in geographical mode, as a sum of separate localisms, as an additive unity, at its outside limit an ideal sum. But since the War, the organic differences from region to region have been increasingly obliterated by standardization; and the organic social unity of each region has been increasingly fragmented and abstracted by the new closed lives of the individual family units, by the breakdown of cities and the dehumanization of transportation and of the media which lead from one monad to another. Communication in this new society is upwards, through the abstract connecting link, and back down again. The isolated units are all haunted by the feeling that the center of things, of life, of control, is elsewhere, beyond immediate lived experiences. The principal images of interrelationship in this new society are mechanical juxtapositions: the identical prefabricated houses in the housing project, swarming over the hills; the four-lane highway full of cars bumper to bumper and observed from above, abstractly, by a traffic helicopter. If there is a crisis in American literature at present, it should be understood against the background of this ungrateful social material, in which only trick shots can produce the illusion of life.

Chandler lies somewhere between these two literary situations. His whole background, his way of thinking and of seeing things, derives from the period between the wars. But by an accident of place, his social content anticipates the realities of the fifties and sixties. For Los Angeles is already a kind of microcosm and forecast of the country as a whole: a new centerless city, in which the various classes have lost touch with each other because each is isolated in his own geographical compartment. If the symbol of social coherence and comprehensibility was furnished by the nineteenth-century Parisian apartment house (dramatized in Zola's *Pot-Bouille*) with its shop on the ground floor, its wealthy inhabitants on the second and third, petty bourgeoisie further up, and workers' rooms on top along with the maids and servants, then Los Angeles is the opposite, a spreading out horizontally, a flowing apart of the elements of the social structure.

Since there is no longer any privileged experience in which the whole of the social structure can be grasped, a figure must be invented who can be superimposed on the society as a whole, whose routine and life-pattern serve somehow to tie its separate and isolated parts together. Its equivalent is the picaresque novel, where a single character moves from one background to another, links picturesque but not intrinsically related episodes together. In doing this the detective in a sense once again fulfills the demands of the function of knowledge rather than that of lived experience: through him we are able to see, to know, the society as a whole, but he does not really stand for any genuine close-up experience of it. Of course the origin of the literary detective lies in the creation of the professional police, whose organization can be attributed not so much to a desire to prevent crime in general as to the will on the part of modern governments to know and thus to control the varying elements of their administrative areas. The great continental detectives (Lecoq, Maigret) are generally policemen; but in the Anglo-Saxon countries where governmental control sits far more lightly on the citizens, the private detective, from Holmes to Chandler's Philip Marlowe, takes the place of the government functionary.

As an involuntary explorer of the society, Marlowe visits either those places you don't look at or those you can't look at: the anonymous or the wealthy and secretive. Both have something of the strangeness with which Chandler characterizes the police station: "A New York police reporter wrote once that when you pass in beyond the green lights of the precinct station you pass clear out of this world into a place beyond the law." On the one hand those parts of the American scene which are as impersonal and seedy as a public waiting rooms: run-down office buildings, the elevator with the spittoon and the elevator man sitting on a stool beside it; dingy office interiors, Marlowe's own in particular, seen at all hours of the clock, at those times when we have forgotten that offices exist, in the late evening, when the other offices are dark, in the early morning before the traffic begins; police stations; hotel rooms and lobbies, with the characteristic potted palms and overstuffed armchairs; rooming houses with managers who work illegal lines of business on the side. All these places are characterized by belonging to the mass, collective side of our society: places occupied by faceless people who leave no stamp of their personality behind them, in short, the dimension of the interchangeable, the inauthentic:

> Out of the apartment houses come women who should be young but have faces like stale beer; men with pulled-down hats and quick eyes that look the street over behind the cupped hand that shields the match flame; worn intellectuals with cigarette coughs and no money in the bank; fly cops with granite faces and unwavering eyes; cokies and coke peddlers; people who look like nothing in particular and know it, and once in a while even men that actually go to work. But they come out early, when the wide cracked sidewalks are empty and still have dew on them.

The presentation of this kind of social material is far more frequent in European art than in our own: as if somehow we were willing to know anything about ourselves, the worst kind of secret, just as long as it was not this nameless, faceless one. But it suffices to compare the faces of actors and participants in almost any European movie with those in American ones to note the absence in ours of the whole-grain lens and the dissimilarity between the product offered and the features of people around us in the street. What makes this somewhat more difficult to observe is that of course our view of life is conditioned by the art we know, which has trained us not to see what the texture of ordinary people's faces is, but rather to invest them with photographic glamour.

The other side of American life with which Marlowe comes into contact is the reverse of the above: the great estate, with its retinue of servants, chauffeurs, and secretaries; and around it, the various institutions which cater to wealth and preserve its secrecy: the private clubs, set back on private roads in the mountains, patrolled by a private police which admits members only; the clinics in which drugs are available; the religious cults; the luxury hotels with their hotel detectives; the private gambling ships, anchored out beyond the three-mile limit; and a little further away, the corrupt local police which rule a municipality in the name of a single family or man, and the various kinds of illegal activity which spring up to satisfy money and its wants.

But Chandler's picture of America has an intellectual content as well: it is the converse, the darker concrete reality, of an abstract intellectual illusion about the United States. The federal system and the archaic federal Constitution developed in Americans a double image of their country's political reality, a double system of political thoughts which never intersect with each other. On the one hand, a glamorous national politics whose distant leading figures are invested with charisma, an unreal, distinguished quality adhering to their foreign policy activities, their economic programs given the appearance of intellectual content by the appropriate ideologies of liberalism or conservatism. On the other hand, local politics, with its odium, its everpresent corruption, its deals and perpetual preoccupation with undramatic, materialistic questions such as sewage disposal, zoning regulations, property taxes, and so forth. Governors are half-way between the two worlds, but for a mayor, for example, to become a senator involves a thorough-going metamorphosis, a transformation from one species into another. Indeed, the qualities perceived in the political macrocosm are only illusory qualities, the projection of the dialectical opposite of the real qualities of the microcosm: everyone is convinced of the dirtiness of politics and politicians on the local level, and when everything is seen in terms of interest, the absence of greed becomes the feature which dazzles. Like the father whose defects are invisible to his own children, the national politicians (with occasional stunning exceptions) seem to be beyond personal self-interest, and this lends an automatic prestige to their professional affairs, lifts them onto a different rhetorical level entirely.

On the level of abstract thought, the effect of the preordained permanency of the Constitution is to hinder the development of any speculative political theorizing in this country, and to replace it with pragmatizism within the system, the calculation of counter-influences and possibilities of compromise. A kind of reverence attaches to the abstract, a disabused cynicism to the concrete. As in certain types of mental obsession and dissociation, the American is able to observe local injustice, racism, corruption, educational incompetence, with a practiced eye, while he continues to entertain boundless optimism as to the greatness of the country, taken as a whole.

The action of Chandler's books takes place inside the microcosm, in the darkness of a local world without the benefit of the federal Constitution, as in a world without God. The literary shock is dependent on the habit of the political double standard in the mind of the reader: it is only because we are used to thinking of the nation as a whole in terms of justice that we are struck by these images of people caught in the power of a local county authority as absolutely as though they were in a foreign country. The local power apparatus is beyond appeal, in this other face of federalism; the rule of naked force and money is complete and undisguised by an embellishments of theory. In an eery optical illusion, the jungle reappears in the suburbs.

In this sense the honesty of the detective can be understood as an organ of perception, a membrane which, irritated, serves to indicate in its sensitivity the nature of the world around it. For if the detective is dishonest, his job boils down to the technical problem of how to succeed on given assignment. If he is honest, he is able to feel the resistance of things, to permit an intellectual vision of what he goes through on the level of action. And Chandler's sentimentalism, which attaches to occasional honest characters in the earlier books, but which is perhaps strongest in *The Long Goodbye*, is the reverse and complement of this vision, a momentary relief from it, a compensation for it: where everything is seen in a single light, there is not much possibility for subtlety of variety of feelings to develop, there is available only the ground tonality and its opposite.

The detective's journey is episodic because of the fragmentary, atomistic nature of the society he moves through. In European countries, people no matter how solitary are still somehow engaged in the social substance; their very solitude is social; their identity is inextricably entangled with that of all the others by a clear system of classes, by a national language, in what Heidegger describes as the *Mitsein*, the being-together-with-others.

But the form of Chandler's books reflects an initial American separation of people from each other, their need to be linked by some external force (in this case the detective) if they are ever to be fitted together as parts of the same picture puzzle. And this separation is projected out onto space itself: no matter how crowded the street in question, the various solitudes never really merge into a collective experience, there is always distance between them. Each dingy office is separated from the next; each room in the rooming house from the one next to it; each dwelling from the pavement beyond it. This is why the most characteristic leitmotif of Chandler's books is the figure standing, looking out of one world, peering vaguely or attentively across into another:

> Across the street was an Italian funeral home, neat and quiet and reticent, white painted brick, flush with the sidewalk. Pietro Palermo Funeral Parlors. The thin green script of neon sign lay across its facade, with a chaste air. A tall man in dark clothes came out of the front door and leaned against the white wall. He looked very handsome. He had dark skin and a handsome head of iron-gray hair brushed back from his forehead. He got out what looked at the distance to be a silver or platinum and black enamel cigarette case, opened it languidly with two long brown fingers and selected a gold-tipped cigarette. He put the case away and lit the cigarette with a pocket lighter that seemed to match the case. He put that away and folded his arms and stared at nothing with half-closed eyes. From the tip of his motionless cigarette a thin whisp of smoke rose straight up past his face, as think and straight as the smoke of a dying campfire at dawn.

In psychological or allegorical terms, this figure on the doorstep represents Suspicion, and suspicion is everywhere in this world, peering from behind a curtain, barring entry, refusing to answer, preserving the privacy of the monad against snoopers and trespassers. Its characteristic manifestations are the servant coming back out into the hallway, the man in the car lot hearing a noise, the custodian of a deserted farm looking outside, the manager of the rooming house taking another look upstairs, the bodyguard appearing in the doorway.

Hence the detective's principal contact with the people he meets is a rather external one; they are seen briefly in their own doorways, for a purpose, and their personalities come out against the grain, hesitant, hostile, stubborn, as they react to the various questions and drag their feet on the answers. But seen another way the very superficiality of these meetings with the characters is artistically motivated: for the characters themselves are pretexts for their speech, and the specialized nature of this speech is that it is somehow external, indicative of types, objective, remarks bounced across to strangers:

> Her eyes receded and her chin followed them. She sniffed hard. "You been drinkin' liquor," she said coldly.
>
> "I just had a tooth out. the dentist gave it to me."
>
> "I don't hold to it."
>
> "It's bad stuff except for medicine," I said.
>
> "I don't hold with it for medicine neither."
>
> "I think you're right," I said. "Did he leave her any money? Her husband?"
>
> "I wouldn't know." Her mouth was the size of a prune and as smooth. I had lost out.

This kind of dialogue is also characteristic of the early Faulkner; it is quite different from that of Hemingway, which is much more personal and fluid, created from the inside, somehow re-enacted and personally re-experienced by the author. Here clichés and stereotyped speech patterns are heated into life by the presence behind them of a certain form of emotion, that which you would feel in your dealings with strangers: a kind of outgoing belligerence, or hostility, or the amusement of the native, or bantering, helpful indifference: a communicativeness always nuanced or colored by an attitude. And whenever Chandler's dialogue, which in the early books is very good, strays from this particular level to something more intimate and more expressive, it begins to falter; for his forte is the speech pattern of inauthenticity, of externality, and derives immediately from the inner organic logic of his material itself.

In the art of the twenties and thirties, however, such dialogue had the value of social schematism. A set of fixed social types and categories underlay it, and the dialogue was itself a way of demonstrating the coherence and peculiar organization the society possessed, of apprehending it in a miniature. Anyone who has watched New York movies of the thirties is aware how linguistic characterization feeds into a picture of the city as a whole: the stock ethnic and professional types, the cabbie, the reporter, the flatfoot, the high society playboy and flapper, and so forth. Needless to say, the decay of this kind of movie results from the decay of such a picture of the city, which no longer presents any convenience as a way of organizing reality. But already the Los Angeles of Chandler was an unstructured city, and the social types are here nowhere near a pronounced. By the chance of a historical accident, Chandler was able to benefit from the survival of a purely linguistic typological way of creating his characters after the system of types that hd supported it was already in decay. A last hold, before the dissolving contours of the society made these linguistic types disappear also, leaving the novelist faced with the problem of the absence of any standard by which dialogue can be judged realistic or lifelike (except in certain very specialized situations).

In Chandler the presentation of social reality is involved immediately and directly with the problem of language. He thought of himself primarily as a stylist, and there can be no doubt that he invented a distinctive kind of language, with its own humor and imagery, its own special movement. But the most striking feature of this style is its use of slang, and here Chandler's own remarks are instructive:

> I had to learn American just like a foreign language. To use it I had to study it and analyze it. As a result, when I use slang, colloquialisms, snide talk to any kind of off-beat language I do it deliberately. The literary use of slang is a study in itself. I've found that there are only two kinds that are any good: slang that has established itself in the language, and slang that you make up yourself. Everything else is apt to be passe before it gets into print . . . .

And Chandler comments on O'Neill's use in *The Iceman Cometh* of the expression "the big sleep," "in the belief that it was an accepted underworld expression. If so, I'd like to see whence it comes, because I invented the expression."

But slang is eminently serial in its nature: it exists as objectively as a joke, passed from hand to hand, always elsewhere, never fully the property of its user. In this, the literary problem of slang forms a parallel in the microcosm of style to the problem of the presentation of the serial society itself, never present fully in any of its manifestations, without a privileged center, offering the impossible alternative between an objective and abstract lexical knowledge of it as a whole and a lived concrete experience of its worthless components.

## III

Part of the appeal of Chandler's books for us is a nostalgic one. They are among a whole class of objects we have come to call "camp," including: Humphrey Bogart movies, certain comic books, hard-boiled detective stories, and monster movies, among other things. Pop art is the principal contemporary manifestation of this nostalgic interest: it is not unlike art about other art, for in spite in its simplicity it has two levels within it, a simplified outer expression, and an inner period atmosphere which is its object and which is evoked by balloon speeches, the enlarged dots of newspaper print, the faded faces of celebrities and well-known imaginary characters. Rather than art about art, it would be more accurate to say that it is art whose content is not direct experience, but already formed ideological artifacts.

Yet the experience of nostalgia remains itself to be explained. It is not a constant of all periods, and yet when it does appear, it is generally characterized by an attachment to a moment of the past wholly different from our own, which offers a more complete kind of relief from the present. The Romantics for example reacted against the growth of an industrial society by recalling examples of pastoral, hierarchically organized ones from history or from travel. And limited sections of our own society continue to feel this kind of nostalgia, for Jeffersonian America, for example, or for the conditions of the frontier. Or else they satisfy their nostalgia in a concrete way by tourism in countries whose life and ways are the equivalent of some pre-capitalistic stage of historical development.

But the nostalgia which gave birth to pop art fastens for its object on the period immediately preceding our own, one apparently from a larger historical perspective not very different from it: its objects all come from a span of years too often referred to simply as the thirties and which in reality extends from the New Deal well across the parenthesis of the Second World War, and up to the beginning of the Cold War. This period is marked by strong political and ideological movements, and with the revival of political life in the sixties these too have been the object of admiration and nostalgia; but they are themselves results and not causes, and are far from being its most significant features.

The atmosphere of a given period is crystallized first of all in its objects: the double-breasted suits, the long dresses of the new look, the fluffy hair-dos, and the styling of the automobiles. But our nostalgia for this particular time is distinct from the evocation of museum-piece objects from the past in that it seeks out not so much the life-style behind them as the objects themselves. It aims at a world like our own in its general conditions, industrialism, market capitalism, mass production, and is unlike it only in being somewhat simpler. It is partly a fascination with dating, again, the passage of time for its own sake: like looking at photographs of ourselves in old-fashioned clothing in order to have a direct intuition of change, of historicity. (And undoubtedly the existence of the movies as a form does much to account for the peculiar intensity of this nostalgia: we can not only see the past alive before us tangibly, without having to rely on our own imagination of it, more than that, we can feel this past personally by seeing actors young whom we ourselves have grown familiar with as older figures, even by seeing movies we dimly remember from our own pasts.) But this historicity is itself a historical thing. It is as far from the ritual cycle of the seasons as is the turnover in clothing fashions. It is a rapid change intimately liked with the production and marketing of objects for sale.

For the beginning of the Cold War also marked the beginning of the great post-war boom, and with it, the prodigious expansion in advertising, the use of television as a more vivid and suggestive way of selling competing and similar products—one that mingles them more intimately with our lives than did the newspaper or the radio.

The older products had a certain stability about them, a certain permanence of identity that can still be captured here and there in farm country, for example, where a few sparse signs point to the attachment to a few indispensable products. Here, the brand-name is still synonymous with the object itself: a car is a "Ford," a lighter is a "Ronson," a hat is a "Stetson." In this early stage of the marketing of industrial products, the brands require a stable, relatively unchanging identity in order to become identified and adopted by the public, and the relatively primary and simplified advertising is merely a way of recalling something already familiar to the public mind. To be sure, the advertisements tend to blend with the image of the brand itself, but for that very reason in this period the advertisements also change very little and have a kind of stability of their own. Thus the older kinds of products remain relatively integrated into the landscape of natural objects; they still fulfill easily identifiable needs, desires which are still felt to be relatively "natural"; lying midway between nature (land, climate, foodstuffs) and human reality, they correspond to a world in which the principal activity is still the overcoming of the resistance of nature and of things, and in which human need and desire arise as a function of that struggle.

But with the post-war boom the premium comes to be placed on rapid change and evolution of products rather than on their stability and identity. In automobiles, in cigarettes, in soaps, among other things, this wild proliferation and transformation of marketable objects can be observed. Nor can scientific or technical advance (the invention of cigarette filters, of the automatic transmission, of the long-playing record) be held responsible for it. On the contrary most of these technical innovations were feasible earlier; it is only when frequent styling changes are desirable that they are appealed to. The cause of this wholesale alteration in our purchasable environment would appear to be twofold: first, the increasing wealth and diversification of the various manufacturing companies which no longer have to depend on a single brand and which can now invent and eliminate brands at their convenience. Second, the increasing autonomy of advertising, which is able to float any number of unfamiliar new objects in a hurry—in a kind of time exposure in which the older, slower familiarity is artificially reproduced by around-the-clock stimuli.

What is being created in these advertising exposures is not so much an object, a new type of physical thing, but rather an artificial need or desire, a kind of mental or ideological symbol by which the consumer's craving to buy is associated with a particular type of packaging and label. Evidently in a situation in which most basic needs have already been satisfied it is necessary to evolve ever newer and more specialized ones in order to continue to be able to sell products. But the change has its psychological dimension as well, and corresponds to the turnover from a production economy to a service one. Fewer and fewer people are involved with objects as tools, with natural objects as raw materials; more and more are involved with objects as semi-ideas, busy marketing and consuming objects which they never really apprehend as pure materiality, as the product of work on resisting things. In such a world, material needs are sublimated into more symbolic satisfactions; the initial desire is not the solution of a material problem, but the style and symbolic connotations of the product to be possessed.

The life-problems of such a world are radically different in kind from those of the relatively simple world of needs and physical resistance which preceded it. They involve a struggle, not against things and relatively solid systems of power, but against ideological fantasms, bits and pieces of spiritualized matter, the solicitations of various kinds of dream-like mirages and cravings, a life to the second power, not heightened and intensified but merely refined and confused, unable to find a footing in the reality of things.

Such a world clearly poses the most difficult problems for the artist trying to register it. It is full of merely spiritualized, or in our conventional terminology, merely "psychological" problems which do not seem to stand in any direct, observable relationship to the objective realities of the society. At their upper limit, presented for themselves alone, these problems lose themselves in super-subtleties and uninteresting introspection; while the presentation of the objective reality itself strikes the modern reader as old-fashioned and without any relevance to his lived experience.

But the most immediate and visible effects of this situation are stylistic. In the time of Balzac manufactured objects, products, have an immediate and intrinsic novelistic interest, and not only because they record as furnishings the taste and personality of their owners. In this earliest period of industrial capitalism, they are in the very process of being invented and marketed by contemporaries, and where some books tell the very story of their evolution and exploitation, others allow them to stand mute around or behind the characters themselves, as testimony to the nature of the world being created at that moment, and to the stage which human energies have been able to reach. In the era of stable products, however, to which Chandler's books belong, there is no longer any feeling of the creative energy embodied in a product: the latter are simply there, in a permanent industrial background which has come to resemble that of nature itself. Now the author's task is to make an inventory of these objects, to demonstrate, by the fulness of his catalogue, how completely he knows his way around the world of machines and machine products, and it is in this sense that Chandler's descriptions of furniture, his description of women's clothing styles, will function: as a naming, a sign of expertise and know-how. And at the limits of this type of language, the brand-names themselves: "I went in past him, into a dim pleasant room with an apricot Chinese rug that looked expensive, deep-sided chairs, a number of white drum lamps, a big Capehart in the corner." "I got a half-bottle of Old Taylor out of the deep drawer of the desk." "The sweetish smell of his Fatima poisoned the air for me." (Hemingway is of course the chief representative of this style of brand-name-dropping, but it has currency throughout the literature of the thirties.)

By the time we come to that cross-country inventory of Americana which is Nabokov's *Lolita*, the attitude to objects has changed significantly. Precisely in order for his descriptions to be representative, Nabokov hesitates to use the actual brand-names of the products: the aesthetic reason, that such language is of a different nature from the language of the narration generally and cannot be crudely introduced into it, is part of a more general realization that the physical product itself has long since been dissolved as a permanence. Like the "substances" of philosophy, of mathematics, of the physical sciences, it has long since lost its essentiality and become a locus of processes, a meeting place for social manipulation and human raw material. Where Nabokov occasionally does use names, they are brand-names invented in imitation of the real, and as such his use is a way of rendering, not the product, but the process of nomination. But in general he describes the jumble of commercial products in the American landscape from the outside, as pure appearance without any reference to functionality, since in the new American culture of the fifties functionality, practical use in the satisfaction of need and desire, is no longer of any great importance.

The famous pop art Brillo box represents a different kind of attitude towards objects: the attempt to seize them, not in their material, but in their dated historical reality, as a certain moment and style of the past. It is a fetish representing the will to return to a period when there was still a certain solidity. The Brillo box is a way of making us stare at a single commercial product, in hopes that our vision of all those around us will be transformed, that our new stare will infuse those also with depth and solidity, with the meaning of remembered objects and products, with the physical foundation and dimensions of the older world of need.

The comic strip drawing does much the same thing for the world of culture, as jammed as the airwaves with bits and pieces of stories, imagined characters, cheaply manufactured fantasies of all kinds, even where newspaper and historical truth have come to be assimilated to the products of the entertainment industry. Now suddenly all the floating figures and shapes are simplified down, stamped with exaggeration, blown up and reduced to the size of children's daydreams. The transfer to the fixed object which is the painting takes place in imitation of the material consumption by the child of the comic books themselves, which he handles and uses as objects.

For the nostalgia for this earlier world operates just as strongly on the forms as on the content of its materials. Humphrey Bogart, for example, obviously stands for the hero who knows how to find his way around the dangerous anarchy of the world of the thirties and forties. He is distinguished from the other stars of his period in that he is able to show fear, and his fear is the organ of perception and exploration of the dark world lying about him. As an image, he is related to Marlowe (indeed briefly coincides with him in the movie version of *The Big Sleep*), of the Hemingway hero of the earlier part of the same period in whom the trait of purely technical know-how was even more pronounced.

On the other hand his revival has its formal dimension as well, whether we are consciously aware of it or not. For in our recognition of Humphrey Bogart as culture hero is also included a regret for the smaller black-and-white ninety-minute movie in which he traditionally appeared, and beyond that, for that period in the history of the medium when work was done in a small, fixed form, in a series of small works rather than isolated, enormous, and expensive production. (This evolution in the movie industry parallels the movement in serious literature away from the fixed form of the nineteenth century towards the personally invented, style-conscious individual forms of the twentieth.)

Thus the perception of the products with which the world around us is furnished precedes our perception of things-in-themselves and forms it. We first use objects, only then gradually do we learn to stand away from them and to contemplate them disinterestedly, and it is in this fashion that the commercial nature of our surroundings influences and shapes the production of our literary images, stamping them with the character of a certain period. In Chandler's style the period identifies itself in his most characteristic feature, the exaggerated comparison, the function of which is at the same time to isolate the object in question and to indicate its value: "She was in oyster-white lounging pajamas trimmed with white fur, cut as flowingly as a summer sea frothing on the beach of some small and exclusive island." "Even on Central Avenue, not the quietest-dressed street in the world, he looked about as conspicuous as a tarantula upon a slice of angel food." "There was a desk and a night clerk with one of those moustaches that gets stuck under your fingernail." "This is the ultimate end of the fog belt, and the beginning of that semi-desert region where the sun is as light and dry as old sherry in the morning, as hot as a blast furnace at noon, and drops like an angry brick at nightfall."

As in the hard-boiled movies, the narrator's voice works in counterpoint to the things seen, heightening them subjectively through his own reactions to them, through the poetry his comparisons lend them, and letting them fall back again into their sordid, drab reality through the deadpan humor which disavows what it has just maintained. But where the movies already present a divided structure of vision and sound ready to be played off against each other, the literary work must rely on some deeper division in its material itself. Such a tone is possible for it only against the background of a certain recognizable uniformity of objects, among which the outlandish comparison serves as a pause, drawing a circle momentarily around one of them, causing it to stand out as typical of one of the two zones of the novel's content, as either very expensive or very shabby. It avoids the flat and naturalistically prosaic on the one hand, and the poetic and unreal on the other, in a delicate compromise executed by the tone of the narration. And because it is a spoken account in its very essence, it stands as testimony, like the records of old songs or old comedians, to what every day life was like in a world similar enough to our own to seem very distant.

## IV

> My theory was that the readers just *thought* they cared about nothing but the action; that really, although they didn't know it, the thing they cared about, and that I cared about, was the creation of emotion through dialogue and description. The things they remembered, that haunted them, was not for example, that a man got killed, but that in the moment of his death he was trying to pick a paper clip up off the polished surface of a desk and it kept slipping away from him, so that there was a look of strain on his face and his mouth was half open in a kind of tormented grin, and the last thing in the

> world he thought about was death. He didn't even hear the death knock on the door. That damn little paper clip kept slipping away from his fingers.

Raymond Chandler's novels have not one form, but two, an objective form and a subjective one, the rigid external structure of the detective story on the one hand, and a more personal distinctive rhythm of events on the other, arranged, as is the case with any novelist of originality, according to some ideal molecular chain in the brain cells, as personal in their encephalographic pattern as a fingerprint, peopled with recurrent phantoms, obsessive character types, actors in some forgotten psychic drama through whom the social world continues to be interpreted. Yet the two kinds of form do not conflict with each other; on the contrary the second seems to have been generated out of the first by the latter's own internal contradictions. Indeed, it results from a kind of formula on Chandler's part:

> It often seems to this particular writer that the only reasonably honest and effective way of fooling the reader that remains is to make the reader exercise his mind about the wrong problems, to make him, as it were, solve a mystery (since he is almost sure to solve something) which will land him in a bypath because it is only tangential to the central problem.

For the detective story is not only a purely intellectual mode of knowing events, it is also a puzzle in which the faculties of analysis and reasoning are exercised, and Chandler here simply generalizes a technique of outwitting the reader. Instead of the innovation that will only work once (the most famous is of course that of Agatha Christie in *The Murder of Roger Ackroyd*, where as is well known the murderer turns out to be the narrator himself), he invents a principle for the construction of the plot itself.

It is of course the presence of this kind of plot construction in all of his books, the persistence of this fixed intellectual purpose, that accounts for their similarity as forms. Yet the two aspects of the works hardly seem commensurable, seem to involve different dmensions that miss each other in passing: the intellectual purpose is a purely temporal one, it abolishes itself when it is successful, and when the reader realizes that he has been misled and that the real solution to the murder is to be found elsewhere. The form is on the other hand more spatial in character: even after the temporal reading of the book is finished we have a feeling of its continuity spread out before us in a pattern, and the earlier, misleading twists of the plot (which the pure mind rejects as illusory filling just as soon as it guesses the secret to the puzzle) remain for the imagination of form as an integral part of the road travelled, the experiences gone through. In Chandler's books we are therefore confronted with the paradox of something slight in density and resonance being at the source of some incomparable larger solid, of a kind of nothingness—creating being, of a shadow projecting three-dimensionality out from itself. It is as though an object designed for some purely practical purpose, a machine of some kind, suddenly turned out to be of interest on a different level of perception, on the aesthetic for example; for the rather negative technical device, the quantitative formula for purely intellectual deception given above in Chandler's own words, is responsible in a kind of dialectical accident for the positive qualitative nature of his forms, their lopsided, episodic movements, the characteristic effects and emotions related to them.

The initial deception takes place on the level of the book as a whole, in that it passes itself off as a murder mystery. In fact Chandler's stories are first and foremost description of searches, in which murder is involved, and which sometimes end with the murder of the person sought for. The immediate result of this formal change is that the detective no longer inhabits the atmosphere of pure thought, of puzzle-solving and the resolution of a set of given elements. On the contrary, he is propelled outwards into the space of his world and obliged to move from one kind of social reality to another incessantly, trying to find clues to his client's whereabouts.

Once set in motion, the search has unexpectedly violent results. It is as if the world of the beginning of the book, the imaginary Chandler Southern California, lay in a kind of uneasy balance, an equilibrium of large and small systems of corruption, in a tense silence as of people straining to listen. The appearance of the detective breaks the balance, sets the various mechanisms of suspicion ringing, as he crosses the boundary lines scooping and preparing to make trouble in a way which isn't yet clear. The upshot is a whole series of murders and beatings: it is as though they existed already in a latent state, the acts that had merited them having already been committed, like chemical substances juxtaposed, waiting for a single element to be withdrawn or added in order to complete a reaction which nothing can stop. The appearance of the detective is this element, allowing the predetermining causes to run their course suddenly, to burst into flame on exposure to the open air.

But as has already been made apparent in Chandler's description of his own plot construction, this trail of bloodshed is a false, scent, designed to draw the reader's attention to guilt in the wrong places. The diversion is not dishonest, inasmuch as the guilt uncovered along the way is also real enough; the latter is simply not that with which the book is directly involved. Hence the episodic nature of the diversionary plot: the characters are drawn in heightened, sharp fashion because we will never see them again. Their entire essence must be revealed in a single brief meeting. Yet these meetings take place on a different plane of reality from that of the main plot of the book. It is not only that the intellectual function of our mind is busy weighing and selecting them (are they related in some way to the search or are they not?) in a set of operations which it does not have to perform on the materials of the main plot (the client and his or her household, the person sought and his or her connections). The very violence and crimes themselves are here apprehended on a different mode: since they are tangential and secondary for us, we learn of them in a manner not so much realistic (novelistic) as legendary, much as we would hear about occasional violence in the newspaper or over the radio. Our interest in them is purely anecdotal, and is already a kind of distance from them. Whether we know it yet or not therefore, these characters of the secondary plot exist for us in a different dimension, like glimpses through a window, noises from the back of a store, unfinished stories, unrelated activities going on in the society around us simultaneously with our own.

The climax of the book must therefore involve a return to its beginning, to the initial plot and characters. Obviously the person searched for must be found. But in a perhaps less obvious way, the guilty party (since a murder, a crime, is always in some way involved in the search) must turn out to be in one way or another a member of the family, the client or a member of his entourage. Chandler's novels are all variations on this pattern, almost mathematically predictable combinations and permutations of these basic possibilities: the missing person is dead and the client did it, or the missing person is guilty and the body found was that of somebody else, or both the client and a member of her entourage are guilty and the missing person is not really missing at all, and so forth.

In a sense this pattern is in itself little more than a variation on the law of the least likely party, since it seems to make little sense that a criminal would go to a detective in the first place and ask him to solve a murder of which he or she was in reality guilty. And then there is a secondary, sociological shock: the comparison between all the secondary, relatively institutionalized killings (gangland murders, police brutality) and the private-life, domestic crime which is the book's central event and which turns out to be just as sordid and violent in its own way.

But the principal explanation of this pattern of a return to the beginning is to be found in the ritual unveiling of the murderer itself. A kind of intellectual satisfaction might be derived from a demonstration of the necessity for such-and-such a minor character, met only briefly in passing, to be the murderer, but we have already seen that the emotional effect of the revelation of the murder depends on a certain familiarity with its innocent mask; and the only characters in Chandler whom we stay with long enough to develop this familiarity, whom we ever get to know in any kind of depth of character analysis, are those of the opening, of what has been called the main plot.

(In ingenious and metaphysical detective stories such as Robbe-Grillet's *Les Gommes* or Doderer's *Ein Mord den Jeder begeht*, the logic inherent in this situation is pushed to its conclusion and the murderer turns out to be the detective himself, in that abstract equation of I = I which Hegel saw as the source of all self-conscious identity. In a more Freudian way, Chandler's imitators have experimented with situations in which, after a search through time as well as through space, the criminal and the victim or the client and the criminal turn out to be related to each other, in one Oedipal variation or another. Yet in all this the detective story plot merely follows the basic tendency of all literary plots or intrigue in general, which is marked by the resolution of multiplicity back into some primal unity, by a return to some primal starting point, in the marriage of hero and heroine and the creation of the original family cellular unit, or the unveiling of the hero's mysterious origins, and so forth.)

On the other hand, it would be wrong to think of Chandler's stories as conforming in their final effect with the description we have given of the unveiling of the murderer in the classical detective story. For the discovery of the criminal here is only half of a more complicated revelation, and takes place, not only as the climax of a murder mystery, but also as that of a search. The search and the murder serve as alternating centers for our attention in a kind of intricate Gestalt pattern; each serves to mask off the weaker, less convincing aspects of the other, each serves to arrest the blurring of the other out into the magical and the symbolic and to refocus it in a raw and sordid clarity. When our mind is following the motif of the murder, the search ceases to be a mere literary technique, a pretext on which to hang a series of episodes, and is invested with a kind of depressing fatality, like a circular movement narrowing down. When on the contrary we focus on the search as the organizing center of the events described, the murder becomes a purposeless accident, the senseless breaking off of a thread, of a trail.

Indeed, it would not be too much to say that there takes place in Chandler a demystification of violent death. The fact of the search tends to arrest the transformation involved in the revelation of the murderer. There is no longer behind the unveiling that infinity of possibilities of evil, that formlessness behind a determinate mask. One character has simply been transformed into another; a name, a label, has wavered and then gone to fix itself to someone else. For the attribute of being a murderer can no longer function as a symbol of pure evil when murder itself has lost its symbolic qualities.

Chandler's de-mystification involves the removal of purpose from the murder-event. The classical detective story always invests murder with purpose by its very formal perspective. The murder is, as we have seen, a kind of abstract point which is made to bear meaning and significance by the convergence of all lines upon it. In the world of the classical detective story nothing happens which is not related to the central murder: therefore it is purposeful, if for no other reason than to organize all that raw material around itself. (The actual purpose, the motive and cause, is worked up after the fact by the author, and never matters very much.)

But in Chandler the other random violence of the secondary plot has intervened to contaminate the central murder. And by the time we reach its explanation, we have come to feel all violence in the same light, and it strikes us as being just a shoddy and cheap, just as physically abrupt and as morally insignificant.

Murder comes to seem moreover in its very essence accidental and without meaning. It was the optic of the classical detective story, the distortion of its formal perspective, that made the murder look like the almost disembodied result of a process of purely mental planning and premeditation, like the jotting down on paper of the results of mathematical operations performed in the head. Now however the gap between intention and execution is glaringly evident: no matter what planning is involved, the leap to physical action, the committing of the murder itself, is always abrupt and without prior logical justification in the world of reality. Thus the reader's mind has been used as an element in a very complicated aesthetic deception: he has been made to expect the solution of an intellectual puzzle, his purely intellectual functions are operating emptily, in anticipation of it, and suddenly, in its place, he is given an evocation of death in all its physicality, when there is no longer any time to prepare himself for it properly, when he is obliged to take the strong sensation on its own terms.

The final element in Chandler's characteristic form is that the underlying crime is always old, lying half-forgotten in the pasts of the characters before the book begins. This is the principal reason why the reader's attention is diverted from it: he assumes it to be a part of the dimension of the present, of the events going on before him in the immediacy of his narrated universe. Instead, it is buried in that world's past, in time, among the dead evoked in the memorable closing page of *The Big Sleep*.

And suddenly the purely intellectual effect of Chandler's construction formula is metamorphized into a result of unmistakable aesthetic intensity. From the point of view of abstract curiosity we might expect the reader to have a reaction not altogether unmixed:

satisfaction at the solution of the puzzle, irritation at having been misled through so much extraneous material which had no real bearing on it. And on the aesthetic level the irritation remains, but transfigured.

For now, at the end, all the events of the book are seen in a new and depressing light: all that energy and activity wasted to find somebody who had in reality been dead for so long, for whom the time of the present was little more than a process of slow physical dissolution. And suddenly, at the thought of that dissolution, and of the mindless lack of identity of the missing person so long called by name, the very appearance of life itself, of time in the present, of the bustling activity of the outside world, is stripped away and we feel in its place the presence of graves beneath the bright sunlight; the present fades to little more than a dusty, once lived moment which will quickly take its place in the back years of an old newspaper file. And our formal distraction at last serves its fundamental purpose: by diverting us with the ritual detective story aim of the detection of the criminal, and of his transformation into the Other, it is able to bring us up short, without warning, against the reality of death itself, stale death, reaching out to remind the living of its own mouldering resting place.

# Raymond Chandler and an American Genre

*E. M. Beekman*

Chandler's method can be more immediately examined by comparing the story "The Curtain" and his novel, his sixth, *The Long Goodbye* (1953), which was recently reprinted in *The Midnight Raymond Chandler*. The germ for the novel (his longest) lies in the first five pages of story. Larry Batzel, sketched briefly in the opening pages of the story, becomes the complex and intriguing character Terry Lennox of *The Long Goodbye*. The comparison illustrates Chandler's method of amplifying a brief sentence or short scene into an elaborate description or into an entire chapter. The action of the first five pages of "The Curtain" is expanded, as a jazz musician builds a solo from a single melody line, into five chapters of the novel. The story starts:

> The first time I ever saw Larry Batzel he was drunk outside Sardi's in a secondhand Rolls-Royce. There was a tall blonde with him who had eyes you wouldn't forget. I helped her argue him out from under the wheel so that she could drive.

That very first sentence alone becomes a paragraph in the book:

> The first time I laid eyes on Terry Lennox he was drunk in a Rolls-Royce Silver Wraith outside the terrace of the Dancers. The parking lot attendant had brought the car out and he was still holding the door open because Terry Lennox's left foot was still dangling outside, as if he had forgotten he had one. He had

From "Raymond Chandler and an American Genre," *Massachusetts Review* 14 (1973): 149-73; pp. 158-68 (footnotes renumbered).

> a young-looking face but his hair was bone white. You could tell by his eyes that he was plastered to the hairline, but otherwise he looked like any other nice young guy in a dinner jacket who had been spending too much money in a joint that exists for that purpose and for no other.

The simple description of the girl in the story's second sentence becomes more precise:

> There was a girl beside him. Her hair was a lovely shade of dark red and she had a distant smile on her lips and over her shoulders she had a blue mink that almost made the Rolls-Royce look like just another automobile. It didn't quite. Nothing can.

The third quoted sentence from "The Curtain" becomes 800 words of description and dialogue in the novel.

Chandler's diction is a mixture of colloquial and poetic language, producing a style which is never purely realistic yet always concrete—Chandler seldom apostrophizes abstraction. This is a hallmark of the American style, of course, from Melville to Hemingway; a direct style of communication which is clear and precise without sacrificing poetic beauty. Such precision can etch a person or a scene very sharply and can create similes or metaphors which are startling either in their beauty or their wit.

Many reviewers have attacked Chandler's "tough-guy similes" which were so cleverly parodied by S. J. Perelman in "Farewell My Lovely Appetizer," but they forget that Chandler intended them to be witty and, more importantly, that he had devised not all of them for humorous purposes only, though humor is very much a part of his work. At times his figurative language is as sharply apt as that of Dickens or Conrad, two authors which whom Chandler has something in common. The stylistic devices look easy enough, but their realization is more difficult. Most often Chandler yokes two incongruous subjects to achieve a startling and fresh observation. Samples:

> 1) I could see, even on that short acquaintance, that thinking was always going to be a bother to her.
>
> 2) The plants filled the place, a forest of them, with nasty meaty leaves and stalks like the newly washed fingers of dead men.

3) A few locks of dry white hair clung to his scalp, like wild flowers fighting for life on a bare rock.

4) The General spoke again, slowly, using his strength as carefully as an out-of-work showgirl uses her last good pair of stockings.

5) There were low bookshelves, there was a thick pinkish Chinese rug in which a gopher could have spent a week without showing his nose above the nap. There were floor cushions, bits of old silk tossed around, as if whoever lived there had to have a piece he could reach out and thumb.

6) Hair like steel wool grew far back on his head and gave him a great deal of doomed forehead that might at a careless glance have seemed a dwelling-place for brains.

7) Under the thinning fog the surf curled and creamed, almost without sound, like a thought trying to form itself on the edge of consciousness.

8) I was as empty of life as a scarecrow's pockets.

9) He looked about as inconspicuous as a tarantula on a slice of angel food.

10) It was a blonde. A blonde to make a bishop kick a hole in a stained-glass window.

11) I lit a cigarette. It tasted like a plumber's handkerchief.

12) The house itself was not so much. It was smaller than Buckingham Palace, rather grey for California, and probably had fewer windows than the Chrysler Building.

13) [A bug crawling over a desk] It wobbled a little as it crawled, like an old woman carrying too many parcels.

14) Its color scheme was bile green, linseed poultice brown, sidewalk grey and monkey-bottom blue. It was as restful as a split lip.

15) Grayson put his bony hand out and I shook it. It felt like shaking hands with a towel-rack.

16) [The elevator] had an elderly perfume in it, like three widows drinking tea.

17) Bright moonlight lay against its wall like a fresh coat of paint.

18) I belonged in Idle Valley like a pearl onion on a banana split.

19) It would have depressed a laughing jackass and made it coo like a mourning dove.

Most often the vehicle negates the tenor of the comparison implying the abjuratory world of Chandler's fiction. (See items 2, 3, 4 above) There is a comic fierceness in the hyperbole which often relies for its effect on the creation of an outrageous grotesquerie so that it becomes similar to surrealism of "black humor" (see 9, 10, 18, 19.)

It seems to me that critics have denigrated these similes simply because they don't expect to find them in this genre of fiction. But I would venture to say that they are no less fittingly-preposterous than Pope's in "The Rape of the Lock," Dickens' famous descriptions, or such similes as Conrad's in *The Secret Agent* : ". . . the Chief Inspector went on peering at the table with a calm face and the slightly anxious attention of an indigent customer bending over what may be called by-products of a butcher's shop with view to an inexpensive dinner." The Inspector, by the way, is examining a pulverized corpse.

Yet Chandler could also get his point across with irony (see 1, 6), just as there are similes of simple poetic beauty which are not so immediately obvious (see 7, 8, 13, 17). How difficult it would be to emulate Chandler's hyperbolic sarcasm can be seen in the work of the many epigones of the hardboiled school of writing, such sorry tradesmen as Spillane, Cheyney, Chase, *et al.*, and in a recent pastiche by a British writer (*Gumshoe*, also made into a film) which only passes muster because the hero is deliberately presented as a bad stand-up comic.

But Chandler's mastery of style is better observed in more expanded rhetorical devices. In chapter 31 of *Farewell, My Lovely*, the aforementioned noticed little bug crawls across the desk of the investigating police officer and falls to the floor. Throughout a conversation about murder Marlowe keeps track of the little bug which is trying to find a way out. When he is leaving, Marlowe picks the bug up and carries him down eighteen floors to put him gently among some vegetation. By referring indirectly to the helplessness of the insignificant insect as a counterpoint to the brutality of the conversation, Chandler implies the inhumanity of the world Marlowe inhabits and, in the final act of off-handed tenderness, he depicts Marlowe's concern for life much better than could many pages of discursive prose. It is a chivalrous act, just a touch insane, since anyone else in that room would have squashed the bug, not necessarily with malice but simply because it would be bothering somebody.

In the same novel Chandler gives a description of a calendar which serves as an indirect metaphor for his gritty, seedy world, and for his hero who will not bow to its malice.

> They had Rembrandt on the calendar that year, a rather smeary self-portrait due to imperfectly registered color plates. It showed him holding a smeared palette with a dirty thumb and wearing a tam-o-shanter which wasn't any too clean either. His other hand held a brush poised in the air, as if he might be going to do a little work after a while, if somebody made a down payment. His fact was aging, saggy, full of the disgust of life, and the thickening effects of liquor. But it had a hard cheerfulness that I liked, and the eyes were as bright as drops of dew.

This is a description that becomes a metaphor for the fictional world and also nicely delineates Chandler's faith in the indomitable spirit of man (and artist), no matter how we are forced to live. The description echoes his remarks elsewhere about Shakespeare.

> Shakespeare would have done well in any generation because he would have refused to die in a corner; he would have taken the false gods and made them over; he would have taken the current formulae and forced them into something lesser men thought them incapable of. Alive today he would undoubtedly have written and directed motion pictures, plays and God knows what. Instead of saying "This medium is no good," he would have used it and made it good. If some people called some of his work cheap (which some of it is), he wouldn't have cared a rap, because he would know that without some vulgarity there is no complete man. He would have hated refinement, as such, because it is always a withdrawal, a shrinking, and he was much too tough to shrink from anything.[1]

This, with a bow to himself as the writer who had "to accept a mediocre form and make something like literature out of it."

In *The High Window* another nonhuman detail is used antithetically as a leitmotiv. A little garden statue of a black boy recurs throughout the novel as a symbol of decency and camaraderie which is lacking in the society Marlowe is embroiled in. Such technical devices and the constancy of the hero carry Chandler's novels from scene to scene. They have a unity which is both technically and poetically "right." The technical contrivances of plot, energized by the conventions of the genre are admirably achieved but they are also subservient to a larger design. Chandler's is a poetry of evil which keeps each book pacing relentlessly to an inconclusive end—certainly a major departure from the melioristic endings of traditional detective fiction. And so one can see that, from the fundamentals of sentences, tropes, rhetorical devices, paragraphs and scenes, a web of fiction is fabricated which is more than the sum of its parts.

*The Big Sleep* is a good example. In the second chapter of that novel Philip Marlowe goes to call on a very wealthy, retired general. The interview is conducted in a hothouse where orchids are cultivated. An arresting notion. But Chandler makes the scene complex metaphor which suggests the entire novel and echoes the theme(s) of the book. The precise details and the striking similes become poetry, metaphors for a claustrophobic artificiality and for a life that is a parasitic death. The flowers are cultivated in an artificial heat where they thrive in profusion. The plants form a jungle of sinister proliferation which surrounds the dying general, who is paralyzed, confined to a wheelchair, brittle, unnaturally cold and barely a living organism. The plants which viciously resemble human flesh, abound in energy and the human being, dried out like a withered leaf, can enjoy life only by proxy; the general can do no more than approximate satisfaction of his vices by greedily watching another man enjoying them for him. Claustrophobia and perversion are enhanced by images of moisture and the sickroom. Life is a travesty here and the contradictions continue. General Sternwood fathered two daughters at an age when incipient parenthood is not the norm. His children are perverse and ruthless; the only member of his family he ever liked was a son-in-law who was a gangster and who turns out to have been murdered. The scene has a Baudelairean touch in the exuberance of the vice described, while the oppressive mood recalls Faulkner who, incidentally, collaborated on the screenplay based on Chandler's book.

These themes of corruption and sinister inversion are mercilessly pursued. The artificial jungle of the hothouse grows into that of a perverse society of sex, money, murder, immorality and betrayal. There is no escape from it, just as there is no escape from a narcosis. The only awakening possible is into the "big sleep" of death,[2] and death is cynical in its democracy. It is nocturnal book and the bleakness of the world depicted is underscored by a persistent rain. All that was intimated in the scene in the hothouse has been developed into a powerful evocation of evil which taints everything, from people to climate, and which is further disclosed in gallery of brilliantly created characters and through a style of forceful poetry.

This book, and the six other novels by Chandler, are in the tradition of negative romanticism which is perhaps the dominant mode of American literature from Hawthorne to our contemporary black humorists—that power of darkness which Hawthorne, Poe and Melville explored, which Mark Twain could not laugh away, and which created a mythical landscape in Faulkner. Poe's "The Fall of the House of Usher" can be regarded as the rehearsal for the saga of the Sartoris-Compson-Sutpen families in Yoknapatawpha County. And the predecessor of Chandler's Californian nightmare had his hero Dupin "be enamored of the night for her own sake." But where Poe brought inductive light to moral darkness, Chandler refuses to cheat his vision in like manner. When Marlowe has solved a dilemma, he has not explained the enigma. All of Chandler's books end on a note of dissatisfaction. The purported solution does not tidy things up since there is no end to a waking nightmare.

This dark vision has lost none of its power today. The excess of violence of which Chandler has been needlessly accused is now hardly noticeable, nor was it lovingly intended to for shock effect, but rather described because life is simply that cheap in this truly egalitarian society: literally, a matter of fact. And so Chandler does not laud death with the lyrical mesmerism of Hemingway, nor does he play metaphysical games with it in Sartrean ingenuity. A death is a waste of life.

A corrupt universe can house no justice or, inversely, justice would be an embarrassing intruder. The forces of authority in Chandler's world are part of an eroding fabric. Justice is a matter of chance and the law a mechanism. As a lawyer in *The Long Goodbye* puts it: "The law isn't justice. It's a very imperfect mechanism. If you press exactly the right buttons and are also lucky, justice may show up in the answer. A mechanism is all the law was ever intended to be." Nevertheless, the parts of this mechanism have power and will grind people down who happen to get stuck in them. The enforcers of the law often look like the machinery they serve and Chandler emphasizes their frightening neutrality, as machines are wont to be.

> They had the calm weathered faces of healthy men in hard condition. They had the eyes they always have, cloudy and grey like freezing water. The firm set mouth, the hard little wrinkles at the corners of the eyes, the hard hollow meaningless stare, not quite cruel and a thousand miles from kind. The dull ready-made clothes, worn without style, with a sort of contempt; the look of men who are poor and yet proud of their power, watching always for way to make it felt, to shove it into you and twist it and grin and watch you squirm, ruthless without malice, cruel and yet not always unkind. What would you expect them to be. Civilization had no meaning for them. (*The Little Sister*)

In *The Long Goodbye* Chandler describes the environment they operate: it is society as a house of detention.

> In the corner of the cell block there may be a second steel door that leads to the show-up box. One of its walls is wire mesh painted black. On the back wall are ruled lines for height. Overhead are floodlights. You go in there in the morning as a rule, just before the night captain goes off duty. You stand against the measuring lines and the lights glare at you and there is no light behind the wire mesh. But plenty of people are out there: cops, detectives, citizens who have been robbed or assaulted or swindled or kicked out of their cars at gun point or conned out of their life savings. You don't see or hear them. You hear the voice of the night captain. You receive him loud and clear. He puts you through your paces as if you were a performing dog. He is tired and cynical and competent. He is the stage manager of a play that has had the longest run in history, but it no longer interests him.

The population which inhabits the grid of the night captain is dead in a different sense.

> We've got the big money, the sharp shooters, the percentage workers, the fast dollar boys, the hoodlums out of New York and Chicago and Detroit and Cleveland. We've got the flashy restaurants and night clubs they run, and the hotels and apartment houses they own, and the grafters and con men and female bandits that live in them. The luxury trades, the pansy decorators, the Lesbian dress designers, the riff-raff of a big hardboiled city with no more personality than a paper cup. Out in the fancy suburbs dear old Dad is reading the sports page in front of a picture window, with his shoes off, thinking he is high class because he has a three-car garage. Mom is in front of her princess dresser trying to paint the suitcases out from under her eyes. And Junior is clamped on to the telephone calling up a succession of high school girls that talk pidgin English and carry contraceptives in their make-up kit. (*The Little Sister*)

Chandler made metropolitan California into a metaphor of America in a manner which has the same harsh clarity as the paintings of Edward Hopper. His fictional world has an unremitting gloom: injustice and the seven deadly sins are paramount and decency is something of a vice.

But, like Faulkner, Chandler fostered a negative heroism. This bleak world is illuminated by the stubborn endurance of his hero, Philip Marlowe, a man who insists on a private code which is not so much one of justice as one of *humanitas*. Marlowe is not a bright shiny volunteer for a superlative of good. He is an angry and bitter man, tainted by the world he invades in his violence, his gallows humor and his melancholy—a melancholy which is at times close to despair since he knows that his efforts are so futile. But he is a man who must endure and who must persist in his defiance against the forces of coercion—a sad man since he realizes the futility; and a noble man because he will not be vanquished.

Marlowe, who was described by Marshall McLuhan as "Chandler's echo of Christopher Marlowe's supermen Tamburlaine and Dr. Faustus," is in a long line of Romantic heroes. He is an outsider, a loner, a man who will not fit the pattern, a character who must not toe the line. If Marlowe were an archetype he would be a somber knight on a never finished quest, recharging his faith by adversity. A Romantic Hero, to be sure, but one who has been mired in reality. As an outsider, in his preference for solitude, in his stubborn defiance and power to endure, Marlowe is very much the archetypical hero of American fiction, from Melville's Ishmael and Bartleby to Hemingway's Frederic Henry and Robert Jordan. In Chandler's novels Marlowe is the only figure with warmth and compassion, but there is a constant infiltration of the autumnal mood, of weariness and futility. That is why these novels are not simple crime fiction: at their close little has been resolved despite the fact that the murderer has been found. All of them end on a note of dissatisfaction.

Marlowe is thus not a simplistic creation. In fact, he is quite subtle and ambiguous. In this character there is a fierce grief which has little opportunity to be assuaged—a grief for a loss, perhaps a primeval Eden, perhaps a community of decent men. Not a grief, however, simply for a loss of innocence, but a bitter frustration about the fact that things *are* as they are though they shouldn't be that way. There is a revulsion for this world yet also a distaste for his own defiant nobility, a nobility very much like a pawned code of honor. In all these particulars Marlowe is a reflection of the most typical American fictional hero, and I think that not enough emphasis has been put on his furious grief which can only escape through a tenuously controlled pathos or though the painfully blasphemous fury of, for example, Frederic Henry at the end of Hemingway's *A Farewell to Arms*. Exiles ever, these characters are not destined to join their fellow men.

In Chandler's angriest and yet saddest novel, *The Long Goodbye*, the conventional vehicle of murder is almost irrelevant. It is basically a novel about friendship and the emotional combat of human relations. Marlowe's affection for Terry Lennox is one of those baffling emotional frauds life is fond of putting over on us. Despite his better judgment, despite the negative qualities of Lennox, despite the trouble this man is fated to visit upon anyone associated with him, Marlowe feels a strong bond and defends him against preposterous odds of circumstantial misfortune. Lennox is weak, cynical, apparently resigned to his fate, yet, though reluctantly, Marlowe finds himself enticed into a bond of fellowship with a man who is a counterfeiter of life in need of protection. This kinship of exile has one flaw: Lennox has no profound relationship left in him to spend. He is a burned-out case fitted with a new exterior by money and modern medicine. Lennox is Marlowe's negative double, and if Marlowe had given in to his feelings he would have had to admit his own defeat at trying to maintain a precarious balance on that edge between despairing ruthlessness and an anger born from a tenuous faith.

Yet Lennox is kin, and it is appropriate that Marlowe pays a silent tribute to this ghostly friendship when he is alone. It is a moving passage, written with superb control of language and emotion, showing how Chandler could handle that most difficult task of the novelist: to create pathos that never gibbers into sentimentality. Marlowe has just finished reading a letter form Lennox who has fled into voluntary exile in Mexico. The letter contained a five-thousand-dollar bill and Lennox asks him to perform a few commemorative gestures.

> I sat there and looked at it for a long time. At last I put it away in my letter case and went out to the kitchen to make that coffee. I did what he asked me to, sentimental or not. I poured two cups and added some bourbon to his and set it down on the side of the table where he had sat at the morning I took him to the plane. I lit a cigarette for him and set it in an ashtray beside the cup. I watched the steam rise from the coffee and the thin thread of smoke rise from the cigarette. Outside in the tecoma a bird was gussing around, talking to himself in low chirps, with an occasional brief flutter of wings. Then the coffee didn't steam anymore and the cigarette stopped smoking and was just a dead butt on the edge of an ashtray. I dropped it into the garbage can under the sink, I poured the coffee out and washed the cup and put it away. That was that. It didn't seem quite enough to do for five thousand dollars.

It is no accident I am sure, that the book deals not only with a counterfeit friendship but also with a counterfeit writer who has prostituted his talents, and with counterfeit love. Nor is it an accident that most of the book takes place in an idyllic valley settled by the very rich. But in modern American fiction every Eden turns out to be a fraud—the only reality is that of the city, and it is one that sours.

In Chandler's work there is Fitzgerald's tone of disenchantment and cynicism, Nathaniel West's exaggerated humor and rueful tenderness, Hemingway's melancholy and brooding, and Faulkner's decadence and stubborn endurance. But unlike Hemingway's heroes, Chandler's Marlowe is not passive. Marlowe pushes against a recalcitrant existence with the quixotic energy of a Bartleby's "I prefer not to." For a man who felt intellectually like a displaced person, at home on neither continent, Chandler wrote a superlative chapter of the American myth.

---

1 *Raymond Chandler Speaking*, p. 82.

2 This expression was Chandler's; when O'Neill used it in *The Iceman Cometh*, the playwright thought he was borrowing a colorful American expression, not realizing who its author was.

# The Complex Art of Raymond Chandler

*George N. Dove*

In his first essay entitled "The Simple Art of Murder," Raymond Chandler took issue with Dorothy Sayers' dictum that the detective story "does not, and by hypothesis never can, attain the loftiest level of literary achievement." Miss Sayers' error, said Chandler, lay in the fact that she defined detective fiction according to a limited formula that produced stories which do not come off artistically as fiction.[1] W.H. Auden, replying to Chandler, paid him a sincere (though qualified) compliment when he wrote that Chandler's "powerful but extremely depressing books should be read and judged, not as escape literature, but as works of art."[2] Both writers miss the point, says Julian Symons in his recent history of crime fiction: "Chandler's books are escape literature of a different kind, that is all."[3] Although he seems unwilling to call Chandler an artist, Symons does say of a later novelist that "at his best, [he] is as good a writer as Chandler, and that should not be taken for light praise."[4]

The question seems to present itself, then, Are Raymond Chandler's novels works of art? Chandler is universally credited (along with Dashiell Hammett) with founding the "tough private eye" school that has almost taken over the detective fiction market during the past three decades, and most critics are willing to praise his depth of psychological insight and his ability to write memorable scenes, but the question of his approach to the art of the narrative needs further exploration.

Leaving aside the matter of literary achievement (here we can take our cue from Chandler, who wrote, "I do not know what the loftiest level of literary achievement is"),[5] perhaps the best approach to the quality of Chandler's art would be to re-phrase the questions

"The Complex Art of Raymond Chandler," *Armchair Detective* 8: (1974-75): 271-4.

something like this: Do the seven novels of Raymond Chandler show evidences of a consistent, conscientious craftsmanship?

Certainly one of the marks of a narrative craftsman is the care with which he puts his stories together, and the structures of the Chandler novels show that he was both an innovator and an experimenter in the art of plot-construction. Chandler himself seemed to regard plot as one of the lesser tools of the writer: of his first novel he said that it was "just another detective yearn that happens to be more interested in people than in plot,"[6] and on another occasion that "plotting may be a bore even if you are good at it."[7] We must not be misled by this cynicism, because Chandler was thinking about the stereotyped whodunit that had been so popular up until his own time, in which most other elements of the story were made subordinate to the plot.

A careful examination of his seven novels will show that Chandler contributed in at least two important ways to the structure of the detective story: he varied his plots in such fashion as to best accommodate his material, and he developed an approach to structure that has been widely imitated by writers of the private-eye school.

At the beginning of *The Big Sleep* (1939) Philip Marlowe, who will be the sleuth-protagonist in all of the Chandler novels, accepts from old General Sternwood a commission to find out who is blackmailing the General's daughter Carmen, and why. Before he leaves the Sternwood residence, however, Marlowe finds out about another family mystery, the disappearance of the General's son-in-law, Rusty Regan. The importance of this complication is that, although he is not being paid to look for Regan and although Regan's disappearance seems to have no relation to the blackmail plot, Marlowe continues to pursue this mystery until the end of the book, long after his original commission has been fulfilled. The form of the story is the familiar Frantic Pursuit: Marlowe tracks down Geiger, the blackmailer, just as Geiger is murdered; then that murderer is found in an automobile at the bottom of the bay; Marlowe reaches the man responsible for this death just a few minutes before he is shot dead; and so on until the final resolution.

*The Big Sleep* represents an historically important departure from the conventional method of plotting detective stories, which was first used by Poe in the Dupin tales, crystallized by Conan Doyle, and employed by writers of detective fiction until it had become standard. Basically, this classic structure embodies seven steps: the Problem, the First Analysis, the Complication, the Period of Confusion, the Dawning Light, the Solution, and the Explanation. Versatile writers could and did vary the sequence (R. Austin Freeman, for example, with his "inverted" stories), but the pattern served as a framework for hundreds of writers, including Dashiell Hammett.

The important features of the structure of *The Big Sleep* can be summarized as follows:

1. What starts out as the main plot (the blackmail of Carmen Sternwood) is solved relatively early.

2. Meanwhile, the minor plot (the disappearance of Rusty Regan) has moved forward independently, with only incidental connection to the blackmail plot.

3. Developments in each plot spawn other plots: e.g., the murder of Geiger is coincidental with Marlowe's discovery of the source of his blackmail of Carmen Sternwood.

4. Solutions occur successively, but (until the final resolution) there are still other problems to be solved.

5. Thus, the solution of each problem leaves questions unanswered and loose ends to be tied up. The story is carried forward by a series of partial successes, with each solution leaving a residue of mystery.

6. After he has cleared up the blackmail plot, Marlowe's curiosity about Rusty Regan leads him on with an investigation that was not part of his original commission. At this point, the "minor" plot becomes the main plot.

Complications, spin-off plots, and reversals of major and minor plots were, of course, not new in 1939. The important development in *The Big Sleep* is one listed as number 5 above, the "residue of mystery," which Chandler successfully employed in this novel and which has been imitated by a number of writers ever since.

I use the term "residue of mystery" to describe a story-line that diverges from the main plot, runs parallel to it, and, after the solution of the original problem, carries forward the element of suspense on its own. Thus a spin-off plot that merges back into the main story, or is resolved at the same time as the solution of the major problem, does not belong in the residue-of-mystery class; to be so classified, it must outlive the original mystery.

I am not sure that Raymond Chandler was the first to use this narrative device, but its popularity among his successors and imitators would seem to indicate that they learned from him its usefulness as a vehicle for suspense. A good example can be seen in Ross Macdonald's *The Chill*: Lew Archer is commissioned to find a missing girl; he finds her before a fifth of the story has been told, but in the meantime he has turned up a whole constellation of related problems, and there is enough reside of mystery to keep the book going for another 150 pages.

In his second novel, *Farewell, My Lovely* (1940), Chandler switched to the parallel-merging plot type of story. In the first chapter, Marlowe involves himself with a released convict, Moose Malloy, who is searching for his lost Velma. "Nothing made it my business except curiosity," say Marlowe, and this curiosity carries us though six chapters, when we are introduced into a new and ostensibly unrelated story, the theft of a jade necklace. For a time the two narratives move ahead apparently independently of each other until Marlowe discovers a relationship between them, and toward the end of the book they are fully merged and are resolved together.

The structure of this novel differs from that of *The Big Sleep* in two ways. There is no residue of mystery in *Farewell My Lovely* and no spin-off plots, and the suspense of the two original mysteries is maintained to the end. Chandler had a different kind of story to tell in this one, and he refused the temptation to repeat a pattern that had proved successful in his first novel.

Having tried two innovative types of structure, Chandler turned in *The High Window* (1942) to the classic, traditional single story-line. The story is every bit as complex as those of his first two novels, with complications, minor plots, and three murders, but Marlowe's original commission to recover the valuable rare coin is the central mystery and is not resolved until the last chapter. There are no spin-off plots and no residue of mystery as in *The Big Sleep*, no parallel plotting as in *Farewell, My Lovely*.

If one judges a detective story in terms of its ability to mystify, Chandler's fourth novel, *The Lady in the Lake* (1943), must be his most successful. The initial situation is the familiar one: Marlowe is commissioned to find Crystal Kingsley, who has been missing for a month. Early in the investigation he comes across the murder of another woman, Muriel Chess. Marlowe works on both cases, motivated partly by his curiosity and partly by a suspicion that they are related. In a startling conclusion, Marlowe is able to demonstrate that the two situations are exactly the reverse of what they originally appeared. It was Crystal Kingsley who was murdered, and the disappearance was that of Muriel Chess.

The remarkable quality of *The Lady in the Lake*, as far as plot construction is concerned, lies in the apparent complexity of the story (the reversal of plots), while the over-all structure is really quite simple. There are only one main plot and two minor ones, with no real spin-offs and no residue of mystery. Actually, the structure of *The Lady in the Lake* can be fitted into the seven-step pattern of the Poe-Doyle formula, complete with the expansive explanation at the end.

After *The Lady in the Lake*, Chandler ceased to experiment with approaches to the problem of story-construction. In the remaining three novels, the structural devices are those he had tried and apparently found satisfactory.

It was not until 1949 that the fifth novel appeared. In *The Little Sister* he repeated the device he had used in *The Big Sleep*, the residue of mystery. The story opens with Marlowe's commission to find a missing person. This job is finished two-thirds of the way through the book, but in the meantime Marlowe has become involved with three new murders, plus one old unsolved one, plus a commission to protect a movie star. It is this last involvement that becomes a genuine residue: while investigating the disappearance of Orrin Quest, Marlowe has almost by accident been commissioned to protect Mavis Weld. Thus, even after the original problem has been solved, there is enough residue of mystery to carry the story forward through another thirteen chapters.

*The Long Goodbye* (1953), Chandler's longest novel and his most complex one, is the work of a writer who by now had so mastered the art of construction as to be able to demonstrate a genuine virtuosity in the handling of plot. In the first dozen chapters we are introduced to two stories (Marlowe's befriending Terry Lennox and his commission to protect Roger Wade) which seem to be unrelated, and we are consequently prepared for a novel of the parallel-merging plot variety like *Farewell, My Lovely*. Actually, the second story is a spin-off of the first, so that we have not parallel-merging plots but a residue-of-mystery structure. The subtlety of this complicated arrangement is cleverly concealed throughout most of the book by Chandler's ability to keep the original involvement alive with a series of hints and suggestions after the apparent death of Terry Lennox.

Chandler's seventh and last novel, *Playback*, though not published until 1958, had been originally put together as a movie script in 1947, and thus belongs in point of conception between *The Lady in the Lake* and *The Little Sister*.[8] Structurally it lacks the complexity and virtuosity of Chandler's late novels. The plot is the classic single story-line; complications there are in abundance, but they are merged back into the main story and are not genuine residue plots.

It would seem, then, that Chandler experimented with a number of kinds of plot-construction and that he varied his structural devices to suit his material, instead of following the customary practice of hitting upon a successful formula and then writing stories to fit that pattern. Let us look now at two other evidences of Chandler's craftsmanship, his use of unifying devices and his ability to handle the problem of coincidence.

Some of Chandler's successors who have tried to imitate his complex plotting would do well to study the skill with which he keeps his reader from getting lost in his more complicated stories. A brief examination of his first, fourth and sixth novels will show how he developed this ability.

There is one point in *The Big Sleep* when Marlowe is investigating five mysteries: blackmail, two disappearances, and two murders. Apparently feeling that this may be too much for the reader, Chandler lets the two murders be solved quickly. There are still the original main plot (the blackmail of Carmen Sternwood) and the spin-off (the disappearance of Rusty Regan), but Chandler ties them into each other through the repeated re-introduction of two characters who are involved in both stories and so preserves the unity of what could otherwise be an awkwardly split novel.

*The Lady in the Lake*, with its reversed mysteries and its theme of appearance versus reality, could also be an extremely difficult book to read, except for the fact that Chandler uses Marlowe's insight as a unifying device. "There's a connection in time," says Marlowe of the (apparent) murder and the (apparent) disappearance. "I don't know of any other connection, but I thought I'd better mention it." He does mention it at least four times while the two stories are moving ahead on separate lines, signalling the reader that all may not be as it appears.

Chandler undertook a difficult narrative problem in *The Long Goodbye*, first introducing and then cutting off a story (the Terry Lennox plot), switching to an entirely different one (the Roger Wade plot), and then re-introducing the original story for the final resolution. The problem, of course, is to keep the reader from forgetting about the first story while the second unfolds, but Chandler was by this time able to control his material like a real master of the craft of the narrative. By using a number of devices, he drops repeated hints that the stories are connected: comparisons between the two cases are made by Marlowe and others, an increasing number of personal relationships are revealed, and finally the shadowy "Paul Marston," Eileen Wade's lover, is revealed as Terry Lennox. When the presumably dead Lennox reappears at the end of the story the reader may be surprised, but he has not been allowed to forget.

One of the temptations a mystery-writer must resist is that of letting sheer coincidence carry too much of the burden in the development of his story. Raymond Chandler succumbed to that temptation in his first and third novels, but in the second one he managed nicely to explain an apparent coincidence by means of investigation. By the time he wrote *The Little Sister*, he had learned not only how to master coincidence but how to use it as a unifying structural device.

"Fate stage-managed the whole thing," says Marlowe at that point in *The Big Sleep* when two tires blow at just the right moment to put him within easy walking distance of the gangster hideout he has been seeking. The reader of this book may feel that Fate intervenes a little too obviously on two other occasions, when Marlowe reaches Geiger's house just in time to hear the shot that kills the photographer, and when he arrives outside the door of Harry Jones' office just in time to overhear a revealing conversation between him and the gangster, Canino. Such things do happen, but three times in one story may make us wonder.

Early in *Farewell, My Lovely* there is what seems to be an incredible coincidence, Marlowe's being called in on a case that proves to be related to one into which he had blundered by pure accident. In this story, however, Chandler turns the apparent coincidence into a parallel mystery, which Marlowe solves by an ingenious piece of detection.

Fate steps back onto the stage as manager in *The High Window*, first when the apartment house manager just happens to quiet a disturbance across the hall from where a murder has been committed and discovers the murder weapon; then when Marlowe just happens to lean down to wipe his hands and finds some incriminating photos he would otherwise have overlooked; and a little later when Marlowe just happens to be at the right place and at the right time to overhear a crucial and revealing conversation.

Such awkwardness is not to be found in the later novels, and in his fifth book, *The Little Sister*, Chandler contrives the use of coincidence as a vehicle for the spin-off plot that provides the residue of mystery: Mavis Weld, whom Marlowe had been paid to protect, turns out to be the sister of the murdered Orrin Quest. This is not purely fortuitous coincidence but careful plotting. It is not Fate but Raymond Chandler who is in control.

Whether Chandler's novels should be considered "works of art" must, finally, depend upon one's definition of art. When we attempt to assess his craftsmanship, however, the evidence is much more tangible, as I have tried to show. The writer who is not satisfied even with a successful formula for the construction of his story but must experiment over and over until he has found several that he can handle with confidence, is a craftsman. The same can be said of a writer who so carefully unifies his novel that even the most complicated narrative hangs together and finally adds up as a story, or who refuses to yield to sheer coincidence but can use it as a structural device. Whatever else he did well, Raymond Chandler was a master in the craft of construction.

---

[1] In *The Art of the Mystery Story*, ed. Howard Haycraft (New York: Simon and Schuster, 1946), p. 231.

[2] "The Guilty Vicarage: Notes on the Detective Story, by an Addict," in *The Critical Performance*, ed. Stanley Edgar Hyman (New York: Vintage Books, 1956), p. 306.

[3] *Mortal Consequences: A History—From the Detective Story to the Crime Novel* (New York: Harper and Row, 1972), p. 14.

[4] Ibid, p. 190.

[5] Op. cit., p. 231.

[6] Philip Durham, *Down These Mean Streets a Man Must Go* (Chapel Hill: The University of North Carolina Press, 1963), p. 33.

[7] Symons, p. 143.

[8] Durham, pp. 136-7.

# Raymond Chandler's Los Angeles

*Tom S. Reck*

No city lends itself more to metaphor than Los Angeles, and no writer has risen to the implicit challenge better than Raymond Chandler. The city is artificial in a quite literal sense. All its features, whether flora, fauna or freeway, have had to be imported because it is built on a desert where nothing grows naturally. Jailed off by the mountains into solitary confinement, it must pipe in its water and pump out is excrement. It is the only U.S. city where the freeways are not mere eyesores but part of the aesthetic (actually unaesthetic) principles of the place. They are organic, as it were. And Los Angeles is excessively vulnerable to the usual symbols of God's wrath: flash flood, fire, earthquake—plus such 20th century plagues as smog, pollution, street violence and hip subcultures. As a former oasis, a paradise gone sour, it begs to be a metaphor. And if its contagious diseases have become common knowledge in the 1970's Raymond Chandler was aware of its symbolic possibilities when he was writing his novels in the 1930's and 1940's.

Chandler is not always taken seriously as a writer because he worked in that suspect genre, detective fiction. The case for detective fiction as serious literature, for murder as metaphor, has been argued by Dorothy Sayers, David Madden and Joseph Wood Krutch, and the verdict in its favor is acceptable to anyone who has really considered the question. There has also been much discussion of Chandler's detective-hero, Philip Marlowe, who has been called an existential hero, a shopworn Galahad and an American Everyman. Finally Chandler's stylistic affinities with Hemingway have been explored.

But Chandler's role as Los Angles laureate, especially interesting because he wrote of the city in scathing ridicule when it was still held to be "an Eden," has never been sufficiently explored. Chandler brings Los Angles into focus. He is superior to Waugh, Fitzgerald, Huxley and West, whose general literary prestige has supported the

"Raymond Chandler's Los Angeles," *Nation* 20 Dec. 1975: 661-63.

assumption that they know best about Southern California. As Lawrence Powell says in *The Raymond Chandler Omnibus*, Chandler stops "the kaleidoscope so that we see the brilliant bits and pieces in perfect register." He fixes the city in a time capsule, so that its details cannot be erased by the ravages of time. His expertise is such that he can perceive the delicate differences between Pasadena, Santa Monica and Beverly Hills that make them separate entities within the larger envelope.

But if Raymond Chandler's Los Angeles has some basis in reality, it is also a kind of hallucination, a returning nightmare—of what that particular city is to him and of what any place is capable of becoming. And he supports his vision by a close cataloguing of surface details, which in turn represent the internal sickness.

To begin with, Chandler the horticulturist sees Los Angeles as a botanical relief map, a kind of Kew Gardens, with specimens noted and labeled, and useful to Chandler's detective-hero in identifying each section of the city. The flora is also used symbolically to represent nature's purity, contrasted with the corruption of the civilization that has overgrown it. For example, this is what opens Chandler's *The Little Sister*:

> The fur stores are advertising their summer sales. The call houses that specialize in 16 year old virgins are doing a land office business. And in Beverly Hills the Jacaranda trees are beginning to bloom.

Besides the vegetation, the architecture of L.A. preoccupies Chandler. His sense of the murder house in *The Lady in the Lake* is not only architecturally typical of the city but symbolically suggests its chaos and its corruption:

> The house was built downwards, one of those clinging vine effects, with the front door a little below street level, the patio on the roof, the bedroom in the basement, and a garage like the corner pocket of a pool table.

The house's furnishings, which Chandler here and always notes with the eye of a decorator taking inventory, are evocative of the city's ostentation and tastelessness (apricot Chinese rugs, deep-sided chairs, white drum lamps, davenports in pale tan mohair, stucco archways with beaded curtains). These garish objects are worlds away from what ordinarily represent home and safety, and they signal danger and depravity. The city's hotels and apartment dwellings, in Chandler's eyes, are festering sores; and if they have fallen from a former elegance, their malevolence is heightened for him. Here is the hotel in *The Little Sister*:

> The memories of old cigars clung to its lobby like the dirty gilt on its ceilings. . . . The marble of the desk had turned a yellowish brown with age.

In *The High Window* Philip Marlowe enters a ratty hotel where nobody except people named Smith and Jones sign the register and where the night clerk is "half watchdog and half pander." It has "hallways you could touch on both sides without stretching," and "rusted screens and dirty net curtains." Such descriptions are talismans of murder to come. The buildings are purgatories for the depraved; their disease is congenital and cannot be hidden by renovation or refurbishing—as the Chateau Bercy from *The Little Sister* proves. It houses the novel's cold-blooded killer despite the fact that it has been "made over" with "glass brick, cornice lighting" and a color scheme of "bile green, linseed-poultice brown, sidewalk gray and monkey-bottom blue." If the Hemingway hero's favorite emotion is that "cool, clear feeling," Marlowe's is disgust. And it is for that reason that he spends so much time in these offensive habitats and transmits their details with such relish. He is feeding his own habit of loathing.

Like the hotels and apartments, the office buildings of Los Angeles are up to no good. In *The Long Goodbye* a massive office building, whose ugliness is "deliberate and expensive," hides the Carne Organization—which specializes in protection for "the carriage trade, protection meaning almost anything with one foot inside the law." The Stockwell Building in *The Long Goodbye* is populated by abortionists and dope pushers posing as "urologists, dermatologists or any branch of medicine in which the treatment can be frequent and the regular use of local anesthetics is normal." The Fulwider Building in *The Big Sleep* has

> . . . plenty of vacancies or plenty of tenants who wished to remain anonymous. Painless dentists, shyster detective agencies, small sick businesses that had crawled there to die, mail order schools that would teach you how to become a railroad clerk or a radio technician or a screen writer—if the postal inspectors didn't catch up with them first.

Chandler's buildings are not ships of fools but of degenerates, contemporary equivalents of Dante's Inferno, with sinners hiding behind the frosted glass doors. In *The High Window* the lettered names on the doors are a kind of heinous refrain that Marlowe reads aloud to himself each time he makes the journey past them down the hall to discover perversion and murder. He repeats to himself as he walks past:

> H. R. Teager, Dental Laboratories, L. Pridview, Public Accountant. Dalton and Rees, Typewriting Service. Dr. E.J. Blaskowitz, and underneath and name in small letters: Chiropractic Physician.

If Chandler makes the architecture of Los Angeles suggest its evil, he uses its odd natural terrain as a stage for assorted beatings and murders and other varieties of violence. There are within the city limits of L.A. mountain tops, deserted canyons, sinister cul-de-sacs, uninhabited and uninhabitable pockets, close to civilization but still apart from it, almost as agreed-upon sites for the murky business at hand, perfect places for profanation. In *Farewell, My Lovely*, Marlowe is taken to one of these sites to be beaten himself and to have his client killed.

> Purisima Canyon has a sort of level shaft at the inner end of it, they say. This is walled off from the road by a white fence of four-by-fours, but you can just squeeze by. A dirt road winds down into a little hollow and we are to wait there without lights. There are no houses around.

L.A. is in area the largest city in the country and its rapid growth has resulted in a cartographer's nightmare. It therefore makes sense that Chandler likes to tell you how to get around within the confines of his city. It is not only a kind of specialty of his but it also suggests the chaos of the city—and suggests the skill that needs to be exercised in his complicated and malevolent world. He tells you just how long it takes to get from one spot in the city to another, as if exaggerated familiarity with the terrain is required for survival in such a place. For example, in *The Big Sleep*:

> The coupe went west on the boulevard; which forced me to make a left turn. . . . I caught sight of him two or three times and then made him turning north into Laurel Canyon Drive. Halfway up the grade he turned left and took a curving ribbon of wet concrete which is called Laverne Terrace.

It is a kind of choreography, for a dance in and around and through a bed of hot coals.

Marlowe's eating habits also contribute to a spiteful vision of L.A. At a time considerably before L.A. became the procreator of "junk food" and franchised eateries, a veritable chorus line of Taco Bells, Dennys, McDonalds and Colonel Sanders, Chandler uses the city's food to represent its rotteness. In *The Long Goodbye*, he writes:

> The coffee was overstrained and the sandwich was as full of rich flavor as a piece off an old sheet.

And in *The Little Sister*:

> Down at the drugstore lunch counter I took time to inhale two cups of coffee and a melted cheese sandwich with two slivers of ersatz bacon imbedded in it like dead fish in the silt at the bottom of a drained pool.

The fact that Marlowe continues to indulge such a diet tells us all about his character. Part martyr and part sociologist, part arrogance and part piety—he seeks out what will reinforce his vision of a world gone awry. His disgust is always part delight, because it supports what he suspects. Los Angeles to a banquet for him.

As for the city's inhabitants, the rich among them are Chandler's special enemies. They are either his malefactors, aggressors in acts of violence and deceit, or they are his wards, unable to keep their houses in order and in need of the competent and responsible Marlowe. Either way, they get his disdain and he is full of little asides about them. In *The Long Goodbye*, Marlowe tells a millionaire, "A man doesn't make your kind of money in any way I can understand." In *The High Window* he writes about Pasadena: "Nobody walked in that neighborhood, not even the mailman."

The California rich weave in and out of a Chandler novel, returning symbols that repel and fascinate him. The detective-martyr willingly lays himself down on their altar for sacrifice, as he does their dirty linen for them and then quietly removes himself without being paid or even thanked. He is a savior sent especially to walk on the water of L.A., offering up his palms for the affluent to drive nails through.

That the physicians of L.A. are among his favorite agents of evil is a nice irony, since Southern California is supposedly a health haven. They are never Marlowe's clients, but are often obstacles in his quest for truth and justice. In *Farewell, My Lovely*, a Dr. Sonderborg force-feeds Marlowe with dope at a swank prison/hospital. Oblivious of their Hippocratic oaths, Chandler's L.A. doctors use their skills to inflict slow torture. Dr. Allmore in *The Lady in the Lake* specializes in "people who are living on the raw edge of nervous collapse from drink and dissipation," and offers aid "as long as the money comes in, as long as the patient remains alive and reasonably sane."

The women of Los Angeles are further symbols of the city's psychosis. They evoke a sinister sexuality that comes from either frigidity of nymphomania, which for Chandler's purposes are not necessarily opposites. Miss Fromsett in *The Lady in the Lake* is typical; her clothing suggests the dangers of her sexuality. She wears "a steel gray business suit and under the jacket a dark blue shirt and a man's tie of a lighter shade. The edges of a folded handkerchief in the breast pocket looked sharp enough to slice bread." Meticulous but mannish, a foreboding fastidiousness, a deadly and diseased eroticism. About Carmen Sternwood from *The Big Sleep* Chandler writes that her eyes "were slate gray and had almost no expression when they looked at me. She came over near me and smiled with her mouth and she had little sharp predatory teeth as white as fresh orange pith or as shiny as porcelain." A woman in *The Long Goodbye* treats Marlowe to a harangue that borders on the obscene: "She opened a mouth like a firebucket and laughed. That terminated my interest in her. I couldn't hear the laugh but the hole in her face when she unzippered her teeth was all I needed."

Chandler sees sex, Los Angeles style, as an evil like medical science: it has been corrupted from its proper functions of love and procreation. Sex is a distraction in Marlowe's quest for truth and purity. In *The Little Sister* Marlowe philosophizes, "Let's leave sex on one side. It's great stuff. Like chocolate sundaes. But there comes a time when you would rather cut your throat." And in *The Long Goodbye* we are given the most concise summary of Chandler on the subject of human sexuality:

> It's excitement of the highest order, but it's an impure emotion—impure in the aesthetic sense. I'm not sneering at sex. It's necessary and it doesn't have to be ugly. But it always has to be managed. Making it glamorous is a billion-dollar business and it costs every cent of it.

Los Angeles, the manufacturer of movie sex fantasies, the center of the country's sexual pulse and the mythic sex capital of the world, has betrayed the high purpose of sexuality.

There is a passage in *Farewell, My Lovely* which finds Marlowe in one of his bitter analytic moods (they usually occur late at night after a day in which he has gotten nowhere or somewhere he'd prefer not to have gotten). It sums up the pestilences of Los Angeles:

> I thought of dead eyes looking at a moonless sky, with black blood at the corners of the mouths beneath them. I thought of

> nasty old women beaten to death against the posts of their dirty beds. I thought of a man with bright blond hair who was afraid and didn't quite know what he was afraid of, who was sensitive to know that something was wrong, and was too vain or too dull to guess what it was that was wrong. I thought of beautiful rich women who could be had. I thought of nice slim curious girls who lived alone and could be had too, in a different way. I thought of cops, tough cops, that could be greased and yet were not by any means all bad. Fat prosperous cops with Chamber of Commerce voices like Chief Wax. Slim, smart and deadly cops like Randall, who for all their meanness and smartness were not free to do a clean job in a clean way. I thought of sour old goats like Nulty who had given up trying. I thought of Indians and psychics and dope doctors.

Although Marlowe is the city's Jeremiah, exposing its fetidness, and prophesying its doom, he sometimes, as this passage suggests, seems himself tainted by his close proximity, as a doctor might contract a disease unawares from an infected patient. But there can be no question about the skill with which his author has etched for us the landscape of his Los Angeles, his city of devils, naturalistic or fantastic, real or imagined. The flora: hydrangea, jacaranda, bougainvillaea. The fauna: the decadent rich, the desperate poor, the corrupt cops. The architecture: stucco bungalows, Santa Monica mansions, sinister office buildings. It is not necessary to verify the accuracy of the Chandler vision. He is a good social critic, but more than that he is an artist. And so, if his Los Angeles is mainly a picture of purgatory, onto which he pinned the label of Los Angles, that does not detract from his portrait of fallen man and the banality of evil.

# Rats Behind The Wainscoting: Politics, Convention, and Chandler's *The Big Sleep*

*Peter J. Rabinowitz*

## I

Despite New Critical claims that works of art are "autonomous," most critics today would probably agree that it is impossible to make adequate sense of a literary text without knowing the assumptions and beliefs controlling it. As the structuralists have demonstrated, literature—like language—operates through signs with no inherent meaning; we can "recover the meaning" of a text only when we have grasped the system of norms behind the signs, a system of norms which comes in part not only from outside the work in question, but even from outside the sphere of art as a whole.

That system, to be sure, is vast; Jonathan Culler, for instance, delineates five separate levels on which such norms operate to allow literature to become "intelligible" to us.[1] But even Culler's elaborate analysis seems to accept implicitly the assumption that there is a clear-cut distinction between those levels which are intrinsic to art and those which are extrinsic. At first glance, that assumption—surely a familiar one[2]—may appear unquestionable. We all recognize that *some* of the norms which allow us to decipher a text come from prior experiences with the world and society, rather than with literature per se; intelligent reading of Tolstoy's *War and Peace* depends in part on knowledge of nineteenth-century history, without which we would miss, for instance, the inevitability of Napoleon's defeat and

"Rats Behind the Wainscoting: Politics, Convention, and Chandler's *The Big Sleep*." Reprinted from *Texas Studies in Language and Literature* 22 (1980): 224-45.

hence much of the novel's irony. And just as certainly, *some* norms appear purely literary; the pleasure we get when a poem fulfills certain expectations of meter and rhyme requires prior experience with conventions of poetry, conventions which have little to do with the world outside the poem.

But is this distinction really that sharp? To be sure, Culler recognizes that there might be some overlap, that there might be a relationship between some literary conventions and some social attitudes, but he continually backs off from discussing it: "We could, of course, speak of such conventions of theories or views of the world, as if it were the task of novels of express them, but such an approach would do scant justice to the novels themselves."[3] And given Culler's critical goal ("to specify how we go about making sense of texts, what are the the interpretive operations on which literature itself, as an institution, is based"[4]), the New Critical bias of the extrinsic/intrinsic distinction and of the phrase "the novels themselves" is probably appropriate, perhaps even necessary. But such an approach oversimplifies the interrelation between literary and extraliterary norms. While it is a useful postulate for certain kinds of inquiry, the assumption that artistic conventions can be treated in purely formal terms obscures the social dynamics at work when real audiences confront art. A formal study of the techniques of the minstrel show might have some explanatory power; but unless you look at the social implications of the genre's conventions, you will never understand why minstrel shows have all but disappeared. The "rules" for reading literature may be similar to the "rules" for playing chess; but they are not entirely analogous because of the very close relationship between the literary conventions of texts and the social and cultural attitudes of readers.

The relationship, needless to say, is complex. To a certain extent, social attitudes *create* literary conventions. The novel, at any rate, is a largely mimetic form, and not only its content, but even its formal characteristics, originate partly in social conditions.[5] But the influence runs simultaneously the other way. Literature, like language, provides one frame through which we come to understand the world, and as John Cawelti has put it, "Our artistic experiences over a period of time work on the structure of our imaginations and feelings and thereby have long-term effects on the way in which we understand and respond to reality."[6] Indeed, the corruption of the "innocent" reader by literary conventions has been a major theme of literature itself: *Eugene Onegin, Madame Bovary,* Lisa Alther's *Kinflicks*. In sum, art and life imitate each other; conventions appear both to reflect (sometimes obscurely) and to affect (sometimes indirectly) the ways we interact with the world.

This essay is an exploration of the relationship between literary conventions and social attitudes. Specifically, I shall show that some conventions that appear to be purely literary have, in fact, deep social roots and that authors who want to challenge popular political assumptions may find a suitable battleground on the field of literary conventions. My case in point is Raymond Chandler's first novel, *The Big Sleep* (1939), a work which makes a serious political argument by vigorously overturning what are generally considered purely aesthetic conventions. I have chosen this book for a variety of reasons: first, because the detective story is a highly conventionalized genre, with specific rules which have been accepted by readers, critics, and writers alike; second, because in the Howard Hawks film based on it, we have what amounts to a reconventionalized version of the novel, a version which underscores the social and political implications of Chandler's original attack on the tradition; and third, because the novel itself is far better than its academic reputation suggests and is worthy of more critical scrutiny than it has received.

## II

Critics from W.H. Auden to S.S. Van Dine have long delighted in tabulating the laws which govern the classic detective story. But most of them view the genre—and criticism of it—as a diversion, and consequently treat the rules like those for any other game. There have been so many of these rules—many of them extremely silly (such as Knox's dictum that "Not more than one secret room or passage is allowable"[7])—that one is apt to agree that they are arbitrary. But if we do a little pruning, if we take off some excess foliage to look for the *essential* rules which show up explicitly or implicitly on every list, then we begin to see that their ramifications extend beyond game playing.

The genre, in fact, hinges on three primary conventions; most of the other rules that critics and authors have enunciated are trivial or else are elaborations or consequences of these three. First of all, as S.S. Van Dine puts it, "There must be but one culprit." Second, the detective must always triumph by restoring order in the end; as Van Dine archly notes, "The detective novel must have a detective in it, and a detective is not a detective unless he detects." Finally, the crime must turn out to be a the result of some idiosyncratic aberration, succeeding temporarily only because it operates under a veil of falsehood; the criminal, therefore, can always be uncovered through simple rational procedures—what Van Dine calls "logical deductions."[8] Although there are violations of these rules, they are rather rare, for many apparent exceptions turn out to be mere variations. For instance, Christie's *Murder in the Calais Coach (Murder on the Orient Express)* appears to have twelve criminals, not one, and they remain unpunished. Actually, though, those twelve are justly avenging a previous crime; it is the victim himself who is the "real criminal," and Poirot's final explanation demonstrates that justice has indeed been served and order restored.

Now these three rules are *not* "purely literary." As soon as we examine the kind of imaginative universe which such rules generate, we can begin to see social underpinnings. For convenience, I will limit myself primarily to the works of Agatha Christie. Of course, there are other practitioners who might serve to represent the genre; but Christie, if not the most accomplished of them, is surely the most widely read, and it seems appropriate to assume that her works have been particularly effective in catching readers. Most of the remarks which follow, however, would apply with only slight modification to Ellery Queen, John Dickson Carr, Ngaio Marsh, and others.

What sort of world *do* the conventions lead to in the novels of Agatha Christie? What are the beliefs at the root of her imaginative landscape? What views of society, politics, and humanity might lead her to construct it, and what social attitudes would such a world foster and encourage? John Cawelti, one of the few critics to have seriously posed such questions, gives us an extremely valuable point of departure. Christie, he claims, develops "the moral fantasy that human actions have a simple and rational explanation and that guilt is specific and not ambiguous."[9] If we push this insight further we can see that Christie's world entails a definite political vision; it reflects particular political biases and encourages readers to take certain political stances. And to those she convinces, her invented world offers a special form of political comfort.

Christie's novels always open with the same conflict: the peaceful, natural social order (often a small country village) is threatened by disruption through a murder or series of murders that seems bizarre and inexplicable. But this specter of social disruption is always laid to rest in the same way. According to the first rule of the genre, the threat always turns out to come from an individual rather than from a social failing; the restoration of order guaranteed by the second rule thus never requires a serious alteration—or even examination—of society. Furthermore, according to the third rule, evil can operate only as long as "the truth" remains concealed. This, of course, simplifies the detective's task of restoration, for once the deviant individual is unmasked, he or she is powerless to operate further. No wonder Poirot can claim, "I have only one duty—to discover the truth."[10] Rarely is physical force required in Christie's world; once the truth is revealed through reason, justice follows as a matter of course. As Harrison R. Steeves puts it, "There is nothing in art . . . more unswervingly optimistic" than a detective story.[11]

Viewing the conventions of the genre in this light helps explain why the detective story has been so popular: whatever their other virtues, Christie's novels also have a cathartic effect. Indeed, her work can be seen as a trivialization of Aristotelian tragedy. Writing for a bourgeois audience tormented by the possibility of social upheaval, she arouses its worst fears and then purges this emotion with the affirmation of both the justice and the strength of the status quo. Since evil springs not from social inadequacies but from antisocial individuals with "a little kink in the brain somewhere,"[12] the existence of evil does not necessitate a change in the social order. The sympathetic reader closes Christie's novels with a sense of profound peace; if anything goes wrong there is no reason to vote the government out of power—just call in Poirot. It is appropriate that so many of her novels take place on country estates, an excellent symbol of the society she wishes to convince us is both desirable and eternal.

Christie's political vision emerges most clearly in her overtly political novels, especially such early potboilers as *The Secret Adversary* (1922). This implausible tale concerns a Labour Party attempt to oust the Conservatives. Catastrophic as this would be, it is but the tip of the iceberg. As her spokesman soberly informs us, "A Labour Government at this juncture would . . . be a grave disability for British trade, but that is a mere nothing to the real danger. . . . Bolshevist gold is pouring into this country for the specific purpose of procuring a Revolution."[13]

Absurd as this sounds today, it probably struck a sympathetic chord in the conservative middle class of 1922. That such a claim was believable is demonstrated by an incident which occurred only two years later. The *Daily Mail* published a letter—supposedly from Zinoviev, but probably a fake—in which the British Communist Party was ordered to start preparations for a military insurrection;[14] and the public's consequent outrage contributed to the conservative backlash of the October 1924 elections. Given the political atmosphere in 1922, such gullibility is not really surprising. The collapse of the British economy following the war had resulted in a virtual depression of 1921; the Empire was threatened by radical agitation in Ireland, and by Gandhi's civil disobedience in India, leading to his arrest in 1922; the labor union movement, moderately sympathetic to the Soviet cause, had grown so substantially that the Labour Party was able, in the 1922 elections, to replace the Liberals as the official opposition. No wonder there was "widespread mistrust and . . . fear" of the Labour Party in the early twenties.[15]

Christie's novel capitalizes on this mistrust and fear; but once she unleashes the threatening prospect of imminent revolution, she reassures us that we really have nothing to fear. She does this with a masterstroke as ingenious as it is naive—she reveals that there is a *single man* behind the "Bolshies." The Revolution can thus be forestalled without recourse either to social reorganization or to political repression. Once this individual is found out—unmasked by a bunch of amateurs at that—the power of the truth is so great that even the abashed Labour Party falls into line to support the status quo.[16]

Needless to say, in her better novels Christie complicates and refines this basic scheme. Her criminals occasionally have accomplices; noncriminals often tell lies in order to protect their loved ones or to cover minor inadequacies which are not quite "crimes"; occasionally, some genteel violence is called for. But her outlook remains generally as I have described it: confident that logic and justice will prevail.

The detective story is simultaneously a reflection of such attitudes and a cause of them, although not in any simpleminded way.

Thus, the conventions of the classical English detective story cannot be considered simply a direct reflection of the attitudes of its actual readers. Detective stories are enthusiastically read by readers who are equally at home with genres built on substantially different conventions; there is nothing unusual about a person who enjoys both Christie and writers whose sociopolitical ideas are thoroughly subversive. Our attitudes are complex, ambiguous, even internally inconsistent enough for us to respond to a variety of works mirroring different strands of our personalities. On the other hand, certain sociopolitical currents—and consequently, certain widespread beliefs—probably made especially fertile ground for the detective story to flourish. The genre, in fact, first took form in the 1840s, at a time when many people felt threatened by the social unrest that produced the *Communist Manifesto*, and it reached its golden age between the two world wars, when fear of the Bolshevik threat was at one of its crests.

Nor could one realistically argue that traditional detective novels "created" the attitudes that led to such events as the execution of Sacco and Vanzetti. And yet, readers who worried about social disruption did find an echo of their fears in these novels; and these novels probably helped reinforce the conservative tendencies in their thoughts, since everything in the novels' imaginative world would nourish the belief that killing the arch-villians disguised as simple, innocent men would push back the encroaching chaos.

## III

Chandler himself criticized the genteel English school for its lack of mimetic realism,[17] but as sympathetic as we might find that argument, it is really a false issue. After all, Christie's novels are as true to her view of reality as Chandler's are to his; and neither of them portrays a world particularly close to the day-to-day one in which most of us live. What is more interesting than the question of photographic accuracy is the way that Chandler's angle of vision influences his art. He sees the world not from a country estate, but rather from the Los Angeles of the union-busting Merchants and Manufacturers Association, a city ruled by what Frank MacShane, in his excellent biography of Chandler, calls a "right wing coalition so repressive that it had no equal elsewhere in the country."[18] This background, and the typically thirties cynicism that went with it, clashed violently with the conventions of the genre and helped make *The Big Sleep* the extraordinary novel that it is. At first, the critics were so impressed with the brutality and degeneracy of the novel's subject matter (it made Hammett "seem as innocuous as Winnie-the-Pooh," quipped the *New Yorker)*,[19] that they overlooked just how far *The Big Sleep* subverted the conventions of the classics. Yet the subversion was serious indeed, for the novel breaks all three of the cardinal rules of the genre. There are many criminals, some of them introduced as such from the beginning; despite both logical explanation and physical carnage, the detective cannot eliminate them; and most important, their crimes cannot be explained away as individual, nonsocial quirks or abnormalities. Thus, the novel ends not with the soothing conservative affirmation of order, but with something more politically unsettling; loose ends, a detective who fails, and a pervasive sense of individual despair, social chaos, and the triumph of evil. While MacShane is correct when he says that Chandler uses "the formulas of detective fiction,"[20] there is a twist to his use of them that MacShane misses.

The events in *The Big Sleep* are so intricate that even Chandler later had difficulty recalling all the details. "I remember," he wrote to Hamish Hamilton, "several years ago when Howard Hawks was making *The Big Sleep*, the movie, he and Bogart got into an argument as to whether one of the characters was murdered or committed suicide. They sent me a wire asking me, and dammit I didn't know either."[21]

The rough outline of the story is as follows. Detective Philip Marlowe is hired by the wealthy, aging General Sternwood to "take care of" Arthur Gwynn Geiger, a pornography dealer, blackmailer, and bisexual who is putting the screws on the General's younger daughter, Carmen. Marlowe eventually learns, however, that the General really wants to track down the husband of his older daughter, Vivian, a former bootlegger named Rusty Regan. Regan has mysteriously disappeared, apparently in the company of Mona Grant, the wife of gambler and local racketeer Eddie Mars. Several seduction attempts by the Sternwood sisters, three or four murders (depending on how you count that ambiguous death), and countless other sensational events take place before Marlowe can discover Mona; in the process, he is himself captured by Lash Canino, Mars' gunman. With the help of Mona—to whom he has given the pet name "Silver-Wig"—he escapes and kills Canino; and he returns to the Sternwood mansion where the denouement takes place. Carmen, furious that Marlowe has resisted her advances, tries to kill him; we learn that she had shot Regan for similar reasons some time ago. Mars and Canino, who had helped dispose of the body in a sump, had been using their knowledge to blackmail Vivian. At Marlowe's insistence, Vivian agrees to put her sister in an institution.

If Christie's country mansions symbolize the essential innocence of her world, and the glass key symbolizes for Hammett the impossibility of returning to that innocence once you have been corrupted, then Raymond Chandler's vision can be crystallized in a phrase Marlowe twice uses to describe Carmen's sinister, moronic giggles: "rats behind the wainscoting."[22] The apparent respectability of the world masks a fundamental core of horror: corruption, perversity, death. Marlowe's world is not one where it is lost, as in Hammett's. In Chandler's world, innocence simply does not exist.

Given that Chandler did not share the political vision implied in the classical detective story, one might well ask why he chose to revamp the genre rather than to write in another genre, such as that of *The Day of the Locust, To Have and Have Not, U.S.A.* One reason may have been the reciprocal relationship between convention and attitude. That the conventions of a genre are morally or politically unsound is reason enough to challenge them on their home ground. Jane Austen began her string of realistic novels with the upside-down gothic of *Northanger Abbey*. And surely similar considerations influenced Pushkin's decision to challenge the moral assumptions of the sentimental novels of his day by his parody of them in *The Belkin Tales* (especially "The Station Master").

Although *The Big Sleep* is not a traditional parody, it does, as I have said, topple all the fundamental conventions of the genre. Most obvious is Chandler's violation of our first rule. In a Christie novel, a string of crimes always has a single source. But here, the number of criminals seems endless; as Harry Jones remarks, "We're all grifters. So we sell each other out for a nickel" (p. 156. Geiger, Brody, Taylor, Lundgren, Canino, Carmen, and Mars: that's enough to populate an entire decade of Christie productions. Guilt is thus impossible to localize in Chandler's urban jungle—and we shall see later on why this is so important.

More startling still is Chandler's violation of the second rule: the detective fails to bring the most vicious of these criminals to justice. To be sure, the novel opens with the promise of his success, for against the grim background of California degeneracy, the virtues of Philip Marlowe stand out in bold relief. With his vigorous intelligence and unusual (although not superhuman) physical stamina, with his honesty, integrity, justice, and even chastity, he is—as Chandler himself often stressed—a modern knight. Marlowe first appears in *The Big Sleep* [23] and the knighthood theme is announced in the second paragraph, which foreshadows Marlowe's later "rescue" of the nude Carmen: "There was a broad stained-glass panel showing a knight in dark armor rescuing a lady who was tied to a tree and didn't have any clothes on but some very long and convenient hair. The knight had pushed the vizor of his helmet back to be sociable, and he was fiddling with the knots on the ropes that tied the lady to the tree and not getting anywhere. I stood there and thought that if I lived in the house, I would sooner or later have to climb up there and help him. He didn't seem to be really trying" (p.1).

But while few readers miss the promises held out by the imagery of Marlowe's knighthood, a curious number have failed to realize that they are never fulfilled. Thus, for instance, Philip Durham argues that Marlowe is the traditional American man of action who brings "fair play and justice where it could not be or had not been administered,"[24] and R.W. Lid claims that he is "Chandler's knight, righting the balance in a wronged and fallen universe. He corrects injustices, stands up for the underdog, speaks out for the little guy."[25] But *The Big Sleep* does not depict the triumph of justice and fair play;

to the contrary, it traces Marlowe's descent from moderately optimistic knighthood to a despairing recognition of his own impotence. For in contrast to the similar virtues of Poirot, Marlowe's virtues are powerless against the vastly superior forces of evil. He may be able to perform a few good acts, such as protecting General Sternwood from heartbreak and avenging Harry Jones's death. But this is a far cry from the administration of justice, which Marlowe comes to realize is not longer possible for an individual in our urban society.

In order to understand how Marlowe fails, we must first understand the plot—no mean feat. Specifically, we must recognize the central villain. Actually, this is more of a problem than might appear. As we have noted, Chandler's world is infected with far more widespread guilt than Christie's; and certainly, many of the evildoers are punished, even overpunished. Geiger, Brody, and Owen Taylor are just as dead for their crimes as the far more vicious Canino is for his: Carol Lundgren is in jail; and Carmen, the kind of traditional "aberrant individual" that Christie would have made the villain (which may explain why so many readers falsely see her as such)[26] is about to be institutionalized. Don't we have enough retribution for a dozen novels?

Chandler's world is more vicious than Christie's, and it is not surprising that his novels end in more bloodshed. But this should not fool us. Chandler, in order to stress the theme of widespread evil, may have given us a large number of criminals; but in order to stress the note of despair, he had made one of them stand out above the rest and has left him quite untouched at the end. This is not a trivial point; it is this structural twist which keeps the plot from resolution and which consequently provides much of its political force. Since so many readers and critics, however, have misread the novel's denouement, it may be necessary to demonstrate that Eddie Mars and not Carmen is, in fact, the closest thing to a central villain in the novel; that Chandler has purposefully structured his novel to make him the evil counterpart to Marlowe's virtue (in effect, he plays the dragon to Marlowe's knight): and that by leaving him unpunished, Chandler puts the capstone on the theme of failure he builds throughout the entire novel.

## IV

Besides the novel itself, there are three sources which cast light on the role of Eddie Mars and significance of his continued power at the end of *The Big Sleep*: "Killer in the Rain" and "The Curtain," two short stories which Chandler "cannibalized" (to use his word) when he wrote the novel; and the film that Howard Hawks made of *The Big Sleep* in the 1940s.

The two stories can be considered as a draft of the novel. As such, they provide the kind of evidence which any draft provides when compared to a polished artistic whole. They are especially revealing with regard to two aspects of the novel: the prose style (which sharpened considerably between 1934, when "Killer" was written, and 1939) and, more relevant to our concerns, the plot structure. Specifically, aside from Marlowe (unnamed in "Killer," Carmady in "The Curtain"), the only character in the novel with an equivalent in both stories is Eddie Mars, who replaced the one-armed Guy Slade from "Killer" and Joe Messarvey from "The Curtain."[27] Mars, then, like Marlowe, is a common denominator of the two old plots—one of the two screws holding the pieces of the new construction together.

But Chandler did more than use Mars' character as a unifying thread; he also increased his importance by shifting the moral responsibility. In the stories, Slade and Messarvey are vicious and disreputable, but they are largely innocent of the actual crimes committed. In *The Big Sleep* Mars, while not a literal killer, is behind most of the violence that takes place. It is Mars' stranglehold on Vivian which makes the blackmail and its consequences possible; it is the need to protect Mars' position that results in Canino's murder of Jones (the second most honorable character in the novel) and his attempted murder of Marlowe.

Marlowe himself is quite aware of the special position of Mars. In the course of the novel, he criticizes the police, the rich, and the racketeers. But of his moral outbursts, the most bitter is the one against Eddie Mars:

> "You think he's just a gambler. I think he is a pornographer, a blackmailer, a hot car broker, a killer by remote control, and a suborner of crooked cops. He's whatever looks good to him, whatever has the cabbage pinned to it. . . . [Jones is] a dead little bird now, with his feathers ruffled and his neck limp and a pearl of blood on his beak. Canino killed him. But Eddie Mars wouldn't do that, would he, Silver-Wig? He never killed anybody. He just hires it done." (pp. 179-80, 182)

Marlowe delivers this speech to Silver-Wig, and its vehemence—which Chandler made far stronger than in the parallel scene from "The Curtain"—is partly due to his growing involvement with her. This is no reason, however, to dismiss his words as anything less than sincere. Indeed, the competition for Silver-Wig's affections, which the novel also develops more fully than does "The Curtain," serves to underscore the adversary relationship between the two men. It is not uncommon in mythology for hero and dragon to compete for the same woman, nor is it uncommon for the wife or daughter of the ogre to become the ally of the hero (e.g., Ariadne and Theseus.)[28] Significantly, Chandler emphasizes Marlowe's failure by inverting the traditional heroic pattern. Although Silver-Wig helps Marlowe escape, he is unable to win her away from her husband. Thus, in the last sentences of both *The Big Sleep* and "The Curtain" we are presented with a Theseus abandoned by his Ariadne: "On the way downtown I stopped at a bar and had a couple of double scotches.[29] They didn't do me any good. All they did was make me think of Silver-Wig, and I never saw her again" (p. 214).

Comparison of the source stories and the final text, then, confirms that Chandler saw Mars as a primary thread linking the disparate plots, and made whatever alterations were necessary to point up his function as Marlowe's antagonist. As a final touch, he gave hero and villain new names to emphasize their respective roles—another sign of his extreme care in writing. The theme of the individual's weakness in the face of evil is doubly reinforced by Marlowe's name, which is surely *not* the "coincidence" MacShane claims it is.[30] First, while *The Big Sleep* is not modeled on *Heart of Darkness* in the same way that Robbe-Grillet's *Les Gommes* is modeled on Oedipus, British-educated Chandler must have had Conrad in mind when he finally chose the name of his detective, for the general drift of the two novels is strikingly parallel. Both tell of idealists who adventures seem destined to bring them in contact with some kind of truth, but who in fact find only a hollowness and a horror. Significantly, both these lovers of truth learn that the only way to deal with the horror they have exposed is to bury it once again with a lie, a lie that leaves the hero perhaps wiser, but also more bitter; and a lie that leaves the evil fundamentally untouched.

In addition, the name harks back to E. C. Bentley's famous detective novel, *Trent's Last Case*. This is a classic, but one that breaks several traditions of the genre: most important, there are two people who act as "detectives," both of whom come up with "solutions," neither of which is correct, as we learn only when the real killer confesses. The names of these two flawed detectives? Philip Trent and Marlowe!

Similarly, as the central force behind the novel's violence, Mars is of course well-named after the god of war; likewise, his position as Marlowe's antagonist is emphasized by having their names begin in the same way. He "mars" everything decent around him. Given all this, it is a delightful coincidence—if coincidence it be—that Kurtz, Marlowe's antagonist in *Heart of Darkness*, is associated too with the planet Mars.[31]

## V

While many readers have failed to appreciate Eddie Mars' function in the novel, there is evidence—indirect but compelling—that Hollywood was not so deceived. Indeed, by comparing the novel with

Hawks' film version, we can learn something about both politics and the aesthetics of the novel's ending.

Hawks's film, despite its romantic elaboration of Marlowe's relationship with Vivian, is largely faithful to the plot of the novel; yet the ending is altered significantly. Why? A general familiarity with popular films of the period suggests an answer. As Chandler—briefly a film writer himself—has remarked, cinematic decisions often result from the need to submit to conservative ethical norms: "Of course most motion pictures are bad. Why shouldn't they be? Apart from its own intrinsic handicaps of excessive cost, hypercritical bluenosed censorship, and the lack of any single-minded controlling force in the making, the motion picture is bad because 90 percent of its source material is tripe, and the other 10 percent is a little too virile and plain-spoken for the putty-minded clerics, the elderly ingénues of the women's clubs, and the tender guardians of that go-dawful mixture of boredom and bad manners known more eloquently as the Impressionable Age."[32] Thus, even the best popular films, at least before the 1960s, were hampered by studio pressure to conform to simplistic ethical patterns to which few sophisticated novels subscribe. Hollywood, for instance, found it difficult to express the notion that crime *should* be punished without falling into the notion that crime always *is* punished. Consequently, when a novel ended with an unpunished criminal, the film version tended to correct the "error," even if it made total hash of the original conception. The film version of Daphne du Maurier's *Rebecca* could not portray a murderer who goes free,[33] yet the alternative solution of killing Maxim was equally unthinkable, for it would require the execution of Laurence Olivier and would bring undeserved suffering upon a stranded Joan Fontaine. Since punishment could not be added to the plot, the only alternative was to remove the crime. Thus the film blithely transformed Rebecca's murder into an unfortunate accident, trivializing the story but preserving the viewers' purity. A similar outrage was perpetrated on the ending of Frances Iles's *Before the Fact* when it was turned into the film *Suspicion*.

The ending of the film of *The Big Sleep* is not so jarring aesthetically; in fact, it is quite effective. but it exemplifies the same mental set. To avoid any hint of immorality, the death of Mars was inserted into the story and made to serve as the movie's climax.[34] Simultaneously, Hawks absolved Carmen, and—more important—expunged the novel's bitterness toward the police, going so far as to use the sound of sirens as a symbol of a return to order at the film's conclusion. The moral universe of Hawks's film is consequently much more soothing than that of the novel; no wonder that Chandler preferred the first half of the film to the second.[35]

Although the film is useful as a demonstration of how Hollywood interpreted the function of Eddie Mars, it is even more valuable as a demonstration of what Chandler had to sacrifice in order to keep his unresolved ending. The killing of Mars is cathartic: Chandler was doubtlessly fully aware of this potential and quite capable of ending his novel with the same dramatic triumph. In ending *The Big Sleep* as he did, then, he consciously sacrificed an audience reaction which would be both powerful and satisfying. Knowing well that a detective story with an unpunished criminal is "like an unresolved chord in music,"[36] he deliberately chose to conclude on a jarring note of irritation.

## VI

Both the multiplicity of the evildoers and Marlowe's failure to restore order are echoed in Chandler's disruption of the third rule of the genre: for the evil in the world of the novel comes less from the quirks of deviant individuals like Carmen than from society itself. Chandler emphasizes this point by his grim portrayal of the environment of his tale: Christie's genteel countryside has been replaced by the dirty sump where the "horrible decayed" (p. 212) body of Regan lies. Chandler himself would argue that his portrayal was more "realistic" than Christie's, but as I have suggested, behind that claim lies a particular view of reality: only if you start with a socially critical attitude toward crime are you likely to view Chandler as more "realistic." And it is to encourage that attitude that he draws the picture he does.

Just as Chandler's reversal of the detective-as-victor convention begins with the traditional image of the hero-as-knight, so his reversal of the convention of individual evil begins with a traditional symbol. At first glance, the Sternwood mansion is reminiscent of the sprawling estates so familiar from Christie's countryside. But from the moment that Carmen enters and throws herself at Marlowe, the image begins to distort. We soon realize that this mansion cannot represent the smooth ordering of society; there are rats behind the wainscoting, and everything is infected.

More important, Chandler's world turns out to be neither logical nor orderly; Poirot's key tool would be useless in this version of Los Angeles, where virtually *everything* is false. Many of Chandler's images for this falsity are comic; he is, despite his gloom, a witty writer. Thus Marlowe can't be sure whether cavalry pennants are bullet-torn or simply moth-eaten (p. 2); Mexican musicians try to impress audiences with their toughness by pretending the mineral water they gulp is really tequila (p. 125); cheap gangsters studiously imitate their Hollywood counterparts (pp. 72, 172). Nothing is solid in California in 1939, as Marlowe ruefully notes while breaking into Geiger's home; "I gave the front door the heavy shoulder. This was foolish. About the only part of a California house you can't put your foot through is the front door" (p. 30).

But were it not for Chandler's stylistic maneuvers, there would be little to laugh about in this Los Angeles where wealth and success stink both literally (Sternwood's foul oilwells) and figuratively

(Geiger's smut bookstore). It is a society where both the legitimate rich and the gangsters have lines into police headquarters, and where the law routinely provides protection for blackmail rackets and a personal guard service for Eddie Mars when he opens his safe each morning (p. 121). And yet the same cops who so oblige the big-timers are likely to "shoot down some petty larceny crook running up an alley with a stolen spare" (p. 101). The police are not embarrassed by their corruption: they see it simply as keeping in step with the rotten times. As Captain Gregory put it, quite sincerely, "I'm a copper. . . Just a plain ordinary copper. Reasonably honest. As honest as you could expect a man to be in a world where it's out of style" (p. 189). Finally, in contrast to Christie's close-knit and chatty environment, Chandler's California is a world of solitary, disconnected individuals; people are so alienated from their neighbors that gunshots in a building go unnoticed, and corruption spreads unimpeded.

## VII

Chandler's disruption of the three basic conventions of the genre, then, correlates with a vision of the world far less comforting than Christie's. Evil cannot be uprooted by logic alone: there is simply too much of it; it is too well organized and too well protected by "legitimate" institutions. It is hard, sometimes impossible, to capture the wrongdoers—and even if you can, society is such that it will continue to spawn them.

Marlowe's journey in the course of the novel is a journey toward the recognition of these social truths. At first, like Poirot, he has confidence in right and justice, and his optimism provides an antidote to the cynicism expressed, for instance, by Vivian Regan and Bernie Ohls. When Vivian notes that Owen "didn't know the right people. That's all a police record means in this rotten crime-ridden country." Marlowe replies, "I wouldn't go that far" (p. 52). And a short while later, he bluntly suggests to Ohls, "You ought to stop some of that flash gambling"—a remark that Ohls finds appallingly naive. "With the syndicate we got in this country? Be your age, Marlowe" (p. 56).

But from the beginning of the novel, there is also a nagging undercurrent of despair. The weather reflects it: the novel opens "with the sun not shining and a look of hard wet rain" (p. 1); the inaction of the knight in the stained-glass window reflects it; even Marlowe's dreams reflect it: "I went to bed full of whiskey and frustration and dreamed about a man in a bloody Chinese coat who chased a naked girl with long jade earrings while I ran after them and tried to take a photograph with an empty camera" (p. 38). And as the novel progresses, Marlowe's thoughts—and in consequence, the whole tone of the narrative—grow more and more somber. Midway through the case he notes, "I was thinking about going out to lunch and that life was pretty flat and that it would probably be just as flat if I took a drink and that taking a drink all alone at this time of day wouldn't be any fun anyway" (p. 117). When Vivian wonders aloud whether there really is a "wrong side of the law" (p. 137), Marlowe is no longer impelled to contradict her. The key moment, however, comes when Marlowe returns to his room to find Carmen waiting impatiently in his bed. Ignoring her, he turns to his chess board: "There was a problem laid out on the board, a six-mover. I couldn't solve it, like a lot of my problems" (p. 143). Symbolically, he tried a knight move, but a few moments later, he recognizes his mistake—both in his game and, by extension, in his perception of the world: "Knights had no meaning in this game. It wasn't a game for knights" (p. 145). He becomes more and more repelled by the society around him: the police, who turn out to be both corrupt and powerless, make him sick; women make him sick (p. 148); the rich make him sick (p. 168). By the end of the book, he doesn't even have an answer to Gregory's cynical defense of his own corruption: "I'd like you to believe that, being a copper I like to see the law win. I'd like to see the flashy well-dressed muggs like Eddie Mars spoiling their manicures in the rock quarry at Folsom, alongside of the poor little slumbred hard guys that got knocked over on their first caper and never had a break since. That's what I'd like. You and me both lived too long to think I'm likely to see it happen. Not in this town, not in any town half this size, in any part of this wide, green and beautiful U.S.A. We just don't run our country that way" (pp. 189-90).

On his final visit to the Sternwood residence, Marlowe notes that "the knight on the stained-glass window still wasn't getting anywhere untying the naked damsel from the tree" (p. 194); but this time, he doesn't offer to help. On the contrary, he refuses payment for "an unsatisfactory job" (p. 195). By pointing out that he is neither a Sherlock Holmes nor a Philo Vance (p. 197), Marlowe seems to admit that the conventional detective has no place in the real world. On might, perhaps, interpret this as the darkness before the light, for it is just before Carmen, trying to kill him, reenacts her murder of Regan. Such an interpretation, however, would distort the story. First of all, Marlowe has already "solved" the mystery and has set the stage for proving it by putting blanks in Carmen's gun. More significant, however, the discovery of the truth does no good whatever. Unlike the last-chapter fireside revelations of Hercule Poirot, this truth is insufficiently powerful to overcome the evil. Nor, for that matter, does this discovery really tell him—or us—anything he did not already know: it only confirms our belief that the rats behind Carmen's wainscoting are predatory, even rabid. Marlowe can now suggest that Carmen be institutionalized—but we have known for some time that this was necessary. What effect does this revelation have on all the questions the book has raised? Since Mars is still free to act, the plague has not been cured. Besides, for Chandler, the perpetrator of evil is not the cause of evil. Even if Marlowe could eliminate Mars, would that make Los Angeles a significantly better place to live? Would it eradicate gambling, murder, and blackmail?

Would it reduce the influence that the racketeers and the rich have over the law? In Chandler's world, evil is fundamentally tied to an overwhelming sickness in the society at large; the capture and punishment of deranged individuals has only a minimal effect.

Ironically, at the end of the novel the best Marlowe can do with this truth is conceal it. Like Conrad's Marlowe, he becomes a preserver of illusion—specifically, General Sternwood's illusion that "his blood is not poison, and that although these two little girls are a trifle wild, as many nice girls are these days, they are not perverts of killers," (p. 211). Far from freeing him, the truth simply helps imprison Marlowe in the nastiness of the world. Rather than bringing Mars to justice, Marlowe finds himself an accomplice—the knight defending the dragon.

The darkest pages of the novel are the last two, where Marlowe contemplates the meaning of death and decides that this world is so ugly that death can only be seen as a liberation. This thought had momentarily flickered through his mind earlier, when he looked on the dead body of Harry Jones, reeking of cyanide and "the sour smell of vomit" (p. 166). The morbidity becomes far stronger, though when he thinks of Rusty Regan lying in the sump: "What did it matter where you lay once you were dead? In a dirty sump or in a marble tower on top of a high hill? You were dead, you were sleeping the big sleep, you were not bothered by things like that. Oil and water were the same as wind and air to you. You just slept the big sleep, not caring about the nastiness of how you died or where you fell. Me, I was part of the nastiness now. Far more a part of it than Rusty Regan was" (pp. 213-14). Once again, we hear the voice of Conrad's Marlow, this time from "Youth": "You simply can do nothing, neither great nor little—not a thing in the world. . . . Youth, strength, genius, thoughts, achievements, simple hearts—all dies. . . . No matter."[37]

## VIII

The conventions of the detective novel, than—like most artistic conventions—can profitably be studied in a social and political context. They serve a formal aesthetic function, but they also serve political ends through their reciprocal relationship with social attitudes. The structure of Christie's novels reflects a passive form of conservatism and encourages us to believe that the problems of violence and social disruption can be eliminated without changing the structure of society. Hers is a soothing voice which holds out promises of harmonious resolution if only we will sit still and let the experts take charge. Chandler's reversal of those conventions reverses the effect. His emphasis on the social origins of crime, and his consequent refusal to resolve his plot in traditional fashion, challenges those conservative assumptions. Instead of calming us. Chandler purposely irritates us, disrupts our peace; at the end of *The*

*Big Sleep* we feel dissatisfied. Chandler forces us to disapprove of the world we live in and demands that we reexamine our political outlook.

Does this make Chandler a "political" writer? Many critics have insisted that he is not, because he does not offer any solutions. As Wilson Pollock puts it, "although some of his works might seem to reveal a political consciousness, it wasn't there. . . . He merely believed that society was corrupt, that the only god was the fast and easy buck, and that that there was not very much anyone could do about it."[38] In a sense, this is true. Although Marlowe's continuing battle against corruption offers a model of behavior which is not as passive as Pollock implies, it certainly is possible to read Chandler's novels as essays in mere negativity, cynical suggestions that things are so bad that there is no point in trying to change them.

But Marlowe as a model of behavior—indeed, the whole question of "solutions—is really beside the point. Chandler is a political writer, not because he promotes a particular political line, but because his novels challenge, in a dynamic and forceful way, the hidden political assumptions of other novels which have been widely read and extremely influential. Such an intellectual challenge may or may not be more important than a political program, but it probably has to precede one, and in many ways, it is the most valuable and important work that a writer can do.

---

1 Jonathan Culler, *Structuralist Poetics: Structuralism. Linguistics, and the Study of Literature* (Ithaca: Cornell Univ. Press, 1975), pp. 140-60.

2 The extrinsic/intrinsic distinction is, or course, a critical commonplace; one major source of its currency is the enormously influential book by Rene Wellek and Austin Warren, *Theory of Literature*, 3rd. ed. (New York: Harcourt, 1956).

3 Culler, p. 146.

4 Ibid. p. viii.

5 See, for instance, Ian Watt, *The Rise of the Novel* (Berkeley and Los Angeles: Univ. of California Press, 1957), esp. ch. 2.

6 John G. Cawelti, *Adventure, Mystery, and Romance* (Chicago: Univ. of Chicago Press, 1976), p. 24.

7 Ronald Knox, "Detective Stories," in *Literary Distractions* (New York: Sheed and Ward, 1958), pp. 180-98. Among the countless other critics who see detective stories as a game is Fredric Jameson: "The detective story, as a form without ideological content, without any overt political or social or philosophical point, permits . . . pure stylistic experimentation." ("On Raymond Chandler," *Southern Review*, n.s. 6 no. 3 [July, 1970], 625.) E.M. Beekman concurs: "The traditional detective novel is not a novel at all, but an intellectual game on the level of acrostics or checkers." ("Raymond Chandler and an American Genre," *Massachusetts Review*, 14 [1973], 149.) So does Jacques

Barzun in "Detection and the Literary Art," in Barzun, ed., *The Delights of Detection* (New York: Criterion, 1961), pp. 9-23.

8 S.S. Van Dine, "Twenty Rules for Writing Detective Stories," in *The Art of the Mystery Story: A Collection of Critical Essays*, ed. Howard Haycraft (New York: Grossett and Dunlap Universal Library, 1947), pp. 190-91. My formulation is quite close to that enunciated by W.H. Auden: "The basic formula is this: a murder occurs; many are suspected; all but one suspect, who is the murderer, are eliminated; the murderer is arrested or dies," ("The Guilty Vicarage," in *The Dyer's Hand and Other Essays* [New York: Vintage, 1948], p. 147.)

9 Cawelti, p. 132. See also John M. Reilly's remark: "The 'classic' mystery conveys the notion that a developed human mind, coupled with will, can maintain order, because, it is implied, society is an aggregate of personal relationships." ("The Politics of Tough Guy Mysteries," *University of Dayton Review*, 10 [1973], 25.) There is much of interest in Reilly's discussion of the role of disillusioned populism in the tough mysteries, and especially in the genre's latent tendencies toward fascism; he does not dwell, however, on our concern here—the relation between politics and convention. See also Mark Gidley's claim that "classic detective fiction . . . usually restores the reader's faith in the ultimate efficacy of justice, in the stability of the social order." (Elements of the Detective Story in William Faulkner's Fiction," *Journal of Popular Culture*, 7, no. 1 [Summer 1973], 106) Finally, note Michael Holquist's study of the convention and its inverse function in contemporary literature: "Whodunit and Other Questions: Metaphysical Detective Stories in Post Modern Fiction," *New Literary History*, 3 (Autumn 1971), 135-56.

10 Agatha Christie, *The Mystery of the Blue Train* (New York: Pocket Books, 1940), p. 204. Originally published in 1928.

11 Harrison R. Steeves, "A Sober Word on the Detective Story," in *The Art of the Mystery Story*, p. 520.

12 Christie, *Mystery of the Blue Train*, p. 172. John Dickson Carr's Dr. Fell elaborates: "this is not, of course, to say that all murderers are mad, but they are in a fantastic state of mind, or they would not be murderers. And they do fantastic things." (*To Wake the Dead* New York: Collier, 1965], pp. 201-02.

13 Agatha Christie, *The Secret Adversary* (New York: Bantam, 1967), p. 29. Originally published in 1922.

14 R.K. Webb, *Modern England from the Eighteenth Century to the Present* (New York: Dodd, Mead, 1968), p. 511. For a good summary of the immediate postwar years, see pp. 486-514.

15 Henry Pelling, *Modern Britain (1885-1955)* (New York: Norton, 1966), pp. 99-100.

16 The notion that a few masterminds control international events underlines a whole subgenre of literature. For decades, Sax Rohmer charged Dr. Fu Manchu with all the upheavals in the Mysterious East. In fact, in *President Fu Manchu* (1936), the arch-fiend engineers the assassination of Heuy Long (called Harvey Bragg)

and nearly succeeds in stealing the 1936 election. Some of Ian Fleming's novels fit this mold, as does Richard Prather's remarkable *The Trojan Hearse* (1964) which seriously argues that Hubert Humphrey (called Horatio Humble) is about to rape the nation with the help of the Communist Party, the Mafia, and an unusually venal impresario. National virtue is preserved only by the individual heroism of Shell Scott, who barrels through the wall of a secret hideout on the steel ball of a wrecking machine. Phallic bravado can go no further.

[17] See especially, Raymond Chandler, "The Simple Art of Murder," [1944] in *The Simple Art of Murder* (New York: Pocket Books, 1952), pp. 177-94.

[18] Frank MacShane, *The Life of Raymond Chandler* (New York: Dutton, 1976), p. 64.

[19] "Mysteries," *New Yorker*, 11 February 1939, p. 84.

[20] MacShane, p. 63. Beekman recognizes that Chandler's novels "use elements of a particular fictional tradition, and in so doing either amplify or destroy established constrictions, not for malice but from superior artistic imagination" ("Chandler and an American Genre," p. 150), but neither examines these changes in detail nor investigates their political implications.

[21] "Letter to Hamish Hamilton, March 21, 1949," in *Raymond Chandler Speaking*, ed. Dorothy Gardiner and Kathrine Sorley Walker (Freeport, N.Y.: Books for Libraries Press, 1971), p. 221.

[22] Raymond Chandler, *The Big Sleep* (New York: Pocket Books, 1950), pp. 60, 143. All further references to this edition are made in the text.

[23] Once the character caught on, Chandler renamed the hero in some of his earlier stories "Marlowe."

[24] Philip Durham, *Down These Mean Streets a Man Must Go: Raymond Chandler's Knight* ( Chapel Hill: Univ. of North Carolina Press, 1963), p. 32.

[25] R.W. Lid, "Philip Marlowe Speaking," *Kenyon Review*, 31, no. 2, (1969), 159. Later he seems to back off slightly from this position, but he never really follows through on his retreat.

[26] Even Cawelti suggests as much, implicitly (Cawelti, p. 174). Philip Durham, in listing the "villains" of the book, includes Geiger, Brody, and Canino—all of whom are dead at the end; but he neglects to mention Mars. (The *Black Mask* School," in *Tough Guy Writers of the Thirties*, ed. David Madden [Carbondale: Southern Illinois Univ. Press, Crosscurrents: Modern Critiques, 1968], pp. 78-79.) Similarly, Herbert Ruhm refers to Carmen as "the villainess" ("Raymond Chandler: From Bloomsbury to the Jungle—and Beyond," in *Tough Guys Writers*, p. 181).

[27] Two others—General Sternwood and Carmen—are involved in incidents from both stories; but as characters, they only have equivalents in one or the other. Thus, for example, the General takes

over some of the plot function of Tony Dravec in "Killer," but in no sense is there any continuity of character between the two.

28 A detailed examination of these themes in the context of the "combat myth" can be found in Joseph Fontenrose, *Python* (Berkeley: Univ. of California Press, 1957).

29 "Double scotches" was originally simply "drinks." (Raymond Chandler, "Curtain" [1934], in *Killer in the Rain* [New York: Pocket Books, 1965], p. 127)

30 MacShane, p. 69.

31 The names of the other characters in *The Big Sleep* have been carefully chosen as well. Almost all have been rechristened from the original stories, and almost all of the names are evocative. Carmen, a literal man-killer, is obviously named after Merimee: *Carmen* was one of Chandler's favorite stories. ("Letter to Hamish Hamilton, December 4, 1949, in *Chandler Speaking*, p. 84). Lash Canino conjures up images of whip and knives, and he is as vicious a dog as literature has produced. Mona Grant, enigmatic as the Mona Lisa, "grants" Marlowe his freedom. And the name Sternwood resounds with quality and solidity, even if we learn that the wood is rotten. Amid all these names full of character, the name of Harry Jones stands out—for he is the nonentity in this world, the little guy with nothing going for him.

32 Raymond Chandler, "Oscar Night in Hollywood," *Atlantic Monthly*, March 1948, p. 25.

33 Of course, Maxim de Winter is "punished" in the novel; but by film-world standards, the destruction of Manderley and the years of miserable wandering were too subtle a retribution for murder.

34 Hollywood's quid pro quo morality is often applied with disarming ingenuity. Marlowe has seen Canino kill Jones—it is therefore acceptable for him to kill Canino in return. But since Marlowe has not seen Mars himself kill anyone, it would not be cricket for Marlowe himself to kill him. Moral scruples are preserved when Marlowe forces Mars out a door and his own men gun him down. There is, apparently, yet a third—and perhaps a fourth—version of the scene as well; see MacShane, p. 125. MacShane's description, however, is confusing, for he seems to have forgotten how the film actually ends.

35 "Letter to Hamish Hamilton, May 30, 1946," in *Chandler Speaking*, p. 216.

36 "Casual Notes on the Mystery Novel (1919)," in *Chandler Speaking*, p. 66 Chandler insists that this is a purely formal matter, having nothing to do with morality; but his dichotomy is a false one. The punishment of the criminal is formally "satisfying" *because* it is morally lulling—that is, because it allows the novel to perform its social function of arousing and then purging our fears of social chaos. In any case, the unresolved conclusion of *The Big Sleep* is a conscious irritant.

---

[37] Joseph Conrad, "Youth," in *The Norton Anthololgy of English Literature*, ed. M.H. Abrams et. al. (New York: Norton, 1968), 2: 1502, 1504.

[38] Wilson Pollock, "Man with a Toy Gun." *New Republic*, 7 May 1962, p. 21.

# Aggressive Reading: Detective Fiction and Realistic Narrative

*James Guetti*

But I am not so much interested in the aggressive strength of the detective within this story [Dashiell Hammett's *Maltese Falcon*] as I am in the perceptual arrangement of a narrative that—for a reader—both requires and justifies that strength. In Hammett, as we have seen, this arrangement may involve the introduction of something new and strange—a character, or a place, or a movement. But I have also suggested that what is strangest of all in *The Maltese Falcon* is not its characters or happenings but rather the way those elements are seen, the way the narrative that includes them is composed. Everything is strange in this story because everything in it is laid out in pieces. The texture of this narrative is that of succession of anonymous and arhythmic fragments, a mess of particulars that may irritate a reader, inclining him to work them over and work them up into something. What Hammett's prose style does, then, is to present the world in such a way that a reader is prompted to treat that world aggressively, as a puzzle to be solved, whose pieces are its clues. It is this presentation that creates the very possibility of aggressive response.

This peculiar way of structuring a narrative that Hammett established and legitimatized for the detective story was to continue after him, in the work of Raymond Chandler. Here is Chandler's hero, Philip Marlowe, discovering that a corpse is missing:

> It was hard bare masculine bedroom with a polished wood floor, a couple of small throw rugs in an Indian design, two straight chairs, a bureau in dark grained wood with a man's toilet set and two black candles in foot-high brass candlesticks. The bed was narrow and looked hard and had a maroon batik

From "Aggressive Reading: Detective Fiction and Realistic Narrative." Reprinted from *Raritan* 2:1 (1982): 133-54; pp. 137-42

> cover. The room felt cold. I locked it up again, wiped the knob off with my handkerchief, and went back to the totem pole. I knelt down and squinted along the nap of the rug to the front door. I thought I could see two parallel grooves pointing that way, as though heels had dragged. Whoever had done it had meant business. Dead men are heavier than broken hearts.

Chandler's eye, through Marlowe, is just as particular as Hammett's. His narratives are founded upon similar series of fragmentary perceptions, connected for the most part only by temporal sequence, which under the scrutiny of both detective and reader, become the clues to a mystery. And Marlowe's characteristic solution, his way of reading this complicated experience, is to turn it into a slick one-liner: "Dead men are heavier than broken hearts." Such declarations do not solve anything, of course, but they sound as if they do, and they are the most habitual action that this detective takes against the confusions of his case.

The narrative of this book—*The Big Sleep*—is full of these confusions, clumps of perceptual pieces like those in *The Maltese Falcon*, strange because unconnected, that both the detective and a reader seem required to sort through and shape, but with the difference that no sequence of them can go on for very long before Philip Marlowe steps in and cuts it off with this sort of remark:

> The General spoke again, slowly, using his strength as carefully as an out-of-work show-girl uses her last good pair of stockings.
>
> She was as sore as an alderman with mumps.
>
> I was as empty of life as a scarecrow's pockets.
>
> The sunshine was an empty as a headwaiter's smile.

Sentences like this do to the succession of Marlowe's perceptions what punch lines to do jokes, organizing that succession into a set of rounded periods, each of which is transformed from a group of strange fragments into Marlowe's own private mental property. It is this process that enables Marlowe to survive his piecemeal experience.

So although he is not physically violent in the way of Sam Spade, this hyperaction of Philip Marlowe's consciousness, by which he is always rounding things up and polishing them off, suggests that he is in fact more aggressive than Hammett's hero, that his need to assemble the world that comes to him unintegrated is greater and more immediate. Later in Chandler's career, in *The Long Goodbye*, we find his detective operating more gracefully but just as insistently in this vein. As before, he does so constantly and casually: of prizefighters on television he says that "Not one of them could hit hard enough to wake his grandmother out of a light doze," while the commercials "would have sickened a goat raised on barbed wire and broken beer bottles." But also as before, Marlowe employs this brand of verbal facility not merely to eas his tensed imagination, but to shape the course of the entire story.

Marlowe's wit is his weapon, not because he is able to think himself out of scrapes and to circumvent danger, but because he actually meets threats of all kinds with his ability to rephrase them. At one point in the *The Long Goodbye*, for example, he is grilled and beaten by a police captain named Gregorius. On his way out he tries as usual to have the last word:

> "No man likes to betray a friend but I wouldn't betray an enemy into your hands. You're not only a gorilla, you're an incompetent. You don't know how to operate a simple investigation. I was balanced on a knife edge and you could have swung me either way. But you had to abuse me, throw coffee in my face, and use your fists on me when I was in a spot where all I could do was take it. From now on I wouldn't tell you the time by the clock on your own wall."

This, as it happens, is more than a bit disingenuous. Marlowe was not "balanced on a knife edge," for it seems most unlikely that he would have told the police captain anything about his friend Terry Lennox. But saying that he was so "balanced" allows him to punish Gregorius verbally. When the latter next accuses him of being "just a little old cop-hater," Marlowe takes another shot: "There are places where cops are not hated, Captain. But in those places you wouldn't be a cop."

Why, that seems almost poetry. What antagonist, no matter how much a "gorilla," could stand up against such a thrust? But it is Chandler's main strength in *The Long Goodbye* that he does not make it easy for his hero. In some of his other cases, perhaps, Marlowe would have been allowed to say this and get out the door, a clear winner. But here he is held up, and the captain has his own version of the last word by spitting in Marlowe's face.

Yet such is the power of his glib formulas that Marlowe still may seem to have got the better of the exchange. Such is their power, in fact, that even in situations where Marlowe himself resorts to physical violence, and wins, it is still his words that really count. To make this clearer, I want now to quote an extended sequence. It begins, as does any passage where Marlowe draws seriously upon his powers of phrase-turning, with a strangeness:

> A man was sitting by the window ruffling a magazine. He wore a bluish-gray suit with an almost invisible pale blue check. On his crossed feet were black moccasin-type ties, the kind with two eyelets that are almost as comfortable as strollers and don't wear your socks out every time you walk a block. His white handkerchief was folded square and the end of a pair of sunglasses showed behind it. He had thick dark wavy hair. He was tanned very dark. He looked up with bird-bright eyes and smiled under a hairline mustache. His tie was a dark maroon tied in a pointed bow over a sparkling white shirt.

This is perhaps a bit smoother than Hammett's prose, but it is very much on the same frequency in its almost complete inattention to niceties of grammatical relief and in its mechanical insistence upon fragmentary visual detail. Something must be done about this fellow, then, once again not merely because he will turn out to be Marlowe's adversary, but because he is part of an entire body of experience that is seen in an adversary way, an object rendered strange by fractured vision.

Typically enough, however, what makes this stranger especially threatening is his own words. He likes a neat phrase himself, and he abuses Marlowe verbally for a page or so, while on his side the detective is able only to show that he knows his visitor's name, and that he's a gambler, and that he "probably started out as a pimp in a Mexican whorehouse." Not bad, perhaps, but not enough. The gambler named Menendez dominates the meeting, needling Marlowe for two pages more, and at the moment in the story that follows, Marlowe is still saying nothing:

> I didn't say anything. After a moment he grinned slowly. "Tarzan on a big red scooter," he drawled. " A tough guy. Lets me come in here and walk all over him. A guy that gets hired for nickels and dimes and gets pushed around by anybody. No dough, no family, no prospects, no nothing. See you around, Cheapie."
>
> I sat still with my jaws clamped, staring at the glitter of his gold cigarette case on the desk corner. I felt old and tired. I got up slowly and reached for the case.
>
> "You forgot this," I said, going around the desk.
>
> "I got half a dozen of them," he sneered.
>
> When I was near enough to him I held it out. His hand reached for it casually. "How about a half a dozen of these?" I asked him and hit him as hard as I could in the middle of his belly.
>
> He doubled up mewling. The cigarette case fell to the floor. He backed against the wall and his hands jerked back and forth convulsively. His breath fought to get into his lungs. He was

sweating. Very slowly and with an intense effort he straightened up and we were eye to eye again. I reached out and ran a finger along the bone of his jaw. He held still for it. Finally he worked a smile onto his brown face.

"I didn't think you had it in you," he said.

"Next time bring a gun—or don't call me cheapie."

"I got a guy to carry the gun."

"Bring him with you. You'll need him."

"You're a hard guy to get sore, Marlowe."

I moved the gold cigarette case to one side with my foot and bent and picked it up and handed it to him. He took it and dropped it into his pocket.

"I couldn't figure you," I said. "Why it was worth your time to come up here and ride me. Then it got monotonous. All tough guys are monotonous. Like playing cards with a deck that's all aces. You've got everything and you've got nothing. You're just sitting there looking at yourself. No wonder Terry didn't come to you for help. I would be like borrowing money from a whore."

For me this is a classic Chandler sequence. In it, what one can say is what matters. Marlowe is able to get the physical upper hand, in the first place, by not talking, by sitting still with his jaws clamped. His domination, furthermore, is absolute; he runs his finger along his opponent's jaw, and Menendez holds still for it. But after such violence and victory, there is yet more to be said. Despite Marlowe's right hook, Menendez continues to call him "cheapie." Despite his evident physical ascendancy, Marlowe has to go on and tell the gambler what he thinks of tough guys in general. He has to go on hitting him with punch lines. And the contest is not over until, after another half-page of one-liners, both Menendez and his bodyguard have been sufficiently silenced to leave, though the latter's jaw muscles "bulge" with anger.

In Raymond Chandler, then, the detective takes aggressive action upon his case by means of a certain kind of talk. The case confronts him as a welter of strange fragments, and he attacks it by verbally recomposing it, by rephrasing it. There is of course nothing new in this. Though there is a traditional line of detective fiction in which the accepted routine is to shoot first and make clever remarks later, it is the opposite tradition that is in fact much larger. From Poe to Conan Doyle to Agatha Christie and on, the detective's power is assertive; he reforms his experience and solves his cases by means of the peculiar polish of his phrasing. And what seems most important about Dashiell Hammett's influential contribution to this tradition in American is the characteristic nature of the experience that confronts his detective as the stimulus for that hero's assertiveness, the experience that provokes the various brands of aggressive talking that amount, in fiction, to detective work. For what Hammett does, once more, is to certify a narrative presentation that seems fundamentally uncomposed and strange, and that therefore invites aggressive translation and composition by whoever runs up against it.

# Howard Hawks's *The Big Sleep*: A Paradigm for the Postwar American Family

*Brian Gallagher*

The fact that most of World War II intervened between the publication of Raymond Chandler's "hard-boiled" detective novel, *The Big Sleep* (1939), and the film Howard Hawks made from it (1945, released commercially in 1946) should not, in itself, be grounds for reading the film as essentially a postwar version of a prewar story.[1] However, when the numerous changes made for the screen are added together and put in the context of the reformulated narrative, it becomes apparent that the film can, on one level, be seen as a parable of the kind (and quality) of family life that would be possible after American society adjusted itself to the irreversible injuries and losses of the war years.

Some of these changes were dictated by the Production Code (e.g., the elimination of Geiger's pornography racket, the overt exclusion of homosexuality from the plot line) and others by box-office considerations (e.g. the addition of the Marlowe-Vivian/ Bogart-Bacall romance). Still others were made to lighten somewhat the grim and sardonic tone of the novel (e.g., the addition of the scene between Marlowe and the sexy book seller, played by Dorothy Malone). Along with the fabled complexity and contrariness of the plot—the film repeats the novel's cardinal sin, for a detective story, of not explaining the death of Owen Taylor, the Sternwood chauffeur — these changes make for a film full of cross-purposes, shifts in mode (at a number of points it resembles Hawk's fast-talking comedies of the 1930s) and inconsistencies, all of these weaknesses counter-balanced, if not overcome, by the wit and verve of the playing and directing. Still, it would seem to take more than mere style to account

"Howard Hawks's *The Big Sleep*: A Paradigm for the Postwar American Family." *North Dakota Quarterly* 51:3 (1983): 78-91.

for the definite unity the film, despite its confusions, possesses. As James Monaco aptly summarizes the matter: "Suffice it to say that a lot of things are happening in *The Big Sleep*; they may be unintentional. But they are no less evident for that."[2] By a careful scrutiny of the film within the context of its production near the end of the war—it is after all filled with four things that would have been everpresent in the minds of returning servicemen and those waiting to greet them: aggression, violence, sex and domestic arrangements—we can discern a sub-text, ultimately ideological, which is productive of that substantial unity lacking in the over-text.

******

Marlowe is at the core of the the novel and film. Although the film makes no formal attempt to approximate the novel's first person point of view, either through a voice-over or the use of a subjective camera,[3] Marlowe is not only in every scene, but each scene begins and ends with him. Yet, Hawks's Marlowe is a very different creature from Chandler's, first and foremost in his relation to women.[4] For Chandler, Marlowe is a cynical idealist who pseudo-chivalric ideals preclude sexual and romantic entanglements; for Hawks, Marlowe is a sexual opportunist whose realistic ideals invite sexual entanglements, and eventually permit a viable romantic attachment.

Moreover, in the film, Marlowe, despite his protestations that he is "just a guy paid to do other people's laundry," takes an active role, really three active roles, in relation to the Sternwood family. For General Sternwood, Marlowe becomes a substitute "son", a replacement for the absent (murdered) Regan, whom the General specifically identifies as "my friend, my son almost,"[5] Marlowe several times admits, to Vivian, how much he likes the General, and his most constant motivation throughout the film is to protect the decrepit old man by caring for the daughters the General is no longer able to control. To accomplish this, he must play "father" to the wild, cruelly childlike Carmen. After his first encounter with her—wearing an absurdly short skirt, she accosts him in the hallway, teases him coyly, "sucking her thumb the while and collapses into his arms ("You're cute")—Marlowe comments authoritatively to Norris, the Sternwood butler, "You ought to wean her. She's old enough." From the moment he discovers a drugged and uncomprehending Carmen in the house of the just murdered Geiger . . . through the last scene—in which he avows to, and with, Vivian, "We'll have to send Carmen away, from a lot of things. They have places for that. Maybe they can cure her. It's been done before"—Marlowe is pledged, as surrogate for General Sternwood, to keeping Carmen from having to face the full consequences of her actions.[6] Most significantly, albeit most slowly, he assumes the role of "husband" to Vivian, herself drastically changed from the novel's neurotic, impossible mate into a woman still able to contemplate and consummate, if warily, an adult romantic relationship. The Marlowe-Vivian relationship is hard-edged, tough, sexy, and, until near the end, very tempestuous.

The film's symbolic interplay with familial relations is epitomized by the leap-frogging role changes made by Marlowe and Vivian in a telephone hoax: First he poses as her "son," then she as his "mother," and finally he as her "father." And at the end of the film's last scene, after stating what "we'll" do with Carmen, Marlowe switches to his "son" role ("We'll have to tell your father about Regan. I think he can take it."), and in his manner of fulfilling both roles (i.e. the "we'll's") Marlowe has already assumed the third, "husband," despite Vivian's mock-protest, "You've forgotten one thing . . . me."

This restructuring of the Sternwood family along more viable, if less than cozy, lines parallels on the personal level the political movement of the Bogart persona in two of his films of the earlier war years, *Casablanca* (1942) and *To Have and Have Not* (1944)—namely, he abandons an isolationist posture for a committed and involved one.[7] Although Marlowe is an extremely tough, and when necessary violent, man, he is not—like General Sternwood or Sternwood's initial choice for "son," Regan, formerly a brigade commander in the Irish Republican Army—a soldier. Rather Marlowe is a type of "citizen-soldier," ready to do battle when aggressed upon, or to defend, on principle, women (even the hardbitten "Sternwood girls") and the defenseless (the paralyzed General). Emblematically, he does not carry a gun, but keeps two, one long-barrelled and one short-barrelled, in his care for emergencies—and ends up having to use both. Tellingly, the chief gangster in the film, Eddie Mars (whose very name is symbolic of war and carnage), alternates between "Marlowe" and "soldier" when addressing him, thereby stressing Marlowe's status as a temporary combatant.

The war in which Marlowe has enlisted—against all those things that ultimately come to be represented by Eddie Mars—demands both physical courage and mental quickness. Marlowe is involved in a number of "losing battles" on his way to find "victory." For example, in one short scene, filmed in Hawks's most viscerally violent manner, Marlowe is trapped in an alley and brutally, efficiently beaten ("This is just our way of sayin' 'Lay off'").

While Marlowe might be, on one hand, a representative of the noble impulses of the citizen-soldier battling against "professional" foes, he is, on the other hand, also a representative of the baser impulses which such a figure may allow himself under extreme conditions: licentiousness, opportunism, even momentary cowardice. That *The Big Sleep* is charged with the high-voltage sexuality of the Marlowe-Vivian relationship—and also, on another epistemological level, that of Bogart-Bacall—should not obscure that fact that Marlowe is, in general, a very sexual creature, willing to take his pleasures, sexual and otherwise, where he finds them, which in this film is almost everywhere. In the bookstore, he announces his intent to Malone with a *double-entendre* ("I'm a private dick on a case"), persuades her to close the shop (it doesn't take much persuading), signals to her to remove her glasses and let her hair down, pronounces his satisfaction at the metamorphosis ("Hell-lo"), shares a drink (and, presumably, in an ellipsis, sex) with her, and bids her a casual adieu ("So long, pal"), all the while having gotten more iformation than he had expected. Many other encounters emphasize the apparently irresistible sexual appeal Marlowe has for women: a woman cabdriver offers to spend her nights with him; a coffee shop waitress gives him an appreciative once over along with the match he requests; the hostess at Eddie Mars's casino throws him a provocative over-the-shoulder look; and shortly after, that hostess and a cigarette girl breathlessly rush up to Marlowe, competing to be the one who delivers a message to him.

The sexual politics of the film are, of course, exclusively male, albeit they disavow, at least retrospectively, a double standard. Although Vivian's sexual past is not detailed and her sexual present is downplayed except in relation to Marlowe, it is clear that she is to be identified with the "busted Valentine" of the song she sings at Mars's casino while the approving Marlowe looks on. For a time, sexual dalliance, the film implies, is normal and healthy.

Around this healthy sexuality—centered in the figures of Bogart and Bacall and epitomized by the "It depends who's in the saddle" interchange at the restaurant"[8]—the film posits, to the extent that censorship allows it, a number of examples of unhealthy sexuality: nymphomania (Carmen), willed abstinence (Eddie Mars hides his wife out to "explain" the disappearance of Regan), and homosexuality (Geiger-Lundgren, and perhaps, Sternwood Regan).[9] If the film eventually forecloses sexual amorality and institutes monogamy as an ideal, it does so in a way that suggests three important things about sexual relations in postwar America: a) that sexual amorality, at least retrospectively, is pardonable; b) that a healthy sexuality can be the basis of, and expressed in, a monogamous relationship; and c) that such a relationship must, in a tough world, have the man as the first among equals.

The movement toward sexual reconciliation starts in the house at Realito when Vivian passionately kisses the bound Marlowe, who immediately begins to presume on his sexual power over her: "That's better. Get a knife and cut these ropes." Canino is killed—with the active help of Vivian, who first plays decoy to allow Marlowe to get to his car for a gun, then misdirects Canino's attention so Marlowe can shoot him. As they ride back to the final showdown at Geiger's, Vivian says, "I guess I'm in love with you"—and Marlowe reciprocates, using exactly the same words. Marlowe then warns Vivian that she will be in "plenty of trouble" if she stays with him, to which she, now committed and so properly subservient, replies. "I don't mind as long as you're around." Only then does Marlowe offer her a gesture of "soldierly" praise: "You looked good, awful good. I didn't know they made 'em like that any more."

The relationship of leader-follower having been established and implicitly recognized by both parties, the film can now proceed to its conclusion in which, to quote Raymond Bellour, "Eddie Mars' death brings the open series of enigma and peripeteia to a close and sets the seal on the emergence of a couple."[10] The iconography of the final scene differs noticeably in its placement of Marlowe and Vivian — instead of being seen beside or opposite him as she almost always was earlier, she now assumes a position *behind* him, as when she stares out the window over his shoulder as they tensely await Mars . . . or when she stands in the curtained doorway between the foreground room (Marlowe's sphere of action) and the background room. . . Even the assignment given her by Marlowe suggests the nature of her new assistantship: "You watch the back."

It may be true, as one critic suggests, that Hawks's "favorite women successfully pursue their men,"[11] or, as another suggests, that "*The Big Sleep* remains a gallery of women who are just as insolent, just as competent and often just as sublimely amoral as any of the men in the film,"[12] but both judgments must be considered in light of the film's denouncement, in which amorality is foreclosed and in which, in this new sexual universe, Marlowe and Vivian emerge as a couple, Marlowe leading ("Wait a minute, let me do the talking, Angel"). That a strong degree of sexuality is to survive into this new ("postwar") relationship is signalled by the final exchange in the film, with its suggestive consonant-vowel play (f-i-x/f-u-c-k):

Marlowe: What's wrong with you?
Vivian: Nothing you can't fix.

******

Overtly, the film version of *The Big Sleep* is a de-politicized version of an only mildly political novel. In Chandler's version there are occasional slurs on the Sternwoods' money ("To hell with the rich") and its exploitative source: "The Sternwoods, having moved up the hill, could no longer smell the stale sump water or oil, but they could still look out their front windows and see what had made them rich. If they wanted to. I didn't suppose they wanted to." More significant is the film's omission of the anti-police subplot—in the novel Marlowe persists with the investigation because of the blatant corruption of the police and the highhanded manner in which they have covered up the case, but in the film Marlowe's relationship with the police, entirely represented in the person of Bernie Ohls, is friendly and, in the main, cooperative. Covertly, though, the film suggests more politically about its historical moment than the novel.

To the extent the film pictures a world at war, it pictures it indirectly—the blackmailers, hoods, gangsters and murderers who people the film's world may be seen as apolitical equivalents of the sinister, bellicose forces at work in the larger world. It is indicative that the most lethal and uncompassionate killer in the story, Canino, is given a name reflective of the lower, more brutal forms of life, of the treacherously aggressive animal side of the human personality. Life in *The Big Sleep* is portrayed in Hobbesean terms—it is "ugly, nasty, brutish and short," particularly for the half-a-dozen characters murdered during its course (seven if Regan is counted), although the most appropriate response to life's brutalities would seem to be the ironic, almost parodistic, quip (Marlowe on Canino: "He'll beat my teeth out, then kick me in the stomach for mumbling").

The film's Hobbesean vision is very much in keeping with Chandler's vision, *except* that in changing Marlowe from Chandler's hopelessly outmoded "knight-errant" into a more practical "citizen-soldier" the film inspires a different ethical stance toward such a world—commitment, on a limited scale, is possible and can be reciprocated. Yet Marlowe's engagement, which centers around his assuming a tripartite role in the Sternwood family, is set within a larger context of mystery—a mystery which often puzzles and thwarts Marlowe and which, in the classic sense of having to fit all the pieces neatly together, is never satisfactorily solved. Marlowe, the type of the citizen-soldier, must act in an aggressive, puzzling universe, or face extinction, although such action often precedes understanding—he is properly, and necessarily, defensive, even when he does not know who is attacking him or why. The nature and logic of the alliances formed against him are often vague—and are likely to be restructured before he can fully grasp them. He is in the position of an intelligent and brave foot soldier, able to discern only hazily the overall forces and strategies at work in the battle. Consequently, he faces the sudden introduction of new forces throughout the film—for instance Jonesy does not appear until two thirds of the way through and Canino until even later. Each new force (each new character) must quickly be evaluated and designated as friend or foe, an activity at which Marlowe is not always adept. It is precisely Marlowe's inability to recognize Jonesy as a potential ally—he mentions to Mars that someone is "tailing me in a gray Plymouth coupe," which puts the murderous Canino on Jonesy's trail—that costs Jonesy his life: Marlowe must stand by "like a sap" as Canino poisons him.

The mise-en-scéne of the film is like that of a battlefield—namely it is marked by its horizonality. Most of the structures it pictures are, or appear to be, a single story high, whether elaborate (the Sternwood mansion, Mars's fancy club-casino) or relatively simple (Geiger's house, the two bookstores). A good deal of emphasis is put on automobile trips in the film, some of them taking up a fair amount of screen time (e.g. Marlowe and Vivian's journey back from Mars' casino) and others merely alluded to (e.g., Norris' telling Marlowe that "Mrs. Rutledge saw you drive up and I was obliged to tell her who you were"). Indeed, the whole sense of the mystery that informs the action depends on a kind of horizontal "mapping"—that is, on connecting one location (and the characters associated with it) with all the other locations (and their characters). Marlowe's ability to map this terrain is never wholly sufficient—many things in the film are left incomplete and unexplained, Owen Taylor's death being only the most obvious one. For instance, we see Marlowe working to decipher the code Geiger used for his blackmail book—but he is interrupted (by Ohls) and the matter is never returned to. Likewise, his persistent question to Vivian—"What does Eddie Mars have on you?"—is never explicitly answered, since the exact nature of the triangular relationship between Mars, Carmen and the murdered Regan is never really explicated, nor is Vivian's precise knowledge of her sister's involvement stated. Conversely, many of the things that can be clearly established—e.g., that no bookseller could have a Chevalier-Audubon 1840 since "nobody would, there isn't one"—are absolutely meaningless in the larger scheme of things. In the face of all this crucial uncertainty (and non-crucial certainty), Marlowe's attitude is one of puzzled cognizance—he takes in whatever information he can without necessarily believing he has all or enough of the facts. His most characteristic gesture throughout the film is his pulling at his ear lobe and murmuring "hmmm" when he learns something.

The horizontality of the mise-en-scéne is paralleled by the film's visual style. Besides Hawks's standard reliance on the eye-level camera (which puts events on a level plane), most of the film's few departures from this norm are likewise characterized by horizontality—one of the few obvious camera movements is a straight, slow dolly in on Marlowe dozing in his car as he waits outside Geiger's house; shortly thereafter, there is an atypical piece of synecdoche; we see Taylor's legs moving horizontally across the screen as he flees the murder scene. Yet, for all the film's movement from place to place, the film's narrative contains not progression but recirculation. As Jacques Rivette notes, "The characters are confined to a few settings, and they move around rather helplessly in them."[13] In the end, most of the surviving characters are back at the scene of the first "battle," Geiger's house, for the final "battle."

This recirculation does, though, have ideological point. Whereas Chandler's novel emphasized the stale, seedy, already decaying quality of the Los Angles cityscape, the film traverses and retraverses a cityscape that is, by turns, bland, bright, tacky, tawdry, and mostly new. This landscape is, in its own way, prophetic—it prefigures the decentered, quasi-urban sprawl that has characterized the unplanned and unregulated development of the American landscape over the last thirty-five years, most particularly in the Sunbelt, of which Los Angeles has remained the El Dorado and spiritual capital. Simply to get anything done, Marlowe must spend a good deal of time driving around what two architectural writers have recently characterized as the "classic non-city. . . a planned non-city,"[14] one which is defined only by its circumference and not its center. What Marlowe manages to accomplish through all this frantic and sometimes misdirected movement is not just to survive, but to survive *into* a new, and presumably permanent, alliance—as the central figure in the reconstructed Sternwood family, a position which is effectively that of being Vivian's mate and, in a hostile world, mentor and guide.

The first shot in the film proper is a close-up of the Sternwood nameplate on the family mansion—and it becomes Marlowe's task as the film unfolds to reintroduce a necessary measure of "sternness" into the life of that family. As a man used to, if not fond of, violence, he knows on which members it must be used (several times he slaps Carmen around) and those on whom it must not (General Sternwood is protected from every blow possible). If Marlowe is a type of the rugged citizen-soldier, willing to be violent when necessary, Vivian is a type of the citizen-soldier's ideal mate, containing a complementary degree of toughness, realism, and unabashed sexuality, without being, like the psychotic Carmen, naturally treacherous or murderous. And she is also willing be subservient and compliant, circumstances permitting. She is, then, very much the type of woman whom many servicemen might expect, were they sufficiently realistic, to encounter on their return home (as opposed to the more prevalent movie stereotype of the faithful sweetheart who spent the war years worrying and waiting without altering her lifestyle or expectations in any essential way). Only strained circumstances have made her cold, self-sufficient and somewhat amoral sexually. On this point the film strikes an implied a bargain—that is, if Marlowe, who himself has been carnal, opportunistic and duplicitous, will allow Vivian the same freedom retrospectively, then she will *projectively* assume her destined role as a monogamous, obedient sexual partner.

The iconography of the credit sequences creates around the film text of parenthesis which suggest the rather compromised (or compromising) nature of the relationship between Marlowe and Vivian. In the opening credits we see the two figures in silhouette, with Marlowe lighting Vivian's cigarette—a figuration that implies both a dark side to their joining and a substratum of physical satiation in that joining. (In Hollywood films of the 1930s and 1940s the ritual give-and-take of cigarette lighting between hero and heroine often stood as a coded allusion to the sexual act.) In the closing sequence, there is an ashtray with two lighted cigarettes side-by-side in it (in lower left of the frame), a symbolic indication that the joining of Marlowe and Vivian, posited in the opening credits and slowly achieved through the narrative, rests as much on physical satisfaction as any other component, that a healthy and acknowledged sexuality can be both the motive force in the checkered sexual past and the basis for monogamous sexual future.

To the extent that the film contained a covert message for returning servicemen (and those to whom they returned), the message was essentially unsentimental: do not expect domestic life to be as it was (or as, ideally, you envisioned it), but rather accept the deprivatons, lapses and compromises of the war years and make do despite.[15] In fact, the Marlowe-Vivian union is, despite its somewhat compromised status, the most positive element in the reconstituted Sternwood family. Carmen is definitely a casualty of the "war," her (probably permanent) exile to a sanitarium paralleling the fate of those many citizen-soldiers who survived the conflict only to become permanent invalids needing continual hospitalization. Similarly, General Sternwood survives in only the most tenuous manner—paralyzed and brought even closer to his imminent death by having to bear the loss of a daughter (Carmen, to madness) and a "son" (Regan, to murder).

Ironically, in the manner of his fulfilling the roles of "son" to General Sternwood and "father" to Carmen, Marlowe has, in principle, upheld the notion of the extended family (spanning three generations), even as he has, in effect, instituted a nuclear family. (Upon the General's death, it will be only he and Vivian.) In this regard, the film is particularly prophetic of the subsequent development of American social life. In the film version of *The Big Sleep*, the nuclear family emerges as a kind of historical inevitability (rising, phoenix-like, form the ashes of the extended family), the logic of its formation being subtractive—with the grandparent soon to perish and the false sister-child ostracized, the couple can and must begin its own natural expansion.

In a capitalist sense, this reconstituted family is something of a new economic unit—having adjusted to the suffering, losses and deprivations of the war years, the family unit of the (film's) future defines itself by the realistically defensive posture it assumes in a world still hostile, if not outrightly aggressive. This family, therefore, looks out for its own welfare first, and, if necessary, at the expense of others—thus, Marlowe finds it most convenient and neat to send Eddie Mars out to die in a hail of his own gunmen's bullets, thereby obviating the troublesome probing into the murky Sternwood family history that would have otherwise resulted.

The subtext of *The Big Sleep* is, then an essential commentary on the nature of the postwar American family and the kind of society in which it would function. In directing our attention, even if subconsciously, to domestic configurations, the film implies that the family unit—as opposed to the class or other unit—is, or will be, the prime reality of social life. In doing so, the film recalls that conjunction of "abundance and total control" which Herbert Marcuse saw as the dominant pattern of the "post-industrial capitalism" which began to emerge after World War II. As Frederic Jameson puts it, summarizing Marcuse, the postwar years have been characterized by

> . . . increased sexual freedom, greater material abundance and consumption, freer access to culture, better housing, more widely available educational benefits and increased social, not to speak of automotive mobility, which are the

> accompaniment to increasing manipulation and the most sophisticated forms of thought-control, increasing abasement of spiritual and intellectual life, a degradation and dehumanization of existence.[16]

Many of the indicators of this abundance are in evidence in *The Big Sleep*—sexual freedom, money, glittering commodities—and there is a great deal of automotive travel back and forth across the emblematic landscape of Southern California. Yet, all these things are seen, all these activities conducted, in a fog of mystification—the individual (here Marlowe) acts in response to forces he cannot fully understand or significantly control. To survive—and to have the considerable spoils that are the survivor's lot (here a Sternwood woman and some share of the Sternwood fortune)—one must become closed-in, hostile, defensive, in a word, alienated. The tightly controlled nuclear family has become the largest viable unit for alliances, the rest of society comprising an alien force against which this family must protect itself and advance its position.

The film's ultimate point—or, more accurately, the ultimate point of its sub-text—seems to be that the returning warrior would not only find his world changed by half a decade of global war, but also that American social life, right down to the family unit, would henceforth be characterized by combativeness not too far removed from that to which he had become accustomed. What the film version of *The Big Sleep* urges on us is the virtue of selfishness—even in the consummation of their union Marlowe and Vivian might be said to use each other. Seen in its historical moment, *The Big Sleep* offers a paradigm for the development of the postwar American family—in a hostile, competitive environment, the family must learn to defend its interests and aggrandize itself, even at the cost of abandoning some of the older, more benevolent views of family life and the responsibility of the family to society. What *The Big Sleep* embodies, almost advocates, is a calculated entrepreneurship of the family.

---

1 The script was written by William Faulkner and Leigh Brackett, with the final scene—rewritten at the insistence of the Production Code censors—by Jules Furthman. As usual with Hawks, he rewrote the reworked scenes day by day as the shooting progressed. According to Bruce F. Kawin, "Warner's liked the picture so much that they decided to hold up its release for more than a year, so that it finally came out as part of Warner's 'twentieth anniversary of sound on the screen.' During the interim, however, it was shown to American servicemen overseas; their reactions led Hawks to write and shoot several new scenes, most of them romantic banter between Philip Marlowe (Bogart) and Vivian Sternwood [sic] (Bacall). When the picture was released, then, it was much faster and funnier than

Brackett and Faulkner had intended" (*Faulkner and Film* [New York: Frederick Ungar, 1977], p. 113).

[2] "Notes on 'The Big Sleep': Thirty Years After," *Sight and Sound*, 44:1 (Winter 1974-75), 35.

[3] The ultimate reference point in this regard is Robert Montgomery's Philip Marlowe film of 1946, *The Lady in the Lake*, in which the camera is totally identified with the position of Marlowe's eyes, our only glimpses of his body being reflections in mirrors, windows, etc.

[4] I use Hawks's name here and elsewhere as a mere convenience in referring to the contriver of the film, chiefly because he was the most central figure in the film's construction, tying together its scripted side and enacted side. Obviously, "Marlowe" is also a creation of Faulkner and Brackett (and Furthman) on one side and Bogart (and those playing opposite him) on the other.

[5] In "Homosexuality and Film Noir," (*Jump Cut*, No. 16, pp. 16-22), Richard Dyer includes General Sternwood in his list of homosexual characters in *film noir*, based on the "hothouse atmosphere" which he inhabits, but Dyer also admits this as his most "tenuous example."

[6] The film's ending, as originally scripted, has Marlowe allowing Carmen to be killed by Mars's gunmen, obviously because, despite all his "fatherly" efforts, he cannot overcome the "corrupt blood" in her veins. Such an ending would have made the "defensive" position of family life I discuss toward the end of this essay an even more cynical and selfish concept—i.e., the family must purify itself of those members who, in capitalist terms, do not return a fair share for the family's investment in them. The ending suggested by the Production Code People—and adopted by Furthman and Hawks—suddenly and illogically implies that Mars may have killed Regan, surely a "fast curve" as Kawin terms it (*Faulkner and Film*, 116).

[7] The second film was partially an outgrowth of the success of the first—and both played on Bogart's ability to suggest the legitimacy of a detached stance ("I stick my neck out for nobody" [*Casablanca*]), akin to the widespread American belief in individualism, only to abandon that stance for the higher legitimacy of anti-Fascist involvement, Fascism being portrayed chiefly as a bullying, anti-individualist force.

[8] This scene was the most important one added after the film was previewed to servicemen. (Originally Norris was to have paid off Marlowe and dismissed him.) Together with the scene where Marlowe returns Carmen to the Sternwood mansion, the one in Brody's apartment and one in Realito, it makes four instances where Vivian is added to a scene in which she is not present in the novel.

[9] There is a good deal of coded allusion to homosexuality in the film—e.g., Geiger's *chinoiserie* house, Lundgren's laying out of Geiger's

body in a candlelit bedroom, the absence of any other motive for Lundgren killing the man he thinks killed Geiger, Brody. Malone describes Geiger as "soft all over" and calls Lundgren, whose first name (Carol) is normally feminine one, Geiger's "shadow" (perhaps suggesting sexual positioning?). In short, for anyone familiar with the novel, it is not difficult to read into the film unspoken lines of Chandler's, like Marlowe's sneer at Lundgren, "You must have thought a lot of that queen." Oddly, but explicably, Bogart's momentary impersonation of a homosexual (when he puts the "bird twitter" into his voice on the first visit to Geiger's bookstore) is the only action fully marked as homosexual in the film. It is a measure of the film's audacity, its heterosexual audacity, that it allows Bogart (whose slight lisp might already be considered of a suspicious nature sexually) to parody himself—and still remain unquestionably and completely heterosexual.

10 "The Obvious and the Code," n.t., *Screen*, 15:4 (Winter 1974-75), 7.

11 Gerald Peary, "Fast Cars and Women," *Focus on Howard Hawks*, ed. Joseph McBride (Englewood Cliffs, N.J.: Prentice-Hall, 1972), p. 115.

12 Monaco, p. 38.

13 "The Genius of Howard Hawks," trans. Russell Campbell and Marvin Pister, in *Great Film Directors*, ed. Leo Braudy and Morris Dickstein (New York: Oxford Univ. Press, 1978), p. 448.

14 David Gebhard and Harriette Von Breton, *L.A. in the Thirties: 1931-1941* (n.p.: Peregrine Smith, 1975), p. 25. The authors go on to argue that Los Angeles by 1941 "came about as close as is humanly possible to realizing the American middle-class view of the ideal environment wherein suburbia was equated with the overpowering rightness of nature and the virtue of rural life, while it was widely suspected that the high-density city was of necessity evil and corrupt" (p. 25). If the authors are correct, then we must count as one of the film's subliminal pleasures for its middle-class audience Marlowe's many journeys from place to place in the film, particularly when we recall that they portend the end of gasoline rationing and restoration of almost total freedom for the singular vehicular unit.

15 A useful, and contrastive, reference point here is William Wyler's *The Best Years of Our Lives* (1946), which deals directly with the lives and problems of a group of returning servicemen. What this film postulates is an *interval*—the returning servicemen at first feel estranged from their families and civilian society, feeling comfortable only with each other—followed by a *reinstitution*— domestic life is returned essentially to its prewar (and presumably permanent American) form. If anything, the war years tested people by a stable standard of domesticity—thus the wife of a young flyer (Dana Andrews) proved to be the tramp "she always was," thereby allowing

him to rectify his mistake and marry a properly innocent and faithful woman.

16 *Marxism and Form: Twentieth-Century Dialectical Theories of Literature* (1971: rpt, Princeton: Princeton Univ. Press, 1974), pp. 107-108.

# Chivalry and Modernity in Raymond Chandler's *The Big Sleep*

*Ernest Fontana*

In this essay it will be assumed that the case for the literary status of Raymond Chandler's fiction has been made.[1] Most notably, perhaps, Fredric Jameson argues that the private detective—Philip Marlowe—is a significant fictive invention, a figure who ties together the "separate and the isolated parts" of "new centerless city, in which various classes have lost touch with each other because each is isolated in his own geographical compartment."[2] Although the conventional, surface plot of Chandler's fiction is directed to the solution of a murder or disappearance, the literary project of Chandler's novels is "organizing essentially plotless material into an illusion of movement."[3] The essential contents of Chandler's books are the "scenic" constituents of the spatially diffused post-industrial city, of which Los Angeles is the American prototype.[4] Marlowe has access to the inaccessible; he connects the apparently disconnected, and he records with lucidity and stylish, verbal economy the formless immensity of a centerless metropolis.[5] Like the freeway system of contemporary Los Angeles, Marlowe's field of perception is a trustworthy and efficient connector, a means of perceptual transit through an urban and social space that has metastasized beyond the confines of the traditional novel.

*The Big Sleep* (1939) is Chandler's first sustained fictive negotiation with post-industrial Los Angeles. Curiously, Chandler here appears to turn to the past, evoking images of chivalry and allusions to romance to define his narrator's relation to this new urban environment and to suggest that Marlowe is not merely an observer, as Jameson argues, but a complex, subjective presence as well. These allusions to romance and chivalry have been recently addressed by

"Chivalry and Modernity in Raymond Chandler's *The Big Sleep*," *Western American Literature* 19:3 (1984): 179-186.

both Jerry Speir and Paul Skenazy. Speir reads *The Big Sleep* as chronicle of the failure of romance,[6] while Skenazy argues that we have instead "a redefinition of romantic roles. Marlowe speaks in a new modern voice, but he is no less heroic"[7] than the traditional chivalric hero of courtly romance. In this essay I intend to pursue Speir's suggestion that *The Big Sleep* is a failure of romance and to examine the reasons why the completion of the chivalric quest ends, in *The Big Sleep*, not with a sense, for both narrator and protagonist, of closure, fulfillment, and renewal, but with a sense of "general uneasiness,"[8] with the hero feeling he is part of the nastiness he had thought he was combatting. The first reason I shall adduce for the failure of romance as genre and of chivalry as personal code is Chandler's perception of the growth of the post-industrial city. This world is delineated in *The Big Sleep* through literal images of disease and physical climate, which, cumulatively, become metaphoric substitutions, suggesting the opacity, pervasiveness, and intractability of the detective-knight's adversaries. A second reason is the absence, in this new urban milieu, of authentic and compelling lords to whom the chivalric knight can swear feudal submission and loyalty.

Over the entrance doors of both the narrative and the Sternwood mansion is an Art Deco stained-glass panel, "showing a knight in dark armor rescuing a lady who was tied to a tree and didn't have any clothes on but some very long and convenient hair."[9] The knight has pushed his visor back and is fiddling with the ropes, not trying very hard to rescue the young lady. Marlowe feel that if he lived in that house he "would sooner or later have to climb up there and help him." Of course, the lady is Carmen Sternwood whom Marlowe will find nude twice in the novel, first in the murdered Geiger's living room and then in his own bed. In the traditional romance, the tied nude "lady" has been abducted and tied by a villain. The knight-hero's rescue of the lady involves slaying her abductor and evil guardian. In *The Big Sleep* there is, however, no external villain, no seamonster for Marlowe-Perseus-St. George to slay in order to rescue Carmen-Andromeda. Carmen Sternwood has been tied by a force within her, her epilepsy. In the work of the influential, turn of the century Italian criminologist, Cesare Lombroso, epilepsy is unscientifically identified as the disease of criminal degenerates,[10] and, in *The Big Sleep* it is presented as a consequence of Sternwood fathering Carmen at an advanced age. The feral monster that the traditional knight slays is, in *The Big Sleep* within his victim, and the maiden cannot be rescued from him without being slain herself. "The hissing sound grew louder and her face had the scraped bone look. Aged, deteriorated, become animal, and not a nice animal" (205). In fact when this internal monster of epilepsy possesses Carmen, it drives her, independently of her will, to acts of sexual excess and murder. Andromeda becomes Medusa.

In the oil-scummed sump, in the proximity of the tired oil wells that are the abandoned origins of the Sternwood fortune, Carmen has murdered Rusty Reagan and attempts to murder Marlowe, her putative rescuer. What Carmen needs is not so much a knight, but a physician. At the end of the novel, Marlowe compromises himself by becoming involved in the conspiracy to hide Carmen's murder of Regan in exchange for her sister's promise that Carmen will be taken away for medical treatment. Marlowe is himself powerless to rescue the lady; he must resign her to medical science and the cost is almost his own life, and finally, the compromising of his professional code.

Throughout *The Big Sleep* Chandler uses disease and weather as motifs to suggest that the adversaries that the modern knight must combat are super-personal, that they are forces which individual acts of heroism are powerless to overcome. Marlowe maintains his honor; he does not sleep with his employer's daughters (though both tempt him), nor does he reveal to the police Carmen's presence at the scene of Geiger's murder. He rejects payment from both Eddie Mars and from Vivian. Yet personal incorruptibility, given the power of the anonymous and collective forces of entropy and degeneration that pervade the book, is ineffectual and irrelevant. In *The Big Sleep*, Marlowe plays the role of a modern knight in a world where conclusive and effectual individual heroism cannot exist. The existential chess game he plays against himself is in fact merely a game that cannot transform the world in which he must act. "Knights had no meaning in this game. It wasn't a game for knights" (146). Yet though Marlowe recognizes this, he continues to play his game of knighthood; it is the only one he knows and there is no other game in sight, except supine submission to a collective entropic adversary. One of the elements of this entropy is the very sudden growth of Los Angeles itself. "Some very tough people have checked in here lately. The penalty of growth" (67). The white frame house of Taggart Wilde, the District Attorney, who comes from an old Los Angeles family, has been literally moved from West Adams or Figueroa Street to Lafayette Park. A traditional, "old fashioned" house has been moved bodily to a new location, and Wilde's traditional, patrician values have been, similarly, translated and compromised. Wilde is aware the Hollywood police have been taking bribes from Geiger to lay off his smut business, but he does not intend to take action. In a similar use of an architectural image of transposition, The Cypress Club, Eddie Mars's illegal gambling operation, is housed in "a rambling frame mansion that had once been the summer residence of a rich man named De Cazens" (121). Its Gothic architecture—"scrolled porches" and turrets—evocative of both a European feudal past and an era of heroic American capitalist production, now has "a general air of nostalgic decay" (121). Later in the novel, Capt. Gregory of the Missing Persons Bureau, who, we are led to believe, has known all along the truth about Regan's murder, tells Marlowe that the possibility of equal justice for rich gangsters and "slum-bred hard guys" is unlikely to happen, "not in this town, not in any town half this size, in any part of this wide, green and beautiful U.S.A. We don't run our country that way" (191). Thus the literal constituents of collective entropy are perceived, the *The Big Sleep*, as rapid urban growth, the decay of patrician values, and the power of wealth to corrupt justice.

Nevertheless, it is not this explicit social analysis that is the source of the novel's intensity, but its use of disease and weather as metaphoric substitutions for never fully defined forces of social and moral menace. These forces are evoked not only by Carmen's epilepsy and use of drugs, by Sternwood's paralysis, by Geiger's homosexuality, by Cobb's alcoholism (all for Chandler forms of disease), but by the October humidity and rain that pervade the book. The greenhouse that sustains the living death of General Sternwood and "the nasty meaty leaves" (5) of the tropical orchids he raises (metaphors for his daughters) is extrapolated, in *The Big Sleep*, to include all of Los Angeles.

> The thunder in the foothills was rumbling again. The glare of lightning was reflected on piled-up black clouds off to the south. A few tentative raindrops splashed down on the sidewalk and made spots as large as nickels. The air was as still as the air in General Sternwood's orchid house." (23)

Encapsulated by humidity, rain, and fog, the Los Angeles of *The Big Sleep* is presented as an environment pervaded by mystery, sickness, and monstrosity. The modern knight is powerless to change the weather of the historical season in which he enacts his quest. Without magical powers, he must learn to keep dry in the rain and to see in the fog—to explicate the world that has become "a wet emptiness" (139). When, finally, the sun does shine at the end of the book, when the mystery of Regan's disappearance has been lifted, the sunshine itself is darkened. Outside, the bright gardens had a haunted look; as though small wild eyes were watching me from behind the bushes, as though the sunshine itself had a mysterious something in its light" (215). The epileptic monster within Carmen survives, unvanquished, to darken the sun and to envelop Los Angeles with intimations of death and decay, of the Big Sleep, which the knight's solution of the mystery of Regan's disappearance cannot dispel. The darkness even enters the knight-hero as he agrees to keep Carmen's guilt a secret, and, likewise, the reader who by virtue of completing the text is implicated in "the secret," which only the dying Sternwood, the king unregenerated by the knight's quest, does not know.

The figure of General Sternwood, descended from a Mexican War general, whose painting hangs above a "big empty fireplace" with its "imperially black mustachios" (2), is a key figure in Chandler's social mythology. He is the lord that Marlowe as knight serves and whom he will not betray: "It is against my principles to tell as much as I've told tonight, without consulting the General" (106). Yet he is a sick, dying lord, who cannot provide Marlowe relevant mastership, but only illusion. The General survives in illusion; the truth about Carmen would kill him, and, as we have seen, Marlowe ends up acting to sustain this illusion.

The world in which Sternwood acted with mastery and effect no longer exists: "he doesn't realize what the world is today" (106). There is no space left for the effective individual action of the masterful and courageous entrepreneur who develops socially beneficial, primary raw materials. Sternwood's original oil wells are exhausted, "no longer piping," and surrounded by "rusted pipe" and "a loading platform that sagged at the end" (204). Instead of energizing the economy of a pristine California frontier, the stagnant, oil-scummed water of Sternwood's original fiefdom is the burial ground for the man who rejected the sexual advances of his epileptic daughter. It is to these men, whom Carmen seeks either to seduce or kill, that Sternwood looks for sons, for heirs to continue the early capitalist ethic of the heroic, individualistic production of empowering energy. But the world of Chandler's post-industrial Los Angeles is a world of enervated consumption, not of heroic production and the development of primary raw materials. It produces not oil, but the decadent pleasures of pornography, drugs, and gambling, which, in turn, generate the collective entropy that envelops the world of the novel. At the end of *The Big Sleep*, the threat the Eddie Mars will blackmail Vivian, when she inherits her father's wealth, remains a real possibility. The future male heir to the dying king's power is neither the knight, Marlowe, nor the gutsy IRA revolutionary, Rusty Regan, but the slick gangster, Eddie Mars.

Rather than enter this post-industrial culture of consumption, Marlowe resists it, living ascetically in his apartment at Franklin and Kenmore, from which he drives Carmen, his nude intruder and seductress, an act for which he will be almost killed. Marlowe's isolation stems from his refusal to enter the new hedonistic economy of consumption, and simultaneously, from Chandler's recognition that the earlier, "heroic" economy of primary production, idealized by Marlowe in the figure of General Sternwood is itself dying and historically superseded. Marlowe, bereft of feudal lord, is a Bedivere without an Arthur.[11]

It is significant, therefore, that Marlowe's problematic relationship to Sternwood is doubled or paralleled by the relationship of "the fag," Carol Lundgren, to the petty blackmailer, Geiger. Lundgren kills Brody, because he mistakenly believes that Brody has murdered Geiger. Deprived of his lord, Lundgren is in a state of despair and incoherence. All he can do is utter meaningless obscenities at Marlowe. One of the two extended single combats in the novel is Marlowe's wrestling with Lundgren after Brody's murder. "We seemed to hang there in the misty moonlight, two grotesque creatures whose feet scraped on the road and whose breathe panted with effort" (93). This combat, with its connotations of physical intimacy, not only suggests that Lundgren's homosexuality is answered by an element within the homophobic Marlowe that he must repress, keep "ironbound" (93), but that Lundgren's maniacal loyalty to Geiger is a grotesque parody of Marlowe's own need to enter into a relationship of chivalric loyalty with a vital and authentic lord. In fact, Lundgren's relationship to Geiger is a metaphor for the dark underside of Marlowe's relationship to Sternwood. The murderous fury of the bereft and disillusioned Lundgren is paralleled by Marlowe's own fury as he tears his bed to pieces "savagely," when he discovers the imprint on his pillow of Carmen's "small corrupt body" (148). To sleep with the daughter of his lord is not only a betrayal of his duty, but the violation of an incest taboo, since the relationship of knight to lord is an unarticulated, repressed homoerotic fantasy that is fully enacted in the Lundgren-Geiger relationship.

A second double figure for Marlowe is Canino, whose name, Little Dog, is echoed by Carmen's name for Marlowe, "Doghouse Reilley." As with Lundgren, Marlowe enters into a nocturnal, single combat with Canino at the desert hideaway in Realito, where Eddie Mars has sequestered his wife, thereby giving the appearance she has run off with Regan. Canino is Mars's knight, his dog, his tool. His relationship to Mars is a debasement of the knight's relationship to his lord and a distorted parody of Marlowe's relationship to Sternwood. Marlowe must kill Canino, not only because of his brutal cyanide poisoning of Harry Jones, but because Canino represents a debasement of the ideal of chivalric loyalty that Marlowe seeks to live by. The nocturnal shooting of the bestial Canino, in which the handcuffed Marlowe uses deception and trickery (he deceives Canino into believing he is in an automobile when he is actually behind it) and violates the rules of gentlemanly combat, is the single time in Chandler's fiction that Marlowe actually kills his opponent. "Perhaps it would have been nice to allow him another shot or two, just like a gentleman of the old school. But his gun was still up and I couldn't wait any longer. Not long enough to be a gentleman of the old school" (189).

This self-mocking violation of the gentlemanly code of modern knighthood suggests that the ideal of chivalry that Marlowe has attempted to live by is no longer relevant to the exigencies of personal survival in a world in which knighthood has been appropriate and debased by "fags" (this is Marlowe's homophobic word) and hoods. The killing of Canino is for Marlowe a rite of passage from the unreal illusions of chivalric romance to the debased realities of the post-industrial metropolis. The lady that Marlowe finally does rescue from a monstrous keeper willingly returns to Canino's lord, her own husband, Eddie Mars. Marlowe becomes "part of the nastiness now" (216), compromising himself further to prevent his dying, ineffectual "king" from knowing the world his own heroic enterprise has engendered. At the end of *The Big Sleep*, Marlowe is stripped of his heroic illusions. His last act of feudal loyalty to Sternwood brings with it the somber and elegiac recognition that his knightly quests will be, henceforth, solitary, lordless, and absurd.

*The Big Sleep*, Chandler's prototypical fiction, is an ironic or failed romance. It establishes a mystery whose solution does not liberate or energize a diseased and entropic world. The solution of the mystery of Regan's disappearance is a process whereby Marlowe discovers the obsolesence of his most cherished values and finds that those he champions are dying and unable to respond with authority to the passion he brings to his task. In this subversion of romance, the knight's only unequivocal victory is textual, the written, retrospective narrative of this subversion. *The Big Sleep* is the confessional narrative of an isolated, publicly insignificant private eye, who in the solitude of his marginality and disillusion, reveals, through words, the opaque, intractable world that survives undiminished by his loyalty, courage, and asceticism.

---

1 See especially, Herbert Ruhm's "Raymond Chandler: From Bloomsbury to the Jungle—and Beyond," *Tough Guy Writers of the Thirties*, ed. David Madden, (Carbondale: Southern Illinois, 1968); Frederic Jameson's "On Raymond Chandler," *Southern Review*, 6 (1970), 624-650; E.M. Beekman's "Raymond Chandler and an American Genre," *Massachusetts Review*, 14 (1973), 149-173; Jerry Speirs *Raymond Chandler* (New York: Frederick Ungar, 1981); Paul Skenazy's *The New Wild West: the Urban Mysteries of Dashiell Hammett and Raymond Chandler* (Boise: Boise State Western Writers Series, 1982).

2 Jameson, p. 629.

3 Jameson, p. 625.

4 On Los Angeles as the prototypical American post-industrial metropolis, see Sam Bass Warner's *The Urban Wilderness* (New York: Harper & Row, 1972), pp. 113-152.

5 "It is neither the violence nor the solution of the mystery Chandler is interested in as it is the city and the people, through the whole range of which, in the solution of the crime, Marlowe moves . . . his adventures being *pittoresque* images of his corrupt society and time." Ruhm, p. 178.

6 Speir, p. 30.

7 Skenazy, pp. 37-38.

8 Beekman, p. 163.

9 Raymond Chandler, *The Big Sleep* (New York: Vintage Books, 1976), p. 1. Hereafter cited in the text.

10 See Gina Lombroso-Ferrero, *Criminal Man* (Montclair, New Jersey: Patterson Smith reprint, 1972), pp. 58-62.

11 Ironically, Marlowe's services as private detective are themselves dependent on the economic activities of the world he seeks, unsuccessfully, to detach himself from. Blackmail, the crime he is originally asked to investigate, is itself a consequence of thriving illegal industries of pornography, drug-dealing, and gambling that serve the inheritors not producers of old wealth. Marlowe is thus tied to an economy he morally abhors.

# The Function of Simile in Raymond Chandler's Novels

*Stephen L. Tanner*

Anyone who has sampled Raymond Chandler's hard-boiled detective novels has discovered that, despite the somberness and often sordidness of the subject matter, the books are very funny. some of the wisecracks of Chandler's detective narrator, Philip Marlowe, are virtually legendary. Probably no American writer since Mark Twain invented so many pungent one-liners. And, of course, much of the humor is produced by the abundant similes that are the hallmark of the Chandler style. His prose is peppered with newly-minted similes and show-stopping metaphors. These distinctive tropes are (using one of them) "as easy to spot as a kangaroo in a dinner jacket." Here are some samples:

as rare as a fat postman
as welcome as a pearl onion on a banana split
a brain like a sack of Portland cement
about as excited as a mortician at a cheap funeral
as sore as an alderman with mumps
tasted like a plumber's handkerchief
as phony as the pedigree of a used car
about as inconspicuous as a tarantula on a slice of angel food
a look that is supposed to make your spine feel like a run in a stocking
debonair as a French count in a college play
a tongue like a lizard's back
enough sex appeal to stampede a businessmen's lunch
stick out like spats at an Iowa picnic

"The Function of Simile in Raymond Chandler's Novels," *Studies in American Humor* 3:4 (1984-5): 337-346.

a face like a collapsed lung
feeling like a short length of chewed string
laughter like a tractor backfiring
a lobby that looked like a high budget musical
with the dignity of an intoxicated dowager
as unlikely to succeed as a ballet dancer with a wooden leg
as restful as a split lip

The effect of some of these is diminished, of course, by being extracted from their context. Some are strained, but the bizarre is Chandler's trademark. On the whole he succeeds so well that when later writers try the same thing, it does not seem original or even natural to them, but a mere imitation of Chandler.

Perhaps his main achievement was a mastery of the American style—a combination of idiom, slang, wisecrack, hyperbole, understatement, and tough talk that in the hands of a man of genius can, as someone put it, make the English language jump through a hoop. Chandler once said he thought Marlowe was an expression of the American mind. In his famous essay on detective fiction. "The Simple Art of Murder," he says. "He talks as a man of his age talks—that is, with rude wit, a lively sense of of the grotesque, a disgust for sham, and a contempt for pettiness."[1] These are the qualities that animate the similes.

The British who generally have taken Chandler more seriously as a writer than have Americans, have been quick to recognize the distinctively American quality of Chandler's style and humor. Somerset Maugham praised his "admirable aptitude for that typical product of the quick American mind, the wisecrack," and said that "his sardonic humor has an engaging spontaneity."[2] Patricia Highsmith observed that "Chandler's similes gave his writing not only vigour and unforgettable personages, but humour of the wild and insolent American Variety."[3] D.C. Russell, in commenting on the prodigality of Chandler's imagery, said, "If they seem more wisecracks than high-flown literary similes, I will point out that Chandler writes the characteristic American humor. In doing this he comes closer to literature than other writers who disdain the native brand of thought and language."[4]

What I wish to establish in this paper is that Chandler was a dedicated and skilled stylist who used figurative language, particularly a kind of comic simile having deep roots in the tradition of American humor, to add poetic resonance and significant new dimensions to the popular and formulaic genre of the detective novel.

It is generally acknowledged that Marlowe is an urban version of the frontier hero.[5] His name is often linked with Leatherstocking, Huck Finn, and the cowboy hero. It is not simply coincidental that Chandler set his kind of detective stories in the West. The West comes into focus in California, the final frontier in geography and expectations. Like the frontier hero, Marlowe is a loner, distrustful of intellectualism, ambivalent toward women and society, possessed of an innate sense of justice, scornful of the artificialities of civilization, indifferent to danger, accustomed to violence, chivalrous in a rude sort of way, and so on. The parallels have been amply delineated. What has not been recognized are the similarities between Chandler's humor and that of the frontier tradition. Even those who remark on the characteristic American quality of Chandler's humor are apparently unaware of the close parallels between Chandler's similes and the style of frontier humor.

As peculiar as the notion appears, Marlowe resembles in significant ways the frontier humorist, that mythic blending of Yankee and backwoodsman whose evolution during the nineteenth century Constance Rourke describes in her classic study *American Humor*. A primary point of similarity is the abundant use of similes that are comically incongruous, but at the same time vividly accurate. The language is concrete, fresh, and colorful, and the detail is stark and realistic. The tropes are often homely, couched in the vernacular, and make generous use of exaggeration and understatement. The tone is anti-intellectual and contemptuous of civilization and sham. There is little respect for delicate sensibilities. The comparisons are often wildly imaginative and manifest a lively sense of the grotesque. Moreover, Chandler's objective method of narration resembles the deadpan delivery of his nineteenth-century counterpart, and the tough talk is reminiscent of the ring-tailed roarers of the old Southwest.

It is surprising enough to discover such elements of the frontier hero and the frontier humorist in Chandler's urban detective novels; and the discovery seems all the more remarkable when one learns that Chandler, although born in the United States, grew up in England and received a classical education at Dulwich, a fine public school. How did the distinctively American patterns of theme, action, and language get into his novels?

The source of his hero is easy to locate. He began writing detective fiction for the pulps, specifically *Black Mask*, and in such magazines the characteristics of the hero were already well defined. In the same year that Chandler published his first story in *Black Mask*, the editor, Joseph T. Shaw, described the moral code of the magazine's desired fictional hero. Chandler accepted these characteristics, and they became part of Marlowe. Shaw's description embodied the traits of the American hero, but, as Frank MacShane, Chandler's biographer, has pointed out, that moral code was not very different from that typified by the product of the English public school. The American hero "is more vigorous and physical, and certainly less intellectual, but a fundamental similarity remains."[6] Consequently, it was easier for Chandler to write pulp detective stories than one might suspect. Chandler himself commented in later life: "It would seem that a classical education might be rather a poor basis for writing novels in a hardboiled vernacular. I happen to think otherwise. A classical education saves you from being fooled by pretentiousness, which is what most current fiction is too full of."[7]

The sources of his distinctive similes are more difficult to trace, but they clearly derive from a combination of his fascination with the American language and his preoccupation with style.

Chandler once said, "I had to learn American just like a foreign language."[8] And in learning it, he fell in love with it. "I'm an intellectual snob who happens to have a fondness for the American vernacular." he wrote in a letter, "largely because I grew up on Latin and Greek. As a result, when I use slang, solecisms, colloquialisms, snide talk or any kind of off-beat language, I do it deliberately."[9] Elsewhere he said, "If I hadn't grown up on Latin and Greek, I doubt if I would know so well how to draw the line between what I call a vernacular style and what I should call an illiterate or faux naif style. That's a hell of a lot of difference, to my mind."[10] Chandler thought of himself primarily as a stylist, and his distance from American English allowed him to do what he did with it. In this respect, as Fredric Jameson has remarked, his situation was similar to that of Nabokov: "The writer of an adopted language is already a kind of stylist by force of circumstance."[11] "All I wanted to do when I began writing," Chandler wrote to a friend, "was to play with a fascinating new language, to see what it would do as a means of expression which might remain on the level of unintellectual thinking and yet acquire the power to say things which are usually said only with literary art."[12] To use the American idiom to its fullest was his fundamental ambition, an objective which led him to a a thorough knowledge of the vernacular traditions in American culture. In a letter to John Houseman, he said, "I have had a lot of fun with the American language; it has fascinating idioms, is constantly creative, very much like the English of Shakespeare's time, its slang and argot is wonderful. . . "[13]

Style was Chandler's principal concern. He aimed to be a "writer of writing" and not simply a "writer of stories." He said that his whole career was based on the idea that "the formula doesn't matter, the thing that counts is what you do with the formula; that is to say, it is all a matter of style."[14] To a young teacher of writing, he counselled that "the most durable thing in writing is style, and style is the most valuable investment a writer can make with his time."[15] On another occasion, he said, "How could I possibly care a button about the detective story as form? All I'm looking for is an excuse for certain experiments in dramatic dialogue."[16] For him, "the mystery and the solution of the mystery are only. . . 'the olive in the martini,' and the really good mystery is one you would read even if you knew somebody had torn out the last chapter."[17]

Chandler's style is memorable because it is poetic rather than prosaic. Ross Macdonald described it as "a highly charged blend of laconic wit and imagistic poetry set to breakneck rhythms."[18] Chandler's particular triumph was that he managed to be hard-boiled and poetic at the same time. He found a style for matching Marlowe to his world. "Vivid language was the decisive element," as Clive James has pointed out, "which meant that how not to make Marlowe sound too good a *writer* was the continuing problem. The solution was a kind of undercutting wit, a style in which Marlowe mocked his own fine phrases. A comic style always on the edge of self-parody..."[19] His theory was that "the public will accept style, provided you do not call it style either in words or by, as it were, standing off and admiring it."[20] Perhaps making style unobtrusive succeeded too well in one sense, because he complained, "Why is it that Americans—of all people the quickest to reverse their moods—do not see the burlesque in my kind of writing."[21]

The elements of burlesque and self-parody bring to mind the tension within Chandler between his commitment to detective fiction and his seriousness as a writer, an artist of language. Peter Conrad has argued that the laconic, scornful, self-deprecating Marlowe "is the incognito of Chandler's lurid, blushful romanticism." According to Conrad, the self-effacing element in Marlowe's narrative voice and in Chandler's letters and statements is "merely the defense of an inordinate literary vanity. He knew himself to be an artist, though he could neither claim to be one nor permit critics to do so on his behalf. He was fastidious aesthete who chose to work in a coarse and brutal form."[22]

Whether Conrad is overstating the case or not, it is clear that Chandler was a deliberate and self-conscious stylist and his use of tropes, particularly similes, reveals and tensions, subtleties, and genius of his preoccupation with style.

Let us consider now the ways in which the similes function. There is not space here for thorough analysis and ample illustration. I simply wish to list and explain briefly some of the main purposes served by Chandler's characteristic tropes.

First of all, pulp fiction was written to amuse and therefore had to be amusing. There was no time for fancy literary effects. The writer had to catch the reader's interest immediately. Chandler's similes amuse and arrest interest at the same time, and more importantly, they allow him to accomplish some rather sophisticated literary effects without calling attention to them. It is a technique that creates visual images, a method in which everything is described and nothing explained. The similes help create the images, and they do so with a conciseness that is a form of wit in itself. Many of the similes have the humor of information conveyed at a blow; they illuminate a character of scene like a flash bulb. Consider this description of General Sternwood in *The Big Sleep*: "A few locks of dry white hair clung to his scalp, like wild flowers fighting for life on a bare rock." That conveys more about the old man than most writers could crowd into several sentences, and even then the nuances would be missing. Marlowe says this of Carmen Sternwood: "Then she lowered her lashes until they almost cuddled her cheeks and slowly raised them again, like a theater curtain." There at one stroke he captures her theatrical flirtatiousness. Or consider this description of

Southern California houses: "Montemar Vista was a few dozen houses of various sizes and shapes hanging by their teeth and eyebrows to a spur of mountain and looking as if a good sneeze would drop them down among the box lunches on the beach."

Chandler was convinced that "the best way to comment on large things is to comment on small things."[23] He wrote to his British publisher: "To say little and convey much, to break the mood of a scene with some completely irrelevant wisecrack without entirely losing the mood—these small things for me stand in lieu of accomplishment."[24] The similes are his primary tool for saying little and conveying much. They are little things which taken together comment on large things; they are fragmentary glimpses of people, places, customs, and behavior that combine to provide a startlingly vivid picture of modern society. Frederic Jameson suggests that a case can by made for Chandler as a painter of American life: "not as a builder of those large-scale models of the American experience which great literature offers, but rather in fragmentary pictures of setting and place, fragmentary perceptions which are by some formal paradox somehow inaccessible to serious literature."[25]

The similes also allow Chandler to say little and convey much because they create perspective through incongruity. Often Chandler yokes two incongruous subjects to achieve a fresh and provocative observation,. The incongruity can launch us beyond our normal perceptions by derailing expectations: along with the laugh comes a reverberation of insight. Chandler admired and learned much from Dashiell Hammett, but he felt there were some things Hammett did not know how to say or did not feel the need to say. "In his hands [the American language] had no overtones, left no echo, evoked no image beyond a distant hill."[26] The evocative poetic quality of Chandler's seemingly offhand prose often enabled him to hint at what was beyond the distant hill.

Another way the similes function is as a means of mediating between a dualism in Chandler's mind, a dualisim that perpetually balanced an innate romanticism against a very self-conscious cynicism, an idealistic longing against an imperfect present. Chandler said, "There must be idealism, but there must also be contempt" and, as Jerry Speir remarks, "it was from his recognition of his own contradictory impulses as emblematic of his own age that his fiction took its unique tone."[27] Ross Macdonald believes "it is Marlowe's doubleness that makes him interesting: the hard-boiled mask half-concealing Chandler's poetic and satiric mind. Part of our pleasure derives from the interplay between the mind of Chandler and the voice of Marlowe. The recognized difference between them is part of the dynamics of the narrative, setting up bipolar tensions in the prose."[28] Like Dickens and Twain, Chandler softened reality by introducing humor. An element of romanticism in all three lent itself to humorous exaggeration, wit, and wisecrack. The similes are a principal means of creating the cushioning humor, and they often consist of a self-deflating wit that disguises the sentimental note in Marlowe and his knight-errantry.

It is Marlowe's voice, of course, that is the essential stuff of the novels. It is the detached, ironic, frequently alienated tone of that voice that awakens and holds our interest and provides interpretive grounds for the stories. And it is largely the similes that define and establish that voice. According to Fredric Jameson, "the narrator's voice works in counterpoint to the things seen, heightening them subjectively through his own reactions to them, through the poetry his comparisons lend them, and letting them fall back again into their sordid, drab reality through the deadpan humor which disavows what is has just maintained." The style "avoids the flat and naturalistically prosaic on the one hand, and the poetic and unreal on the other, in a delicate compromise executed by the tone of the narration."[29]

The tone becomes a principle of control for the Chandler-Marlowe narrator. As David Smith points out, "Chandler turned to a highly-wrought language because he needed a snare to entrap a complex, specific reality that was, in its material existence, insupportable if human integrity was to be preserved."[30] The similes allow Chandler a way of ordering and controlling a disjointed, corrupt, and bewildering world. The world of southern California with its sordidness, vulgarity, violence, fraud, and cruelty is turned, when it enters the language of the novel, into a series of triumphant comic simplicities. Marlowe's capacity to deal with that world is vested, according to Jonathan Raban, in his control "of language that mixes hyperbole and understatement in equal parts—hyperbole for the nightmare violence, understatement for cutting through the highly coloured tissue of lies and false reasons in which violence comes dressed."[31] David Smith describes Marlowe as a truth-teller who requires an arcane linguistic magic composed of slang and simile to ward off the sham he frequently encounters: "Marlowe has to mint his own words fresh to avoid being articulated by the words and attitudes money has minted. So long as Marlowe can tell us that he can listen to 'spring rusting in the air, like a paper bag blowing along a concrete sidewalk" then we know his mind can cope with, and see though any inflated boosterism that the world claims as reality."[32]

Chandler made a study of slang and kept lists of various kinds of slang in notebooks. One purpose of slang is defensive, to protect insiders. Peter Conrad suggests that this aspect of slang provided "a model for the private, defensive use of language by Marlowe, who trusts to a precarious, wittily disgusted style to keep the foulness of the world at bay."[33]

Finally the similes often furnish a between-the-lines social commentary. Note the negative implications of these: a voice that "faded off into a sort of sad whisper, like a mortician asking for a down payment"; someone "looking as unperturbed as a bank president refusing a loan"; someone who "lifted his hands off the desk and made a steeple of the fingers, like an old time family lawyer getting set for a little tangled grammar"; accounts of an affairs that "came as close to the truth as a newspaper stories usually come—as close as Mars is to Saturn"; "a screen star's boudoir, a place of charm and seduction, artificial as a wooden leg"; something "as gaudy as a chiropractor's chart"; something "as flat and stale as a football interview." It is the satirical resonance of such similes that may have prompted David Smith to refer to Chandler as "a social pathologist and Marlowe was his scalpel, only the body was not dead."[34]

Are the similes overworked? Chandler admitted to his publisher, Alfred A. Knopf, that he had run them into the ground in *The Big Sleep*.[35] But even with that admission he continued to use them generously. Did he really want to eliminate them from his writing? After publication of *The Little Sister* in 1949, he wrote to a friend that his tendency to gag resulted from his writing for movies: "It comes from that noxious habit of writing lines for actors which are overpointed for effect, so that the line is really said to the audience rather than to the character in the play. Of course Shakespeare does it too, does it all the time. He just does it better."[36] Chandler was too conscientious a stylist to continue overcooking the comic similes unless he had a reason. The mention of Shakespeare may be a tipoff. It was his stance to play down the detective genre and the kind of writing he did, yet it is very likely that the self-deprecation in this case concealed a conscious strategy. He knew that although he was working in a second-rate genre and using the vernacular, his methods were essentially those used by the finest authors. Despite his denigration of the similes, he never really wanted to eliminate them, because he was aware—an awareness probably ranging from clear consciousness to unexamined hunches—that they served the kind of functions mentioned above. As crude as they sometimes appear, the similes are a more significant literary accomplishment than is usually recognized. They are a main ingredient in a style which enabled Chandler, as he once put it, to take "a cheap, shoddy, and utterly lost kind of writing" and make of it "something that intellectuals claw each other about."[37]

---

[1] Raymond Chandler, *The Simple Art of Murder* (Boston: Houghton Mifflin, 1950), p. 533.

[2] Quoted in Frank MacShane, *The Life of Raymond Chandler* (New York: Dutton, 1976), pp. 183-84.

[3] Introduction to *The Word of Raymond Chandler*, ed. Miriam Gross (New York: A & W Publishers, 1977), p. 4.

[4] "The Chandler Books," *The Atlantic*, March 1945, p. 123.

[5] See, for example, J.C. Porter, "End of the Trail: The American West of Dashiell Hammett and Raymond Chandler," *Western Historical Quarterly*, 6 (1975), 411-24; Philip Durham, *Down These Mean Streets a Man Must Go: Raymond Chandler's Knight* (Chapel Hill: Univ. of North Carolina Press, 1963), pp. 5-6, 80-81; MacShane, *The Life of Raymond Chandler*, pp. 52, 69, 207.

[6] *The Life of Raymond Chandler*, pp. 46-47.
[7] Jerry Speir, *Raymond Chandler* (New York: Ungar, 1981), p. 3.
[8] *The Life of Raymond Chandler*, p. 49.
[9] Frank MacShane, *The Letters of Raymond Chandler* (New York: Columbia Univ. Press, 1981), p. 158.
[10] *The Life of Raymond Chandler*, p. 10.
[11] "On Raymond Chandler," *The Southern Review*, 6 (1970), p. 625.
[12] Speir, p. 118.
[13] John Houseman. "Lost Fortnight" in *The World of Raymond Chandler*, p. 66.
[14] Speir, p. 117.
[15] *The Life of Raymond Chandler*, p. 137.
[16] Speir, p. 141.
[17] Speir, p. 10.
[18] "The Writer as Detective Hero," in *On Crime Writing* (Santa Barbara: Capra Press, 1973), p. 18.
[19] "The Country Behind the Hill," in *The World of Raymond Chandler*, p. 117.
[20] Dorothy Gardiner and Katherine Sorley Walker, eds. *Raymond Chandler Speaking* (London: Hamish Hamilton, 1962), p. 61.
[21] Speir, p. 133.
[22] "The Private Dick as Dandy." *Times Literary Supplement*, 20 January 1978, p. 60.
[23] *The Life of Raymond Chandler*, p. 220.
[24] *Raymond Chandler Speaking*, p. 223.
[25] Jameson, p. 626.
[26] *The Simple Art of Murder*, p. 530.
[27] Speir, p. 1.
[28] Macdonald, p. 19.
[29] Jameson, p. 643.
[30] "The Public Eye of Raymond Chandler," *Journal of American Studies*, 14 (1978), 38.
[31] *The Society of the Poem* (London Harrap, 1971), p. 169.
[32] Smith, p. 437.
[33] Conrad, p. 60.
[34] Smith, p. 424.
[35] *Raymond Chandler Speaking*, p. 212.
[36] *Raymond Chandler Speaking*, p. 224.
[37] *Raymond Chandler Speaking*, p. 74.

# The Mind of the Hardboiled: Ross Macdonald and the Roles of Criticism

*T. R. Steiner*

Macdonald wrestled constantly with Chandler's ghost. Whatever his ambivalence toward [the] detective story, he was singleminded in the intention to supplant this "father." To establish his place in the field, he contrasted himself with and belittled Chandler. Even Dr. Watson would recognize the symptoms of a classic anxiety of influence.

Assertions of Chandler's value and importance to Macdonald can be found in his statements (for example, IJ 37, 41), but very much of the opposite is there as well. Mention of Chandler seems to have been a red flag which often provoked Macdonald to charge. For the trained critic that he was, he made too many misstatements and misjudgments of his predecessor. These "strategies" were augmented by another, overpraise of Hammett and claiming a close attachment to him which is little borne out in practice.

"Raymond Chandler . . . wrote like a slumming angel, and invested the sun-blinded streets of Los Angeles with a romantic presence" (SP 27). To his appreciation of Chandler's alchemy, he often added the typical praise for Chandler's language. He also approved of the late Archer-like turn to loneliness and sensibility (SP 119-120). But his notice of Chandlerian romance can be double-edged, for Macdonald also criticized the romance hero as he called for more realistic and more discriminatingly moral detective novels. Even the approval of Chandler's idiom that I cited comes in the context of Macdonald proposing a wider, less rigidly stylized language for the hardboiled.

By contrast the slurs and negative judgments pile up. The brilliant essay, "Simple Art of Murder," on which Macdonald leans for

From "The Mind of the Hardboiled: Ross Macdonald and the Roles of Criticism" (Section 7), *South Dakota Review* 24:1 (1986): 46-50.

his own discussions of detective fiction is called "not very illuminating criticism." Chandler's vision, we are told, lacks the "tragic unity" of Hammett's; his "central weakness" is his insistence on the hero as sole agent of redemption—to get this Macdonald had to misread the relevant passage in "Simple Art." With for me considerable irony, the prissy Macdonald slams Chandler for his "angry puritanical morality" (SP 117-118). It appears that Macdonald even went out of his way to pick fights with this persona, "Chandler."

One early misjudgment I find insufferable in the wrongness of its donnish arrogance: Chandler's "mind. . . , for all its enviable imaginative force, is uncultivated and second-rate," followed in the draft by a passage that Macdonald had the tact to strike out, "my own mind is neither" (Bruccoli 48, IJ 38).

The interplay gets weird at times. Macdonald may have intended a parallel to Chandler himself by the titular character of *The Ferguson Affair*, who "gain[s] his hopes" only after the author has "put him through the direst ordeals inflicted on anybody in the canon" (Wolfe, 200-01). There may be more mischief in *The Chill.* Two years before publication of the novel, the posthumous *Raymond Chandler Speaking* revealed through its private letters both Chandler's putdown of the first Lew Archer book and his suffering with his wife, a querulous old woman in her decline. When thirty years earlier Cissy Hurlburt Bowen had left her husband to marry Chandler, Ray was thirty-seven, she fifty-three. The December and May couple of *The Chill*, Roy (!) and Tish Osborne Macready Bradshaw, in several particulars resemble the Chandlers.

Macdonald kept repeating the criticisms. Chandler's biggest "mistake" was presented as the unconcern for narrative unity. Over and over Macdonald cited Chandler's downplaying of plot against his own sounder method. Since "plot" and "scene" are abstractions, dialectical aspects of a narrative rather than cleanly severable entities, this begins to sound like a mere quibble. Chandler's plottings, especially after *Farewell, My Lovely*, are much sounder than Macdonald's repeated sallies, or Chandler's self-disparagement, suggest. Furthermore, Macdonald's basic plot, the investigative search that initiates a murder sequence which is by the end fully united with the search, is patterned on Chandler's.

Particularly argumentative is Macdonald's letter to Alfred Knopf (August 1952) defending *Meet Me at the Morgue* against the dismissive Chandlerizing of a Pocket Books editor. For the unestablished author this was a bread and butter issue as well as esthetic—Pocket Books had to contract for paperback reprint before Knopf would accept the book—and one cannot blame him for having objected to preformed artistic constraints. Macdonald's draft (IJ 37-42, from original MS) even more reveals him than the somewhat chastened, diplomatic, but also prouder, letter that he finally sent (Bruccoli 48-50, extracts). A concession that his mysteries are "not as good as Chandler's perhaps" and diffidence about "let[ting] my hair down" do not appear in the letter. "I owe a lot to Chandler, and to

Hammett" becomes "I owe a lot to Chandler (and more to Hammett)." Between the draft and the letter, Macdonald's humility was toned down. Much of the passing praise of Chandler for his "intensity" and "brilliant," "remarkable" world was sunk while the criticisms were heightened. Macdonald excised, "I don't want to give the impression that he's my *bete noire*." While Chandler is called in both versions "one of my masters," in the letter the phrase leads to analysis of their difference. As he reworked his statement, Macdonald became more combative: "My literary range greatly exceeds his"; "I like it better than a Chandler book, and think I can point out various ways in which it is superior to a Chandler book"—neither of which had been in the draft.

Chandler had to be topped—or was it to be bypassed? I think that Macdonald remained ever anxious about his stature relative to Chandler's and ever ambivalent toward the "hardboiled," which was his starting point but would not be—he hoped and trusted—his end.

Why continue to write detective novels, he would ask on occasion (IJ 26). The explanations came thick and fast, with more or less validity and more or less apparent honesty. The detective story is a worthy "democratic" mode; Archer is a welder's mask or protective lead with which I can handle hot, dangerous material (SP 3, 36); I cannot write the semi-autobiographic straight novel without getting bogged down in the feelings (SP 35). Detective novels sell. Detective fiction can be made to carry the heaviest freight of meaning and literary style.

With *The Doomsters* he claimed that he made the anticipated "break" with the Chandler tradition (Bruccoli 55), but I think that he overestimated it. In the novels of the sixties, continuities from the tradition far predominated over changes in the detective, the psychology of murder and the attitude toward the murderer. Macdonald's experiments to extend the genre were few and limited by the standard of his own early ideas, or of detective-story tradition, or contemporary mainstream fiction. If Chandler was trapped by the form, as he sometimes implied, how much more Macdonald, with three time as many "identical" works, and with no work so new to his own line as *The Long Goodbye* to Chandler's.

Whether Macdonald's critique of Chandler was "mostly" disinterested criticism or "mostly" rationalization through dispraise of arts he could not reach, it shows a certain insensitivity to Chandler's value, which is not wholly in the breezy, witty style and flamboyant romance, though "imaginative force" is the key.

Realistic fictions make meanings relevant to historical and philosophic understanding more often through character, representation of social life, and action than by discourse, whether the novelist's or that of his "mind" within the novel. Detective fiction develops character, mimesis, and discourse to the degree that they promote, or at least don't detract from, mystery and its solution. This constraint is a principal challenge to writers aiming for the mainstream. As Macdonald recognized, one way that mysteries may gain depth is obliquely through making symbolic their conventional elements. Yet, neither his not Chandler's narrative structures can be read to say very much—or, rather, they keep repeating the message of appearance vs. reality. Their common form, particularly in Macdonald's convoluted plots, pertains more to genre and the pleasures of reading than to a "world out there" or to metaphor. How great the difference between an Archer novel and the searching openended symbolism of mystery and investigation in, say, Borges or Robbe-Grillet, or to cite examples in the typical realistic mode of detective fiction, Symons or Lem.

What Macdonald couldn't see or wouldn't admit about Chandler is that his books have despite all the stylization the "texture" of life, probably from Chandler's unforced responsiveness to what's "out there." ("Texture" was one of Chandler's favorite buzz-words—SL 87: what he prized in writing, sought, often achieved.) In stripping the Chandler model, perhaps to promote narrative unity, Macdonald lost much of that texture. One notable distinction of detective writing from Doyle to Robbe-Grillet has been its quality of material fact, "clues," the veracious signs to be interpreted—or in the problematic postmodern stories, ambiguous signs. With Chandler who imaged with gusto, we have a dense world to understand and, if we wish, to explore. Because Macdonald's realization is thinner, despite a certain understanding through his favorite psychological or mythic formulae, there is not nearly as much to be made sense of.

Chandler's *The Long Goodbye* seems to me the masterpiece that Macdonald wanted for hardboiled detective fiction, the substantial work congruent with mainstream novels. Except for family tragedy, Macdonald's real contribution in detective-story subject, it presents most of what we find in the mature Macdonald novels: heroes, real and fake; the embittered murderousness of disappointed romanticism; money, class, sex, love in contemporary America; the interplay of Anglo and American societies; ancient histories that require detective investigation. And much more, including some deep stuff on friendship and on a successful author's naked self-evaluation that we don't find in the Archer books. Macdonald's best detective novel, which reveals where its fake hero spent the war, in striking irony to Chandler's daring Paul Marston, in many ways has the *Goodbye* look.

## WORKS CITED

Bruccoli, Matthew J. *Ross Macdonald.* San Diego: Harcourt Brace, 1984.

Chandler, Raymond. *Selected Letters of Raymond Chandler.* Ed. Frank MacShane. New York: Columbia UP, 1981.

Macdonald, Ross. *Self-Portrait: Ceaselessly into the Past.* Ed. Ralph B Sipper. Santa Barbara: Capra, 1981. (SP)

_____, and others. *Inward Journey: Ross Macdonald.* Ed. Ralph B. Sipper. Santa Clara: Cordelia, 1984. (IJ)

Wolfe, Peter. *Dreamers Who Live Their Dreams.* Bowling Green: Popular Press, 1976.

# Raymond Chandler and the Business of Literature

*Johanna M. Smith*

Although best known for his detective novels, Raymond Chandler in fact had several careers: in London from 1908 to 1912, he wrote poetry and Saki-like sketches for *The Westminister Gazette* and essays and reviews for the weekly *The Academy*; from 1924 to 1932, he was an executive of South Basin Oil Company in Los Angeles; during the 1940s and 1950s, he wrote screenplays and several essays for *The Atlantic Monthly* as well as his novels. This mixture—the "very snooty" *Academy*,[1] the "hard-boiled" oil business (*Letters*, 445), and writing and marketing snooty essays as well as hard-boiled novels—informs Chandler's conflicted view of his writing as both a business transaction and an art. The distinction he attempted to maintain between the two may be formulated as that between an economy of exchange and one of expenditure. The former should be a just and mutual exchange established by bargaining; one cedes one's productions only for an equivalent return (e.g., writing is ceded for money). An economy of expenditure, on the other hand, operates on a principle of unconditional expenditure (e.g., one writes for the sake of writing); one produces and gives or sacrifices one's productions in a gift rather than bargaining economy.[2] I will argue that Chandler's difficulties in perceiving himself as a writer—broker of his writing in an exchange economy, yet as an artist detached from this trade—emerge in his novels in the ambivalent professionalism of Philip Marlowe, himself a broker in an exchange economy who attempts to reformulate that economy as one of expenditure.

Chandler's writing had to be marketed, and he prided himself on being "not exactly a baby in these matters" (*Letters*, 444); negotiating "the top price" for his *Atlantic* articles, for example, he considered

"Raymond Chandler and the Business of Literature," *Texas Studies in Language and Literature* 31 (1989): 592-610.

"part of my job as a businessman" (*Letters*, 105). Indeed, for him "a writer who cannot face the rather cynical realities of his trade is lacking in more than popularity" (*Letters*, 481). On the other hand, he regarded himself as an intellectual[3] whose novels aimed at "the creation of emotion through dialogue and description" (*Letters*, 115). At such times, "to me writing is not a business or a racket, it is an art" (*Letters*, 434). The conflicting statements suggest doubts about a commercial success that might seem to undermine his standing as an artist, yet critical judgments which shored up that standing gave Chandler not reassurance but additional conflicts. At times he would insist that detective fiction "can be literature," once literature is defined as "tak[ing] the current formulae and forc[ing] them into something lesser men thought them incapable of" (*Letters*, 477, 172). But he was often made uncomfortable when literary critics took this view, for he had doubts about the manliness of "primping second-guessers who call themselves critics" (*Letters*, 229).[4] On the principle that such reviewers take care of their own, he seems to have worried that critical approval might impugn his own manhood. Much struck by J.B. Priestley's view of the British literary scene—including "practically all the literary critics"—as "completely dominated by homosexuals," Chandler estimated that three-quarters of America's "flossy and perceptive book reviewers" were gay, and his comments on Priestly conclude with a cross-gender image of himself "looking for [gay writers] under the bed like an old maid looking for burglars" (*Letters*, 268). Finally, writing itself occasionally seems insufficiently manly—one should "leave it to the women" now that "the technique of marketable fiction has become almost entirely epicene" (*Letters*, 72).

As we have seen, however, Chandler took pride in writing marketable fiction; thus his own techniques must be presented as eminently non-epicene. He insisted, for instance, that his early pulp fiction for *Black Mask* and *Dime Detective* be differentiated from *Saturday Evening Post*-type "slick stories," for "the superficial neatness of slick writing [is] only natural when it [is] feminine" (*Letters*, 87). And his essay "The Simple Art of Murder" shows critic-novelist Chandler distinguishing himself form more effete critical brethren by virtue of his manly novels. He first defends Dashiell Hammett, his predecessor in the hard-boiled style, against detractors who are "flustered old ladies—of both sexes (or no sex)."[5] By thus conflating wrong-headed critical judgments with effeminacy, Chandler makes writing Hammett-like novels seem a guarantee of masculinity. That accomplished, he can go on to praise the less "spare, frugal" aspects of Hammett's work (190); under this rubric *The Maltese Falcon* becomes "the record of man's devotion to a friend" (188). In this way Chandler sets up a paradigm for the quality he valued in his own work, "the creation of emotion": Hammett is a manly man whose story of "devotion to a friend" can validate Chandler's novels of detection and masculine friendship.

But as a detective, Philip Marlowe shifts uncomfortably between exchange and expenditure economies. Both Marlowe's professional and friendship relations participate in a complex exchange economy, whose dual principle is that a client/friend must always pay in some way for what he gets from Marlowe and that Marlowe must receive an equivalent return for his own investments. In his professional exchanges, Marlowe is, like Chandler, a businessman; as he puts it, "I'm selling what I have to sell to make a living." But what Marlowe sells is not simply "guts and intelligence"; he also offers more tangible moral qualities such as "principles" and "a willingness to get pushed around in order to protect a client."[6] Even if these latter fall under the heading of professional ethics, they are marketable, so it is important to Marlowe (and Chandler) that they be free of commercial taint. Hence, they are often recast in an expenditure economy: Marlowe attempts to replace professional exchanges—services rendered for money—with the unconditional expenditures of masculine friendship. But friendship is also a matter of exchanges. In any exchange economy, power rests with the person who defines which items of exchange are equivalent; for this reason, even though exchange appears a "model of justice and equality," in fact it "grows out of an imbalance of power, which it in turn reconstitutes."[7] While the client/friend "gives" his problems to Marlowe, he generally pays to do so and thus has an employer's power. If Marlowe then gives friendship, this commitment often prompts him to return the money, thereby establishing the primacy of his emotions over the client's financial power; if he does not receive sufficient acknowledgment, however, he feels victimized by an exchange that has become an expenditure.

This troubled relation of client/friend exchanges is analogous to Chandler's view of himself as at once financial power broker and artist. Chandler attempts to participate in both a businessman's exchange economy and an artist's expenditure economy; similarly, Marlowe attempts to be both a hard-boiled professional and a friend. Chandler's difficulties in depicting this masculine friendship seem to me to arise from his discomfort with the respect given him by "gay" critics. I have already suggested Chandler's fear that the critical respect of gays might be perceived as undermining his masculinity, and a similar difficulty appears in the novels' problematic friendships. At issue is what Eve Kosofsky Sedgwick calls the double bind of male homosocial desire. While "homosocial" usually describes same gender bonds *exclusive* of sexuality, Sedgwick uses the term "homosocial desire" to reeroticize these bonds, to suggest that there is an unbroken continuum between homosocial and homosexual relations.[8] As Sedgwick phrases the double bind of this continuum, only "an invisible, carefully blurred, always-already-crossed line" separates the homosocial bond from the homosexual (89).

Marlowe's insistent heterosexuality might seem to clarify the line between homosocial and homosexual desire, but this very insistence indicates Chandler's worry that Marlowe's masculine friendships might be perceived as homosexual rather than homosocial.[9] The problem of masculine friendship is to distinguish between attractions to men and to women when the *structures* of desire—Marlowe's attraction to another—are identical. For Sedgwick the term "desire" includes any "affective of social force" that shapes a relationship (2); in this sense homosocial desire indicates not only attraction but also the resulting structure of men's relations with other men. Furthermore, Sedgwick postulates a "special relationship" between homosocial desire and the social structures that maintain and transmit patriarchal power, so that the status of women is inscribed even in a homosocial structure that appears to exclude them (25). In the Marlowe novels, it is this "special relationship" that moves friendship, which might otherwise appear to be homosocial desire, back into a structure of professional exchange. Ultimately Marlowe's dual exchanges with masculine client/friends, no matter how conflicted, play off against and protect him from his even more tangled heterosexual relations.

In *The Big Sleep* (1939) and *Farewell, My Lovely* (1940), women of threatening sexuality are discovered to be criminal and may therefore be punished; homosocial commitments then become professionally sound. By *The Long Good-bye* (1953), however, Marlowe's dual exchanges with client/friends are extremely uneasy. As he attempts to transform an exchange economy of client relations into an expenditure economy of homosocial friendships, he sees loyalty and commitment become professional commodities; for sale, they are subsumed into the economy they are meant to oppose. Friendship's expenditures are finally indistinguishable from professional exchanges, and homosocial desire becomes a debased currency in an inescapable exchange economy; in this novel, then, friendship must be redefined in terms of professional toughness.

## 1

*The Big Sleep* creates in Marlowe the detective whose professional principles point up the corruption of his world. As Chandler later put it, "Down these mean streets a man must go who is not himself mean, who is neither tarnished nor afraid"; hence, Marlowe must be "the best man in his world" ("Simple," 193). Yet Chandler also knew that Marlowe's professional life is an "impossible struggle" to "make a decent living in a corrupt society" (*Letters*, 197). Marlowe, that is, cannot fully detach himself from his culture; indeed, its very corruption creates the need for his services, which are "themselves dependent on the economic activities" of "an economy he morally abhors."[10] Moreover, this dependence on corruption undermines the activities of detection, calling into question the detective's stance as somehow outside the events he detects. Through the figure of Marlowe as knight, *The Big Sleep* explores this interpenetration of a corrupt economy and the untarnished professional.

During his initial visit to the Sternwood mansion, Marlowe's role as knightly savior is prefigured in his response to a stained-glass window: seeing a knight "not getting anywhere" as he tries to free a naked woman bound to a tree, Marlowe decides that "I would sooner or later have to climb up there and help him" (1). General Sternwood, who is being blackmailed about the unsavory activities of his daughter Carmen, hires Marlowe to make terms with Arthur Geiger, the blackmailer; as he attempts to do so, Marlowe discovers Carmen naked and drugged in the dead Geiger's house and rescues her from this compromising position. This rescue enacts Marlowe's view of himself as a knight, for he has appointed himself Carmen's champion; the fact that she has "gone very, very wrong" and that nobody was doing anything about it" causes him to exclaim, "To hell with the rich. They made me sick" (60). But since he has taken the general's money and thereby associated himself with "the rich," that exchange remains morally and professionally sound only so long as Carmen remains the victim of the rich. When her "small corrupt body" (150) turns up in his bed, however, this erstwhile damsel in distress is now perceived as sexual victimizer; only "professional pride" keeps Marlowe from succumbing to her advances, and he now realizes that "knights had no meaning in this game" (147). Yet Marlowe reconstitutes himself as a knight through his relation to General Sternwood.[11] Having discovered that Carmen is a murderer, he returns the general's fee; by thus "refus[ing] payment for an unsatisfactory job" (201), he recasts their professional exchange as a relation of personal loyalty. He then fulfills his knightly pledge to "protect what little pride a broken and sick old man has... in the thought that his blood is not poison" (216) by concealing Carmen's guilt from the general and extracting her sister's promise that she will be institutionalized. Saving Carmen from the police in this way, Marlowe realizes, means that "I was part of the nastiness now," but, he concludes, "the old man didn't have to be" (219).

While it would appear that Marlowe is now tarnished by the corruption around him, his statement actually attests to his continuing purity. That is, simply by knowing that he is "part of the nastiness," Marlowe in effect testifies to a moral discrimination so fine as to negate his self-condemnation. In addition, by sacrificing himself to keep the general pure, Marlowe has further removed himself from an exchange economy into one of unconditional expenditure, of absolute loss.[12] And his sacrifice in turn validates the "professional pride" that shifted his loyalty away from Carmen to the general. The putative victim of corruption in the economy of the rich, Carmen finally becomes merely a medium of exchange in Marlowe's relationship with her father, part of a traffic in women whose purpose is "cementing the bonds of men with men."[13] By handing

Carmen over to her sister, Marlowe protects her from the police, but his deeper commitment is to his bond with General Sternwood—specifically, to protecting the general's belief in the purity of his "blood" or lineage.

But this commitment to a dying patriarchal aristocracy of blood is widely different from Marlowe's earlier cynicism about the general's (new) money.

> The Sternwoods, having moved up the hill, could no longer smell the stale sump water or the oil, but they could still look out of their front windows and see what had made them rich. If they wanted to. I didn't suppose they would want to. (17)

The oil sump returns at the end of the novel, when Marlowe discovers in it the body of Carmen's murder victim. This irony makes clear to the reader what even Marlowe at one point has suggested: having "more or less written [his daughters] off" (203), the general is one of the irresponsible moneyed class that Marlowe had once castigated for victimizing Carmen. Yet in the early passage, Marlowe satirizes the upward mobility of "the Sternwoods" rather than the general, and his concluding words further take the general off the hook.[14] General Sternwood *is* "part of the nastiness"; that Marlowe fails to so perceive him, thereby remaining his knight, performs two related functions. By uniting Marlowe and the general in the protection of the latter's lineage, it sets up the "special relationship" that Sedgwick hypothesized between homosocial desire and patriarchal social structures; the Sternwood patrilineal purity is maintained through the exclusion of the general's actual "blood," his daughters. More important, Marlowe's skewed perception of the general validates his professionalism, which is ultimately invested not in the satisfactory performance of his employee role in an exchange economy but rather in his remaining emotionally committed to his employer. Already in this first novel, then, the line between professional and personal loyalty is so blurred as to call into question the possibility of uninvolved detection.

## 2

This possibility is further undermined in *Farewell, My Lovely*, where Marlowe's detection is bound up with homosocial and heterosexual desires. At first pursuing and then repudiating these desires, he comes to take an almost masochistic pleasure in his role as solitary professional. Where the Marlowe of *The Big Sleep* accepted his own "nastiness," however, ambiguously, this later

Marlowe presents himself as the uninvolved detective. Yet it becomes clear that this principled isolation allows Marlowe to perceive himself as discoverer of rather than participant in his self-implicating narrative.

While Marlowe often admits the sordidness of his own behavior, such episodes function as moral disinfectant by emphasizing his disgust with his actions. Having primed Jesse Florian with bourbon to pump her for information about Moose Malloy, for instance, Marlowe admits that "getting her drunk for my own sordid purposes" makes him "a little sick at [his] stomach."[15] Later, when the aged Grayle discovers Marlowe kissing his wife, Velma, instead of questioning her about Lindsay Marriott's murder, Marlowe again expresses self-dislike: "I felt nasty, as if I had picked a poor man's pocket" (114). As these examples show, Marlowe's professional integrity no longer consists in acts of self-sacrifice—his behavior is as squalid as others'—but in his *regret* for those actions; by punishing him for falling short of his own standards, this regret validates his sense of professional morality. And when Marlowe dwells on the several beatings that he receives, these recapitulations become an additional self-punishment whose purpose is to further emphasize his commitment to his professional code. Because the beatings are already known to the reader through exposition, this obsessive reiteration of his sufferings suggests not only a whining bid for sympathy but masochistic enjoyment. Marlowe, it seems, adheres to his professional code not only from conviction but also from an enjoyment of the punishment and consequent acknowledgment he receives for being "the best man in his world."

Like these instances of regretful self-disgust and welcomed self-punishment, the three potential friends and allies that Marlowe rejects dramatize his need to reinforce a professional purity. He extends a faltering and finally abortive friendship toward two men, Lieutenant Randall and Red Norgaard, in a pattern of attraction and repulsion which demonstrates both professional distrust and an uneasy homosocial desire. A similar advance-and-retreat pattern with Anne Riordan testifies to Marlowe's discomfort with heterosexuality when it threatens his stance as uninvolved detective.

Initially Marlowe is attracted to Lieutenant Randall because the policeman shares his sense of social corruption. When Randall admits that the police are sometimes forced to solve crimes only "for the record," Marlowe responds by sharing his theories about Lindsay Marriott's murder (164-71). After they browbeat a witness in tandem, however, Marlowe experiences another moment of self-disgust—"I don't like being rough with old ladies" (176)—and he intentionally alienates Randall by pooh-poohing his theories about the Malloy and Marriott cases. Eschewing both friendship and professional collaboration with Randall, Marlowe mutes his sense of guilty complicity in the other's brutality and averts further contamination by police methods. In so doing, Marlowe signals the heightened value of his professional isolation; despite the moral concerns they share, Randall cannot be allowed to measure up to him. In *The Big Sleep*, Chandler localized the guilt for social corruption (albeit not unambiguously) in the rich; in this novel he locates it in vague concepts of "society" and "the system." Once responsibility is generalized in this way, of course, the possibility of individual accountability disappears, yet any functionary of the local power apparatus is nonetheless tainted by it.[16] As a police man, Randall is "caught in the system" (196); hence although he recognizes its evils, he is automatically "not free to do a clean job in a clean way" (202). Once a potential ally, he gradually becomes unfit for his role and leaves Marlowe in the isolated position of the only "clean" professional. Despite his own lapses, then, Marlowe can see himself as the one possible alternative to "the system"

Marlowe's belief in the necessity of both personal and professional isolation is most evident in his relations with Red Norgaard. Like Randall, uncorrupted, in fact cleaner than Randall because he has been ejected from the Bay City police force, Red at first looks like a comrade for Marlowe, and they form a tentative professional association when Red ferries him to Laird Brunette's gambling ship. Marlowe's sensual fascination with Red appears in a description that lingers over his new friend's feminine beauty: "He had the eyes you never see, that you only read about. Violet eyes. Almost purple. Eyes like a girl, a lovely girl. His skin was as soft as silk" (209). This description is noteworthy in a man whose feelings for Velma Grayle are relentlessly heterosexual; detailed and lyrical, it stands in sharp contrast to his jocular view of the seductive Velma as "[a] blonde to make a bishop kick a hole in a stained glass window" (78). Just before he meets Norgaard, however, Marlowe has described several kissing couples "chew[ing] each other's faces" and then "[taking] their teeth out of each other's necks" (206-07). This cannibal and vampire imagery indicates at least a passing distaste for heterosexual behavior; if Marlowe already suspects that Velma murdered Marriott, these images may suggest a fear that his earlier sexual interest in her has sidetracked him from that suspicion. But his interest in her has clearly indicated his heterosexual preferences, so Marlowe now apparently feels free to admire the "lovely girl" in Red without raising questions about his own tastes or being hampered in his work. While we shall see that Marlowe maintains his tough-guy stance toward Anne Riordan, then, he lets down his guard with Red. "It must have been his eyes" (213), he says, that led him to tell Red" a great deal more [about the Malloy case] than I intended to." He admits to Red, "I'm afraid of death and despair, . . . [o]f dark water and drowned men's faces and skulls with empty eyesockets. I'm afraid of dying, of being nothing, of not finding a man named Brunette." This intimate confession indicates a homosocial desire for Red's companionship; in response, Norgaard offers his theories on the Malloy case and on racketeers being "just like other business men"

(215-16), a monologue that reinforces his political correctness on this issue. Yet, despite his attraction to and confidence in Red, Marlowe refuses his proffered help: "either I do it alone or I don't do it" (220).

This alternating attraction and repulsion indicate the double bind I suggest earlier, the perceived correspondence between "the most sanctioned forms of male-homosocial bounding, and the more reprobated expressions of male homosexual sociality."[17] Of course, the furtive nature of Marlowe's time with Red, their soft whispers and unspoken understandings, is necessitated by the danger in Marlowe's professional investigation of Brunette. But it also hints the secrecy of unadmitted homosocial desire, a desire that presents its own dangers. Marlowe has twice characterized the murdered Lindsay Marriott as a "pansy" (53, 80), a homophobic term connoting weakness; if Marlowe feels that men attracted to other men are too feeble to defend themselves from murderous women like Velma, it makes sense that he would refuse a friendship which might put him similarly at risk.[18] Hence, Marlowe is sufficiently unsettled by his attraction to Red to insist that he must "do it alone," that is, to stress and reaffirm his professional isolation.

Like his embryonic friendship with Red, although in a different way, Marlowe's thwarted affair with Anne Riordan demonstrates his obsessive commitment to professional detachment. Initially Marlowe admires Anne's nerve and prefers her "honest little face" to Velma's more steamy allure: "glamoured up blondes" like Velma "were a dime a dozen," he muses, but Anne's "was a face that would wear" (81). Yet he repeatedly refuses her offers of professional help, even though (or perhaps because) she is a competent investigative reporter. In addition, he resists his own desire for the companionship and stability that she represents, in order to protect her, he tells himself, from the enemies who might follow him to her house. But this rationale is unconvincing (we have seen no one following Marlowe), and more plausible explanations can be advanced. One is that, although Marlowe feels Anne's superiority to Velma, she is equally dangerous as a sexual distraction; if he responds to Anne as he has to Velma, he might again be sidetracked from his work. The second explanation recurs to an aspect of Marlowe that I have already mentioned, his tendency toward self-punishment. When he rejects Anne, releasing her hand "slowly as you let go of a dream when you wake up with the sun in your face and have been in an enchanted valley" (158), the exaggeratedly fairy-tale quality of this language suggests that Marlowe renounces Anne, at least in part, for the pleasure of renunciation. Like his self-sacrifice for General Sternwood, this romantic sacrifice moves him into an expenditure economy of absolute loss; thus it pleasurably heightens and reinforces his now bittersweet sense of professional isolation.

Not until the end of the Malloy case does Marlowe feel free to respond to Anne sexually. Yet it is necessary that this rapprochement be distinguished from the heterosexual romance that precedes it

(Moose's love for Velma and her betrayal and murder of him) and be purified from Marlowe's involvement in this romance. As William W. Stowe points out, in this novel Marlowe is not only narrator but participant, so that his "interpretive activities produce something more than, and very different from, simple knowledge of previously existing facts; they produce murders."[19] In effect, for instance, Marlowe engineers Velma's murder of Moose. All his acts—the five words, hidden from the reader, of the note that brings Moose to his apartment; Velma's subsequent arrival at the apartment, a timing perhaps coincidental but possibly arranged by Marlowe; his telling Velma's story in Moose's hearing—hint at his complicity in Moose's murder. Yet Marlowe need not take responsibility for the death of this "soft-voiced big man I had strangely liked" (209), since it is Velma who does the actual killing. Like Carmen Sternwood, Velma is literally a femme fatale; for her crimes against men, which include seduction as well as murder, she must be disposed of. Although Moose too is a murderer, Marlowe's affection for and loyalty to him again issue in the special relationship between homosocial desire and patriarchal social structures, a masculine bond that makes women seem guiltier than men for the same crimes.

Marlowe's primary emotional investment, however, must be perceived as heterosexual; hence, the importance of his final conversation with Anne, which is both professional and romantic. Telling Anne about the outcome of the Malloy case enables Marlowe to present himself as the uninvolved narrator. When Anne objects at one point, "That's just guessing," Marlowe can riposte, "It had to be that way" (243); that is, her challenge allows him to emphasize that he has uncovered rather than constructed this story. And Anne contributes to his narrative in ways that further lessen Marlowe's culpability. By insisting that it was Moose's love for Velma that led to his death, she mutes Marlowe's complicity in it; when she jokingly asks, "What makes you so wonderful?" and adds, "I'd like to be kissed" (246), this tone of bantering sexuality distinguishes their romance from love stories that are "dark and full of blood" (242). Moreover, her nonthreatening sexuality is a safe alternative not only to Velma's attractions but to Red's. Finally, Marlowe must see himself as he saw General Sternwood in *The Big Sleep*, untarnished by "nastiness"; approbation from Anne, who has been determinedly fenced out of his professional life and is therefore still the untainted nice girl, accomplishes this aim. As I have suggested, however, the very carefulness of this conclusion has the opposite effect: it forces the reader to interrogate Marlowe's ethic of detached detection.

3

*The Long Goodbye* further questions this ethic through an extended examination of what one might call hard-boiled friendship. As Marlowe commits himself to Terry Lennox despite the dangers and disappointments of this friendship, his professionalism is at first undermined, yet the professional toughness necessary to shield this friendship is also heightened. At the same time, Marlowe develops a client/friend relationship with Roger Wade that eventually results in Wade's death, and this death dramatizes the difficulties inherent in professional friendship. Like Marlowe's commitment to General Sternwood in *The Big Sleep*, these two friendships present a problematic shift between exchange and expenditure economies, a shift stabilized only by a redefinition of friendship. Thus Marlowe's friendship with Bernie Ohls, albeit tense, outlasts his feeling for Terry because it depends finally on mutual professional toughness.

Chandler's comments on *The Long Goodbye* show him aware of having written a less hard-boiled Marlowe and, in so doing, a more complex version of the detective novel. He defends the first draft of the novel to his agent by saying that "one becomes interested in moral dilemmas, rather than who cracked who on the head" (*Letters*, 315). He later admits that she might be right in thinking Marlowe had become "Christlike and sentimental" and in suggesting that Marlowe "ought to be deriding his own emotions"; perhaps, he adds half ironically, "I have let emotion enter my life in a manner not suitable to the marts of commerce" (*Letters*, 315-16). But he also insists that the changes in Marlowe were intentional "because the hardboiled stuff was too much of a pose after all this time" (*Letters*, 315). In addition, "You write in a style that has been imitated, even plagiarized, to the point where you begin to look as if you were imitating your imitators. So you have to go where they can't follow you." In *The Long Goodbye*, Chandler goes beyond not only his imitators but also his own earlier work. When Marlowe judges Terry Lennox as "a little weak" and "a kept poodle"[20] yet continues to befriend him, this commitment is a measure of his distance from *The Big Sleep*, where he required a stainless client; similarly, his willingness to accept the consequences of friendship with Terry contrasts with his chosen isolation from Randall and Red in *Farewell, My Lovely*. While Marlowe's professional friendship with Terry softens "the hard-boiled pose," then, it also raises concomitant problems.

From the beginning, Marlowe's relationship with Terry inextricably joins professional with personal responses. "Terry Lennox made me plenty of trouble," Marlowe says after their first encounter, "but after all that's my line of work" (3). "I'm supposed to be tough," he reflects, "but there was something about the guy that got me" (5). The disparity between this professional self-assessment and his personal response to Terry indicates Marlowe's unease with these unreconciled stances, and this professional-personal mix becomes increasingly complex. Suspected of killing his wife, Sylvia, Terry comes to Marlowe for professional help, but Marlowe "ha[s] a living to earn, a license to protect" (22) and fears to endanger this professional standing. Hence, although he does drive Terry to Tijuana, he does so because "we are friends" (25). He refuses to answer the consequent police questions for personal reasons: "Terry Lennox was my friend" (33) and "no man likes to betray a friend" (38). Yet these also become professional reasons; for Marlowe, going to jail rather than betraying Terry is "practical," for no one would hire a private detective who "finked on his friends" (52). Finally, friendship is subsumed into business, in fact becomes a constituent of Marlowe's professionalism.

As a result, the exchange economy of a client relationship gradually takes over the friendship. Driving Terry to Tijuana had been a simple act of friendship, Marlowe says, because "you're not paying me anything" (25). In fact, in Marlowe's view it is he who pays. He refuses to reveal Terry's whereabouts to Sergeant Green, for instance, because "I've got a reasonable amount of sentiment invested in him" (33). As a result, he later decides, having "invested time and money" in his friend means that he "owned a piece of him" (58). But after Terry invests money in Marlowe, their power positions are reversed. Marlowe now feels that is is Terry, who, having twice paid for an act of friendship (the $500 he leaves in Marlowe's apartment and the $5,000 he send through the mail), owns a piece of his friend. In return for his $5,000, Terry has requested that Marlowe reenact their last morning together; Marlowe does so, "sentimental or not," but "it didn't seem quite enough to do for five thousand dollars" (69). Terry's money becomes for Marlowe a kind of potlatch, a gift whose goal is "humiliating, defying, and *obligating* a rival"; the recipient can discharge this obligation only with a more valuable gift, or in other words by "return[ing] with interest."[21] Since Terry is now presumed dead, Marlowe can redress the power imbalance in this exchange economy only by mourning his friend, but he finds it impossible to reach the emotional equivalent of $5,000. Finally, then, the money becomes a taunt: "What was it supposed to buy? How much loyalty can a dead man use?" (179).

As he judges his friendship according to an exchange economy and finds it lacking, and as he comes to fear that "if I hadn't been a nice guy to Terry Lennox, he would still be alive" (124), Marlowe becomes increasingly committed to repaying Terry professionally. At first his sense of personal guilt is heightened by professional failure: pressure from the police and Terry's father-in-law prevents him from proving that someone other than Terry killed his wife. By forcing Eileen Wade to confess that she murdered Sylvia Lennox and by leaking her confession to the press, Marlowe salves both senses of failure: clearing Terry is "a personal matter" (196), but it has been accomplished by professional means. But the professional act intended to right the balance of payments between them instead results in the final souring of his affection for Terry. Because the police gave Eileen's confession to Marlowe for their own purposes, he feel that he has been used by them as well as by Terry: friendship, then, translates into "once a patsy, always a patsy" (270).

This disillusion with their friendship is confirmed when Terry returns from the dead with a new identity as Cisco Maioranos. Clearing Terry as a murder suspect has been Marlowe's "long good-bye" to his dead friend, but this mourning becomes the pointless act of a patsy when Terry reappears as someone else. To Terry's plea that "we were pretty good friends once," then, Marlowe replies, "That was two other fellows" (309). "You bought a lot of me" (311), he admits, but now the money "has too much blood on it" (310). He now returns Terry's $5,000, thereby terminating their professional relationship and severing their friendship; in this way he completes the potlatch exchange and takes the moral high ground in their relationship. In addition, although Marlowe clearly suffers by giving up his friendship with Terry, in this way he gains the rewards of unconditional expenditure, the same pleasure of loss he achieved by renouncing Anne Riordan. But the fact remains that Marlowe's commitment to Terry has dangerously heightened his tough-guy stance toward another client/friend, Roger Wade. Here, as in *Farewell, My Lovely*, Marlowe's interpretive activities uncover facts but also produce murders; again professional friendship undermines the possibility of uninvolved professionalism.

Initially, Marlowe responds personally to Roger Wade, admiring his ability to "take a long hard look at himself" (152). In his professional efforts to uncover Wade's connection with Sylvia Lennox's murder, however, Marlowe uses this quality against Roger, several times forcing him into self-appraisal which results in self-destructive drinking. Occasionally, Marlowe's behavior causes him moments of disgust like those in *Farewell, My Lovely*; after one session with Roger, for instance, he characterizes himself as "the heel to end all heels' (172). After another, however, he recasts his investigation of Roger as professional rigor.

> Part of me wanted to let him get good and drunk and see if anything came out. . . The other part of me wanted to get out and stay out, but this was the part I never listened to. Because if I had I would have stayed in the town where I was born. . . with a brain like a sack of Portland cement. (204)

That is, Marlowe is a professional, not a heel. In *Farewell, My Lovely*, the Marlowe who "wanted to get out" established his regret for momentary lapses from his code and thus reinforced that code.

Here the mix of business and emotion in his relation to client/friend Terry has superseded the earlier professional ethic that mandated proper behavior even to nonclients. Such lapses demonstrate that his friendship for Terry, which requires that he use Roger to "see if anything came out," has produced professional methods as brutal as those of Lieutenant Randall.

Once this professionalism, coupled with his friendship for Terry, produces murders, Marlowe must again reaffirm both values. The first murder is Roger's: goaded into drinking by Marlowe's interrogation, Wade passes out and is killed by his wife, Eileen. As Marlowe himself suggests when he "blame[s him]self a little" (231), he can be said to be indirectly responsible for this murder. The related death, Eileen Wade's suicide, is more directly the result of Marlowe's professional activities. Having detected the evidence that Eileen killed both Sylvia Lennox and her own husband, he confronts her with it so that she, like Roger, will "take a good long quiet look at herself" (278); consequently, she kills herself. It is fitting that Marlowe turns against Eileen the same weapon that he had used against her husband, because here he is not only avenging Wade's death but also clearing himself of complicity in it. His defense of his technique—"I wanted to clear an innocent man"—is thus double-edged. Engineering Eileen's suicide and confession does clear the innocent Terry from suspicion in his wife's murder, but it also clears Marlowe of any responsibility for Roger's death. Like Carmen Sternwood, Eileen attempts to seduce Marlowe, and like Velma Grayle she is attractive to him: so like these earlier femmes fatales, Eileen must be punished not only for murder and felonious allure but to mask Marlowe's complicity in her crimes.

In contrast, when Marlowe's quondam friend Bernie Ohls draws him into yet another murder, this sense of shared responsibility solidifies their friendship. Initially it seems that Bernie, like Terry, has forfeited Marlowe's friendship by using him; although both Terry and Bernie capitalize on Marlowe's friendship, however, only Ohls is a fellow professional. Hence, Marlowe's and Ohls's professional partnership against the criminal Menendez restores their once-shaky friendship.

Early in the novel, Marlowe and Ohls reminisce about their days as colleagues in the Los Angeles district attorney's office and joke together as friends. Once they are on opposite sides of the Terry Lennox case, however, the resulting professional tension is exacerbated by Marlowe's "romantic" commitment to Terry (229). As he tells Bernie, "I hear voices crying in the night and I go see what's the matter. . . . You wouldn't do it. That's why you're a good cop and I'm a private eye" (229-30). Like his attraction to Lieutenant Randall in *Farewell, My Lovely*, Marlowe's friendship with Ohls "sour[s] a little" because of this attitude; as Ohls puts it, "No cop likes it when a private citizen does police work behind his back" (277). Although it is Bernie who gives Marlowe access to the confession that clears Terry, he seems to do so at least in part to punish Marlowe for "doing police work behind his back." At this point, then the two are no longer friends, for Marlowe sees himself as Bernie's patsy, while Ohls regards him as a private citizen with romantic ideas rather than as a hard-boiled professional. From this power position, he sets up Marlowe as a decoy so that he can capture the gambler Menendez; when Menendez pistol-whips Marlowe, Bernie tells him that "you had it coming" for meddling in police work (286). Indeed, his sneering "Did the nasty mans hit your facey-wacey?" indicates his contempt for what he perceives as Marlowe's weakness. But once Menendez is disposed of and Bernie and Marlowe rediscover a shared hatred for organized crime, Ohls's attitude changes.

> "You looked pretty good walking in that door," Ohls said.
> "You looked better when Mendy pulled the knife on you."
> "Shake," he said, and put his hand out. (290)

Recognition of equivalent manliness, then, restores their friendship.

This emphasis on "looking good" or being tough distinguishes Marlowe's position as Bernie's patsy from his similar position vis-a-vis Terry. Because Terry is "a little weak," Marlowe feels weak himself when his friend puts him in the position of patsy; like his fascination with Red in *Farewell, My Lovely*, this friendship threatens to feminize or enfeeble him.[22] In contrast, even though Ohls shows his power over Marlowe by tricking him, eventually Ohls acknowledges and thereby validates Marlowe's toughness; in fact, if Marlowe continued to resent his position as Bernie's patsy, he would in effect reinstate Ohls's earlier view of his weakness. The last line of the novel, Marlowe's admission that "no way has yet been invented to say goodbye" to the police, contrasts with his "long goodbye" to Terry; in so doing, it reinforces Marlowe's companionship with Ohls in the toughness that Terry lacked.

This new alliance with the police measures *The Long Goodbye*'s distance from Chandler's two earlier novels. In *The Big Sleep*, Marlowe sees his fealty to General Sternwood as separating him from the corrupt police who "oblige their friends or anybody with a little pull" (107); although he is in fact obliging his own friends by not turning Carmen in to the police, my point is his perceived distinction from police corruption. In contrast, in *The Long Goodbye* Marlowe feels little compunction about joining what is in effect Ohls's personal vendetta against gamblers. His acceptance of Bernie's rationale—"it was a dirty job and it had to be done dirty" (288)—indicates the change from *Farewell, My Lovely*, where Marlowe insisted on separating himself from police who were "not free to do a clean job in a clean way." Like Randall, Ohls shares with Marlowe a hatred of social corruption; unlike him, he is not seen as a tainted instrument of "the system." Insofar as the later Marlowe is less self-isolated from corruption than the earlier version, this change comes about through his alliance in toughness with police.

But against this insistence on toughness is the Marlowe whose friendship with Terry is insistently presented as "sentimental." This seeming paradox may be illuminated by referring to Chandler's rejection of "the hardboiled pose." In this novel Chandler examines the hard-boiled stance as a pose, an act. Terry's view of himself as lacking a stable identity—for him, "an act is all there is" (311)—may be applicable to Marlowe as well. If Terry's belief that "there isn't anything" inside his self is also true for Marlowe, then we can see him as moving among poses: from the professional who is "supposed to be tough," to the friend who is willing to be sentimental, to the disillusioned patsy, and finally back to the hard-boiled professional. Finally, however, it is the hard-boiled pose that seems validated: accepting Bernie's friendship and rejecting Terry's means choosing a manly bond that valorizes toughness rather than a feminized position of weakness and unequal exchange.

4

Nevertheless, as a detective, Marlowe remains tied to an exchange economy; similarly, as a writer, Chandler is tied to a financial system that brands him as a commercial or nonserious writer. We are now in a position to reevaluate the economies of Chandler's self-presentational shifts between the businessman and the artist. It is significant here that Roger Wade is an author of marketable fiction; he writes best-selling historical novels, a genre that Wade himself despises and that Chandler refers to slightingly as "goosed history" (*Letters*, 120, 134). Like Chandler (although more overtly), Wade suspects that literary critics are "all queers, every damned one of them" (215). If Wade is, as Natasha Spender suggests, Chandler's "bad self,"[23] then *The Long Goodbye* may be intended as a farewell to the popular money-making Chandler in favor of the serious author who transcends the taste of "a public that is only semi-literate" (*Letters*, 173).

Even before this penultimate novel, however, Chandler constructed an artistic code that would remove him from an exchange economy. Writing is "a business transaction" for Chandler when he demands from *The Atlantic Monthly*'s assistant treasurer "the top price" for his articles, "as I am accustomed to getting the top price" (*Letters*, 105). Here his work is a counter in writing's exchange economy: if the principle of exchange is that one must pay for what one gets, then *The Atlantic* must pay for Chandler's essay, and top-quality merchandise deserves the top price. But to another audience, the magazine's associate editor, Chandler complains about having to market his wares; he presents himself as "a hater of power and of trading" who must nonetheless "trade brutally and exploit every item of power I may possess" (*Letters*, 47-48). He goes on to locate in his *Atlantic* essays an aesthetic code that functions to place his writing outside such an exchange economy: "I do not write for you for money or for prestige, but for love, the strange lingering love of a world wherein men may think in cool subtleties and talk in the language of almost forgotten cultures" (*Letters*, 48). Such a description of his transactions with *The Atlantic* is an attempt both to exploit and to escape his commercial success. Like the hard-boiled executive he once was, Chandler insists that he does not need money or prestige from *The Atlantic* because he already has both. He points out that "I can make $5000 [the same amount that later so troubles Marlowe] in two days"; in addition, he has achieved the "greater prestige" of turning formulaic pulp fiction, "a cheap, shoddy, and utterly lost kind of writing," into "something that intellectuals claw each other about." But in effect Chandler can *afford* to write essays for love because he has already "traded brutally" to achieve both money and the "commercial value" of prestige (*Letters*, 254). As a writer Chandler, like Marlowe, moves uneasily among poses in an attempt to establish firm ground for professional expenditure. Like Marlowe's world of professional detachment, however, *The Atlantic*'s world of "almost forgotten cultures' is a superstructure whose base is the commercial world of an exchange economy.

---

1 Raymond Chandler to Charles Morton, 20 Nov. 1944, in *Selected Letters of Raymond Chandler*, ed. Frank MacShane (New York: Columbia University Press, 1981), 34; hereafter cited as *Letters*.

2 See Georges Bataille, "The Notion of Expenditure," in *Visions of Excess: Selected Writings, 1927-1939*, trans. Allan Stoekl, Theory and History of Literature 14 (Minneapolis: University of Minnesota Press, 1985), 118-23. My thinking on economies in Chandler's work was shaped by this essay and by conversations with Celeste Goodridge.

3 "I am not only literate but intellectual, much as I dislike the term" (*Letters*, 238; see also 150, 155, 269). Chandler's insistence on his classical education—the phrase "raised on Latin and Greek" recurs throughout the letters like a tic—also indicates an uneasiness lest as a popular writer he be though low-brow.

4 Natasha Spender notes "the overt and vehement aversion [Chandler} always went out of his way to express" toward gays ("His Own Long Goodbye," in *The World of Raymond Chandler*, ed. Miriam Gross (New York: A & W, 1977), 131. While Spender and several of Chandler's women friends in London believed this dislike arose from

"strenuous repression" of his own homosexuality, this seems to me—as Spender herself suggests—"too facile a conclusion" (131).

5 Raymond Chandler, "The Simple Art of Murder" (1944), in *The Simple Art of Murder*, 3rd ed. (New York: Pocket Books, 1964), 192; hereafter cited as "Simple."

6 Raymond Chandler, *The Big Sleep* (1939; New York: Knopf, 1966), 107.

7 See Wai-Chee Dimock, "Debasing Exchange: Edith Wharton's *The House of Mirth*," *PMLA* 100 (Oct. 1985): 784; Dimock is, of course, speaking of Wharton's novels rather than Chandler's.

8 Eve Kosofsky Sedgwick, *Between Men: English Literature and Male Homosocial Desire* (New York: Columbia University Press, 1985), 1.

9 Of a reader who found a "homosexual angle" in Chandler's script for *The Blue Dahlia*, he fumed: "these Hollywood people are so filthy-minded themselves that they smell dirt even where there is none" (*Letters*, 123). This heated response parallels Chandler's worry that readers of his novels would be equally filthy-minded. On this discomfort see Michael Mason's "Marlowe, Men, and Women," In Gross, *World*, 90-101.

10 Ernest Fontana, "Chivalry and Modernity in Raymond Chandler's *The Big Sleep*," *Western American Literature* 19 (1984): 186; my thinking on this point was clarified by Peter Carafiol.

11 Although my view of this relationship differs from his, I have benefited from Fontana's remarks on it and on similar masculine pairings in the novel (183-85).

12 Bataille notes that etymologically "sacrifice" means "the production of *sacred* things" and that things are constituted sacred "by an operation of loss" ("Notion of Expenditure," 119).

13 Sedgwick, *Between Men*, 16.

14 And perhaps Chandler as well: although the few letters on his years with the South Basin Oil Company stress his purely managerial role, his own upward mobility in the company appears to have begun with the removal of a senior auditor for embezzlement, and Chandler may well have felt some residual taint. On his career as an oil executive, see Frank MacShane, *The Life of Raymond Chandler* (New York: Dutton, 1976), 34-40; see also *Letters*, 443-45.

15 Raymond Chandler, *Farewell, My Lovely* (1940; New York: Ballantine, 1971), 26.

16 On this aspect of Chandler's novels, see F.R. Jameson, "On Raymond Chandler," in *The Poetics of Murder: Detective Fiction and Literary Theory*, ed. Glenn W. Most and William W. Stowe (San Diego: Harcourt, 1983), 129-30.

17 Sedgwick, *Between Men*, 89.

18 On correspondence among Marlowe, Marriott, and Moose Malloy, see Leahna K. Babener's illuminating "Raymond Chandler's City of Lies," in *Los Angeles in Fiction: A Collection of Original Essays*, ed. David Fine (Albuquerque: University of New Mexico Press, 1984), 124.

19 William W. Stowe, "From Semiotics to Hermeneutics: Modes of Detection in Doyle and Chandler," in *The Poetics of Murder*, 376.

20 Raymond Chandler, *The Long Goodbye* (1953; New York: Ballantine, 1980), 16, 33.

21 Bataille, "Notion of Expenditure," 121.

22 It is worth noting that in similar one-down situations, when Marlowe feels that Eileen Wade has made a fool of him, he reasserts his masculine potency by directing such racial slurs as "cholo" and "greaseball" at her powerless Chilean houseboy (158, 176).

23 Spender, "His Own Long Goodbye," 135.

# Narrative Symmetries in *Farewell, My Lovely*

*J. K. Van Dover*

In a letter of 2 July 1951, Raymond Chandler explained his unpremeditated approach to plotting his novels: "I do my plotting in my head as I go along, and usually I do it wrong and have to do it all over again. . . . With me plots are not made; they grow. And if they refuse to grow, you throw the stuff away and start over again."[1] In an earlier letter, Chandler had used the same metaphor: "With me a plot, if you could call it that, is an organic thing. It grows and often overgrows."[2] But Chandler's consistency only emphasizes his peculiarity. Images of organic growth seem inappropriate when applied to the highly artificial plot conventions of the mystery and detective story. This is, after all, the most inherently teleological of genres: since Poe, its practitioners have recognized the advantage of beginning with the end, and then, working backward, of inventing the action which necessarily leads to that preordained end. How can the clues be logically placed (and cleverly obscured) until the conclusion toward which they must point has been defined?

The results of Chandler's unusual organic approach have not received much attention or praise. It has been the other qualities of his fiction—his characters, settings, and above all his language and style—that have made his reputation as one of the greatest of detective story writers, and even as one of the major writers of twentieth century American fiction. "The plots," writes Julian Symons, "are firm and adequate, but they are not what we take away from the books."[3] And yet there is more to the structure of Chandler's novels than he or his critics allow. The example of *Farewell, My Lovely* (1940) may serve to illustrate the very definite architecture which underlies the "organically" proliferating action of the novel.[4]

*Farewell, My Lovely* was Chandler's second novel, and like his first, he constructed it from pieces of short stories which he had published earlier. For this one he used roughly 48 of the 54 pages of "Mandarin's Jade" (*Dime Detective*, November 1937) and about half each of "The Man Who Liked Dogs" (*Black Mask*, March 1936) and "Try the Girl" (*Black Mask*, January 1937). Chandler expanded whatever he took from the stories, and he added large sections of new material (he also added a bit from a fourth story, "Trouble Is My Business" [*Dime Detective*, August 1939]): the assembled novel runs to 252 pages. The process through which the characters and plots of three quite different stories were gathered into a single narrative has been analyzed by Maldwyn Mills.[5] Chandler's term for this process of gathering the pieces together was "cannibalization"—another organic metaphor, of a sort. My purpose here is merely to lay out the artful (and apparently inorganic) symmetries which underlie the structure of the novel that grew from the digestion of the stories.

There are four principal murders in *Farewell, My Lovely*. The first occurs in the second chapter when Moose Malloy breaks the neck of Sam Montgomery, the black proprietor of Florian's bar. This leads to the first problem of detection: Marlowe, who stood in the bar while Moose killed Montgomery in his office, agrees to help the police locate Malloy. Lindsay Marriott, who hires Marlowe as a bodyguard in what seems to be an unrelated action, is beaten to death in Chapter Eleven; Marlowe, having been attacked by the killer, was lying unconscious nearby. Marriott's death presents a genuine mystery, and identifying his killer becomes Marlowe's second assignment. Then, in Chapter Thirty, Marlowe comes upon the body of Jesse Florian. Her death begins to lead to the resolution; it confirms that Marlowe's two assignments are somehow related. The fourth murder is that of Moose Malloy in Chapter Thirty-Nine; it occurs as Marlowe completes his exposition of the connected cases. He describes how Velma Valento, aka Helen Grayle, killed Marriott and Malloy killed Mrs. Florian. This fourth murder, Velma's killing of Malloy in Marlowe's apartment, proves his case. (She escapes, and brief coda, Chapter Forty-One, is needed to tie up the last loose end—the fate of Velma—by relating how she kills a corrupt detective and then commits suicide.)

These crimes may indeed seem organic in their sequence. As experienced, they appear to comprise a plausible, if crowded, sequence of dramatic accidents. As explained by Marlowe's exposition, they become a logical sequence of events, all following predictably from the moment when Moose Malloy happened to put his huge hand on Marlowe's shoulder outside Florian's bar. The four main murders are certainly various in their quality. There is no mystery at all about the first: Marlowe is in the next room when Moose Malloy brutally breaks the bar-owner's neck. It is a spontaneous and crude action, and Malloy can, with some justice, partially excuse it as self-defense: in the face of Moose's aggressive questions, Montgomery was reaching for a gun. The death of the effeminate Marriott is, by contrast, surrounded with mysterious circumstances. Who killed him? Why? Why in Purissima Canyon? Why was Marlowe spared? What truth is there in Marriott's account of the theft of his woman friend's Fei Tsui jade? And not only has the crime been carefully calculated, its execution has been uncommonly vicious, the killer repeatedly smashing Marriott's face with a blunt object. Its source turns out to lie in the complex history of the relations between Moose, Velma, Jesse Florian, and Marriott. Marlowe's sense of responsibility for Marriott's fate provides a major drive for his ongoing investigation.

Mrs. Florian, the third victim, is strangled and has her head smashed in. (Head trauma does seem to be a recurring feature. As Lieutenant Randall observes, "Brains on her face. . . . That seems to be the theme song of this case."[6]) Moose Malloy commits the first and third murders, and in the case of Jesse Florian as in the case of Sam Montgomery, the killings are virtually accidental, the consequence of Moose acting on impulse and seeing his great strength lead to fatal results. In both instances he sought information, not death, though the deaths do not bother him much. Velma's beating in of Marriott's head, on the other hand, was deliberate; she needed him dead and she conscientiously arranged the opportunity to execute him. Her second murder, the novel's fourth, is as spontaneous as the first and the third, and like the first two, it occurs in Marlowe's presence, but again Velma sets herself apart from Moose. Her weapon is a gun (and she shoots Malloy in the abdomen, not the head). Though her action may be impulsive, she is not defending herself or seeking information; rather, she is evading his embrace and silencing his voice. Velma needs and wants the two murders she commits.

There is then a varying pattern of interwoven, contrasting motifs in the sequence of murders—accidental/deliberate, spontaneous/ premeditated, Marlowe present/Marlowe absent, known culprit/ mysterious culprit, beatings/shootings, head wound/abdominal wound. The similarities are the natural result of two killers following their modus operandi; the differences are the natural result of differing circumstances. The narrative does seem organic in the apparently haphazard sequence of the narrative weave.

But there is, by contrast, an interestingly symmetrical pattern to the placement of these crimes in the chapters of the narrative, as the following diagram shows.

| **Chapter #** | | **2** | | **11** | | **30** | | **39** | | **41** (Coda) |
|---|---|---|---|---|---|---|---|---|---|---|
| **Intervening Chapters** | (1) | | (9) | | (19) | | (9) | | (1) | |
| **Victim** | | Sam | | Marriott | | Mrs. Florian | | Moose | | (Cop, Velma) |
| **Murderer** | | Moose | | Velma | | Moose | | Velma | | (Velma) |

The most obvious symmetry appears in the last line, the alternation of killers: Moose-Velma-Moose-Velma (with Velma putting a period to the sequence in the coda). But the line of "intervening chapters" is most significant. Chandler has punctuated the narrative with an very neat spacing of crimes in his chapters: 1-9-19-9-1. The point is not that Chandler mechanically laid out the mathematical sequence prior to composing the novel, but rather that his instinct for the proportions of the narrative led him to place the crises at regular intervals, using them to frame the first and last quarters of the novel and building suspense in the middle half of the novel by focussing upon the melodramatic experiences of his detective as Marlowe encounters a Hollywood Indian, a psychic, some brutal policemen, and a corrupt doctor.

That the novel opens and closes with a murder is no surprise; the mysterious murder which lies at the core of the mystery novel naturally occurs at the beginning of the narrative, and the conventional identification and isolation of the killer at the end is often achieved by having the villain killed rather than captured or imprisoned. But Chandler has extended the symmetry, placing the two middle complicating murders equidistant from the ends of the novel. The first of these, Marriott's, provides a radical complication; it has no apparent connection to the initial murder of Sam Montgomery; in order to solve the crime, Marlowe must discover the concealed connection. (Put another way: Chandler must create a connection for Marlowe to discover. The Montgomery murder (Chapters 1-5) comes from "Try the Girl"; the Marriott murder (8-11) comes from "Mandarin's Jade. "The middle nineteen chapters comprise Chandler's suturing of the two plots). The second complicating murder, Jesse Florian's, provides solid evidence that the plots *are* connected, leaving the final nine chapters for Marlowe to work out the details and to arrange a confrontation with Moose Malloy and Velma Valento/Helen Grayle. There the frame is completed, as the culprit in the initial murder—Moose—meets his just fate, killed by Velma. Velma, the culprit in the even-numbered murders (two and four), brings herself to justice with her suicide (murder six) in the coda.

This neat structure can be appreciated from another perspective. *Farewell, My Lovely* transpires over a five day period, Thursday, 30 March to Monday, 3 April (the year, therefore, is presumably 1939). The first two and last two days are full of investigation; Marlowe spends Day 3 semi-conscious (and parts of Days 2 and 4) in Dr. Sonderberg's nefarious sanatorium. The narrative divides roughly as follows: Day 1—Chapters 1-12; Day 2—Chapters 13-24; Day 4—Chapters 25-28; Day 5—Chapters 29-40. (Chapter 41, the coda, takes place over three months later.) When the murders are plotted on this line, another interesting pattern emerges:

| Day | 1 | 2 | [ 3 ] | 4 | 5 | |
|---|---|---|---|---|---|---|
| | Thurs | Fri | [ ] | Sun | Mon | |
| Chaps | x2xxxxxxxx11x | xxxxxxxxxxxx | [ ] | xxxx | x30xxxxxxxx39x | (41) |
| | \| \| | | | | \| | \| |
| Victim | Montg. Marriott | | | | Florian | Moose |

The four main murders are set symmetrically in the first and last days of the investigation, in the second and the penultimate chapter assigned to each day.

This pattern is surely not accidental, but in the forward rush of events, it may not be noticed. The hard-boiled detective story characteristically relied upon such a rushing action. Chandler studied the practice of the master, Erle Stanley Gardner, whose narratives leap from confrontation to confrontation with only the slightest (and most improbable) indication of the succession of days. Chandler provides the tumble of action—his decision to incorporate three long short stories into a single novel reflects the need to provide continuous action and proliferating complications.

But Chandler also counted the days, and the careful reader can count them as well.[7] That Marlowe endures so much in five days—he is twice beaten unconscious and later drugged unconscious—may seem highly improbable. When Johnny Dalmas, the detective in one of the source stories, "Mandarin's Jade," is beaten unconscious, he requires two weeks to recuperate, including ten days in the hospital. Marlowe's resilience may be astonishing, but it allows Chandler to plot his action neatly in a short sequence of days. And within this sequence (defined by chapters or by days), Chandler constructed a carefully balanced narrative.

Chandler's are not the only hard-boiled novels which half-conceal an articulate structure. The narratives of Hammett and Cain, if analyzed, also reveal surprisingly regular proportions. John Dickson Carr, whose locked room mysteries exhibit the traditional end-oriented, byzantine plots of the British tradition, denigrated the "construction" of Chandler's mysteries.[8] And from the traditional point of view he was not entirely wrong. The architecture of Chandler's fiction depends upon the placement of actions and crises, not of clues and red-herrings. For Carr, the "construction" of a detective story resembles the construction of a maze, with its series of right (and wrong) turns leading to a single, inevitable exit.

Chandler's sense of form was indeed more organic and more qualitative. Rather than narrate his fiction according to a blue-print of intellectual directions and misdirections, he relied upon a sense of emotional and experiential weights to shape his stories. In *Farewell, My Lovely*, these balanced weights can be neatly measured either by the narrator's experience of time (days) or by the reader's experience of time (chapters). Both experiences reveal the novel's structural symmetries.

And, not to miss the obvious point, these structural symmetries mirror the novel's moral symmetries. The narrative bell curve that arcs from the accidental encounter on Central Avenue to the mysterious but explicable murders of the pair of blackmailers and then descends to the self-destruction of the murderers reflects the curve of Marlowe's understanding (and misunderstandings) of the moral situation he has become involved in. Sam Montgomery's death is a mere misfortune; Nulty's dismissal of it as insignificant—"Another shine murder"—accurately describes its importance in the novel as well as in the society. It draws Marlowe dramatically into the action, and it supplies a plot element insofar as it obligates Malloy to conceal himself throughout the remainder of the action, but it is not a mystery or even, apparently, much of a crime. Bringing Montgomery's killer to justice never becomes a motive for action in the novel. Neither Marlowe nor the police seem to hold it against Malloy (those who might hold it against him—Montgomery's fellow Blacks—have no voice in the novel). The remaining crimes—the crimes which constitute the real mysteries of the novel—however, are not accidents. And Marlowe does find himself increasingly involved in detecting the criminals; he feels professionally and morally compelled to apprehend the killers of Lindsay Marriott and Jesse Florian. These crimes are the organic consequences of the eight year old transformation of Velma Valento into Helen Grayle. Marriott and Jesse Florian have been the intermediaries in the plot to blackmail Velma/Helen for her past connection with Moose. Marriott provides the link to Velma, and Velma beats his head in; Jesse provides the link to Moose, and Moose beats her head in. The two ends of the chain Velma-Marriott-Jesse-Moose thus collapse against the middle. The neat (and neatly spaced) middle retributions leave the ends—Velma and Moose—to confront one another. Velma, the killer of one, executes Moose, the killer of two. In the coda, far away in Baltimore, Velma kills a detective and herself. Her suicide, whether sentimentally motivated as Marlowe suspects or not, neatly erases all of the criminals in *Farewell, My Lovely*.[9]

She thus closes the moral circle of action, and because she, rather than the police and the social justice system accomplishes the closure, the effect is one of a self-annihilating conclusion. The plot extinguishes itself. And the extinction may be pressed one step further. The narrator and series protagonist, is necessarily a survivor. But by shooting the "Baltimore detective with a camera eye" Velma may also be erasing, by substitution, the only other important principal in this history of betrayals and murders, the Los Angeles detective, Philip Marlowe, thus collapsing the entire symmetrical structure of the narrative. The investigated and the investigator are alike eradicated. And Velma achieves this dissolution through a sequence of diminishing shots: she shoots Moose five times, the detective three times, and herself twice ("the second shot must have been pure reflex"). The final, single shot in this sequence of annihilations is presumably fired by the reader as he closes the book.

Even if this last suggestion finds metafiction where none was intended, it remains clear that Chandler's sense of the shape of his narrative was far from naive. A last, simple illustration of his construction of significant parallels may be cited. Marlowe happened to meet Moose Malloy because, as he explains in the novel's first paragraph:

> I had just come out of a three-chair barber shop where an agency thought a relief barber named Dimitrios Aleidis might be working. It was a small matter. His wife said she was willing to spend a little money to have him come home.
>
> I never found him, but Mrs. Aleidis never paid me any money either. (7)

Though the sexes are reversed and a robbery and a prison term make Malloy's search less of a "small matter," Moose, like Mrs. Aleidis, wants to recover his beloved (who, however, was his fiancee, not his spouse). And Moose's beloved, like Dimitrios Aleidis, does not want to be recovered (though she, unlike Dimitrios, fails to evade Marlowe's search). Like Mrs. Aleidis, Moose enlists Marlowe in his search (and like her, fails to pay any money). Mrs. Aleidis professed herself "willing to spend a little money to have him come home"; Velma has been spending a good deal of money in payment to Marriott and Mrs. Florian to prevent Moose (and her past generally) from coming home. In the Aleidis case, Marlowe acts upon a tip that Dimitrios might have resumed his hair-cutting career (but he didn't, and so he escaped); in the main action, Velma does resume her torch-singing, and this leads to her being identified by the Baltimore detective. The parallels (and the inversions) between this six-line opening vignette and the 245 page case that follows surely suggest that the narrative structures of Raymond Chandler's novels are far from an accidental. The symmetries that underlie *Farewell, My Lovely* demonstrate the deliberate craft with which he went about inventing his art of fiction.

---

1 Letter to H.R. Harwood, in *Selected Letters of Raymond Chandler*, F. MacShane, ed. (NY: Columbia UP 1978): 279.

2 Letter to James Sandoe, 23 September 1948, in *Selected Letters of Raymond Chandler* : 129.

3 Julian Symons, *Bloody Murder* (NY: Viking, 1985): 131.

4 *Farewell, My Lovely* also offers one of the more elegant examples of Chandler's practice of the traditional, puzzle plotting in detective fiction. The business card which Marlowe hands to Mrs. Florian (and which she inadvertantly marks with her empty glass) in Chapter 5 (p. 29) turns up on the body of Lindsay Marriott in Chapter 12 (p. 71) and is finally recognized as linking the novel's two plots in Chapter 40 (249). This is one of Chandler's better clues.

5 "Chandler's Cannibalism" in *Watching the Detectives*, Bell and Daldry, eds. (London: Macmillan, 1990): 117-133.

6 Raymond Chandler, *Farewell, My Lovely* (Harmondsworth: Penguin, 1988): 183. All future references to this edition.

7 The count of the days does not, as it often does in classical detective stories, provide an essential clue to the identity of the

murderer; Chandler does not, therefore, *need* to keep such a scrupulous account. It is noteworthy that he does. On Day 2 Marlowe observes that the next day will be April Fool's Day (99), and a few pages later Jesse Florian notes that a week ago yesterday was a Thursday (114). Day 4 is a Sunday (156) and Day 5 is a Monday (195).

8 *New York Times Book Review* 24 September 1950: 36.

9 And it provides a further symmetry to play against the others. When the coda is included, the novel involves six murders. The first three result from beatings; the last three from shootings.

# Bibliography


## I. PRIMARY SOURCES: THE WORKS OF RAYMOND CHANDLER

### A. Novels

*The Big Sleep*. NY: Knopf, 1939.
*Farewell, My Lovely*. NY: Knopf, 1940.
*The High Window*. NY: Knopf, 1942.
*The Lady in the Lake*. NY: Knopf, 1943.
*The Little Sister*. Boston: Houghton Mifflin, 1949.
*The Long Goodbye*. Boston: Houghton Mifflin, 1954.
*Playback*. Boston: Houghton Mifflin, 1958.
*Poodle Springs*. (Completed by Robert B. Parker.) NY: Putnam, 1989.

### B. Principal Short Story Collections

*Five Murderers*. NY: Avon, 1944. ("Goldfish," "Spanish Blood," "Blackmailers Don't Shoot," "Guns At Cyrano's," "Nevada Gas")
*Five Sinister Characters*. NY: Avon, 1945. ("Trouble Is My Business," "Pearls Are a Nuisance," "I'll Be Waiting," "The King in Yellow," "Red Wind")
*Finger Man and Other Stories*. NY: Avon, 1946. ("Finger Man," "The Bronze Door," "Smart-Aleck Kill," "The Simple Art of Murder")
*Red Wind*. NY: World Publishing, 1946. ("Red Wind," "Blackmailers Don't Shoot," "I'll Be Waiting," "Goldfish," "Guns At Cyrano's")

*Spanish Blood*. Cleveland: World Publishing, 1946. ("Spanish Blood," "The King in Yellow," "Pearls Are a Nuisance," "Nevada Gas," "Trouble Is My Business")

*The Simple Art of Murder*. Boston: Houghton Mifflin, 1950. ("Introduction," "Finger Man," "Smart-Aleck Kill," "Guns At Cyrano's," "Pick-Up on Noon Street," "Goldfish," "The King in Yellow," "Pearls Are a Nuisance," "I'll Be Waiting," "Red Wind," "Nevada Gas," "Spanish Blood," "Trouble Is My Business," "The Simple Art of Murder")

*Trouble Is My Business*. Harmondsworth: Penguin, 1950. ("Trouble Is My Business," "Red Wind," "I'll Be Waiting," "Goldfish," "Guns At Cyrano's")

*Pick-Up on Noon Street*. NY: Pocket, 1952. ("Pick-Up on Noon Street," "Smart-Aleck Kill," "Guns At Cyrano's," "Nevada Gas")

*Smart-Aleck Kill*. London: Hamish Hamilton, 1953. ("Smart-Aleck Kill," "Pick-Up on Noon Street," "Nevada Gas," "Spanish Blood")

*Pearls Are a Nuisance*. London: Hamish Hamilton, 1958. ("Pearls Are a Nuisance," "Finger Man," "The King in Yellow")

*Killer in the Rain*. Boston: Houghton Mifflin, 1964. ("Killer in the Rain," "The Man Who Liked Dogs," "The Curtain," "Try the Girl," "Mandarin's Jade," "Bay City Blues," "The Lady in the Lake," "No Crime in the Mountains")

## C. Other Books

*Raymond Chandler Speaking*. Dorothy Gardiner and Kathrine Sorley Walker, eds. Boston: Houghton Mifflin, 1962.

*Chandler Before Marlowe: Raymond Chandler's Early Prose and Poetry*. Columbia: U South Carolina P, 1973.

*The Blue Dahlia*. NY: Popular Library, 1976.

*The Notebooks of Raymond Chandler*. Frank MacShane, ed. NY: Ecco, 1976.

*Selected Letters of Raymond Chandler*. Frank MacShane, ed. NY: Columbia UP, 1977.

*Chandler Before Marlowe. Raymond Chandler's Early Prose and Poetry 1908-12*. Matthew J. Bruccoli, ed. Columbia: U South Carolina P, 1973.

*The Notebooks of Raymond Chandler and English Summer: A Gothic Romance*. Frank MacShane, ed. NY: Ecco Press, 1976.

*The Blue Dahlia: A Screenplay*. Matthew J. Bruccoli, ed. Carbondale: Southern Illinois UP, 1976.

*Raymond Chandler and James M. Fox: A Correspondence*. Santa Barbara: Neville-Yellin, 1978.

*Selected Letters of Raymond Chandler*. Frank MacShane, ed. NY: Columbia UP, 1981.

*Raymond Chandler's Unknown Thriller: The Screenplay of "Playback."* NY: Mysterious Press, 1985.

### D. Screenplays

*Double Indemnity*. Paramount, 1944. (With Billy Wilder; Billy Wilder, director; featuring Fred MacMurray, Barbara Stanwyck, and Edward G. Robinson)

*And Now Tomorrow*. Paramount, 1944. (With Frank Partos; Irving Pichel, director; featuring Alan Ladd and Loretta Young)

*The Unseen*. Paramount, 1945. (With Hagar Wilde; Lewis Allen, director; featuring Joel McCrea, Gail Russell, and Herbert Marshall)

*The Blue Dahlia*. Paramount, 1946. (George Marshall, director; featuring Alan Ladd, Veronica Lake, and William Bendix)

*Strangers on a Train*. Warner Brothers, 1951. (With Czenzi Ormonde; Alfred Hitchcock, director; featuring Farley Granger, Ruth Roman, and Robert Walker)

### E. Unproduced Screenplays:

*The Innocent Mrs. Duff*. Paramount, 1946.

*Playback*. Universal, 1947-48.

## II. SECONDARY SOURCES

### A. Bibliographies of Chandler's Work and of Works about Chandler

Albert, Walter. *Detective and Mystery Fiction: An International Bibliography of Secondary Sources*. Madison, IN: Brownstone Books, 1984: 357-367.

Bruccoli, Matthew. "Addenda to Bruccoli, *Raymond Chandler* : Chandler's First American Publication." *Papers of the Bibliographical Society of America* 78:3 (1984): 300-01.

_____. *Raymond Chandler: A Checklist*. Kent, OH: Kent State UP, 1968.

_____. *Raymond Chandler: A Descriptive Bibliography*. Pittsburgh Series in Bibliography, No. 11. Pittsburgh: U Pittsburgh P, 1979.

Johnson, Timothy W. and Julia Johnson, eds. *Crime Fiction Criticism*. NY: Garland, 1981: 140-49.

Newlin, Keith. "Raymond Chandler: A Critical and Biographical Bibliography." *Clues* 6:2 (Fall/Winter 1985): 61-72.

Skinner, Robert E. *The Hard-Boiled Explicator: A Guide to the Study of Dashiell Hammett, Raymond Chandler, and Ross Macdonald*. Metuchen, NJ: Scarecrow, 1985: 101-05..

## B. Biography

MacShane, Frank. *The Life of Raymond Chandler*. NY: Dutton, 1976.

## C. Critical Studies

The following list inevitably contains omissions. Some are unintentional. Only English language items are included. Entries in reference works (e.g., *The Dictionary of Literary Biography* or *Twentieth Century Literary Criticism*) have been excluded. Most of the many surveys of detective fiction (and often those of film noir) include a few pages on Chandler; generally, these have been excluded. Articles that refer only slightly to Chandler have been excluded, but this is a matter of judgment. Dissertations are listed separately.

Abrahams, Etta C. "Where Have All the Values Gone? The Private Eye's Vision of America in the Novels of Raymond Chandler and Ross Macdonald." *Armchair Detective* 9 (1976): 128-31.

Aldrich, Pearl G. "The Glimmer of Magic." *PCS* 1:1 (1977): 52-56.

Apostolou, John L. "A.K.A. Philip Marlowe." *Armchair Detective* 17:2 (1984): 201-202.

Arden, Leon. "A Knock at the Backdoor of Art: The Entrance of Raymond Chandler." In *Essays on Detective Fiction*. Bernard Benstock, ed. London: Macmillan, 1983.

Auden, W.H. "The Guilty Vicarage." *Harper's* May 1948: 406-12; reprinted in *The Dyer's Hand*. NY: Vintage, 1948.

Babener, Liahna K. "California Babylon: The World of American Detective Fiction. *Clues* 1:2 (1980): 77-89.

_____. "Raymond Chandler's City of Lies." In *Los Angeles in Fiction*. David Fine, ed. Albuquerque: U New Mexico P, 1984: 109-131.

Barzun, Jacques. "The Aesthetics of the Criminous." *The American Scholar* 53 (1984): 239-41.

_____. "The Illusion of the Real." In *The World of Raymond Chandler*. Miriam Gross, ed. London: Weidenfeld and Nicolson, 1977: 159-63.

_____. "Preface to *Lady in the Lake*." In *A Book of Prefaces*. NY: Garland, 1976: 29-30.

Becker, Jens P. "Murder Considered as One of the Fine Arts." *Literatur in Wissenschaft und Unterricht* 6 (1973): 31-42.

Beekman, E.M. "Raymond Chandler and an American Genre." *Massachusetts Review* 14 (1973): 149-73.

Benstock, Bernard. "Dashiell Hammett and Raymond Chandler: An Anatomy of the Rich." In *All Men Are Created Equal: Ideologies, reves et realities*. Jean Pierre Martin, ed. Aix-en-Provence: Pubs. U. de Provence, 1983: 181-89.

Berry, Jay R., Jr. "Chester Himes and the Hard-Boiled Tradition." *Armchair Detective* 15:1 (1982): 38-43.

Binyon, T.J. "A Lasting Influence?" In *The World of Raymond Chandler*. Miriam Gross, ed. London: Weidenfeld and Nicolson, 1977: 171-83.

Bishop, Paul. "The Longest Goodbye or the Search for Chandler's Los Angeles." *Mystery* 1:2 (1980): 33-36.

Blades, John. "*The Big Sleep*." *Film Heritage* Summer 1970: 7-15.

Brackett, Leigh. "From *The Big Sleep* to *The Long Goodbye*." *Take One* 23 Jan 1974: 26-28.

Brewer, Gay. *A Detective in Distress: Philip Marlowe's Domestic Dream*. San Bernardino: Borgo, 1989.

_____. "Raymond Chandler Without His Knight: Contracting Worlds in *The Blue Dahlia* and *Playback*." *The Mystery Fancier* 13/3 (Summer 1992): 37-49.

Bruccoli, Matthew J. "Afterword: Raymond Chandler and Hollywood." In Raymond Chandler. *The Blue Dahlia*. Carbondale: Southern Illinois UP, 1976: 129-37.

Carr, John Dickinson. "With Colt and Luger." *NY Times Book Review* 24 Sep 1950: 36.

Cawelti, John G. "Hammett, Chandler, and Spillane." In *Adventure, Mystery, and Romance*. Chicago: U Chicago P, 1976.

Chastain, Thomas. "The Case for the Private Eye." In *The Murder Mystique: Crime Writers on Their Art*. Lucy Freeman, ed. NY: Ungar, 1982: 27-32.

Christianson, Scott R. "A Heap of Broken Images: Hardboiled Detective Fiction and the Discourse(s) of Modernity." In *The Cunning Craft: Original Essays on Detective Fiction and Contemporary Literary Theory*. Ronald G. Walker, ed. Macomb: Western Illinois UP, 1990.

Conrad, Peter. "The Private Dick as Dandy." *TLS* 10 January 1978: 60.

Cook, Bruce. Review of *The Life of Raymond Chandler*. *New Republic* 12 June 1976: 26.

Crombie, Winifred. "Raymond Chandler: Burlesque, Parody, Paradox." *Language and Style* 10:2 (1983): 151-68.

Davies, Russell. "Omnes Me Impune Lacessunt." In *The World of Raymond Chandler*. Miriam Gross, ed. London: Weidenfeld and Nicolson, 1977: 31-51.

"Dead Men Do Talk." *Newsweek* 14 May 1945: 95-97.

DeVoto, Bernard. "The Easy Chair." *Harper's* December 1940:36-37.

Dove, George. "The Complex Art of Raymond Chandler." *Armchair Detective* 8: (1974-75): 271-4.

Durham, Philip. *Down These Mean Streets A Man Must Go. Raymond Chandler's Knight.* Chapel Hill: U North Carolina P, 1963.

_____. "Introduction." In Raymond Chandler, *Killer in the Rain.* Boston: Houghton Mifflin, 1964.

Eames, Hugh. "Phillip Marlowe." In *Sleuths, Inc.* Philadelphia: Lippincott, 1978: 185-221.

Elliott, George P. "Country Full of Blondes." *Nation* 23 Apr 1960: 354-60.

Ferncase, Richard K. "Robert Altman's *The Long Goodbye*: Marlowe in the Me Decade." *Journal of Popular Culture* 25.2 (Fall 1991): 87-90.

Finch, G.A. "From Spade to Marlowe to Archer." *Armchair Detective* 4 (1971): 107-10.

_____. "Marlowe's Long Goodbye." *Armchair Detective* 6:1 (1972): 7-11.

Fine, David. "Nathanael West, Raymond Chandler, and the Los Angeles Novel." *California History* 68:4 (1989-90): 196-201.

Fleming, Ian. "Raymond Chandler." *London Magazine* 6 (Dec 1959): 43-54.

Flint, R.W. "A Cato of the Cruelties." *Partisan Review* 14 (1947): 328-30.

Fontana, Ernest. "Chivalry and Modernity in Raymond Chandler's *The Big Sleep.*" *Western American Literature* 19:3 (1984): 179-186.

French, Philip. "Media Marlowes." In *The World of Raymond Chandler.* Miriam Gross, ed. London: Weidenfeld and Nicolson, 1977: 67-79.

Gallagher, Brian. "Howard Hawks's *The Big Sleep*: A Paradigm for the Postwar American Family." *North Dakota Quarterly* 51:3 (1983): 78-91.

Gilbert, Michael. "Autumn in London." In *The World of Raymond Chandler.* Miriam Gross, ed. London: Weidenfeld and Nicolson, 1977: 103-14.

Gregory, Charles. "Knight Without Meaning?" *Sight and Sound* Summer 1973: 155-159.

Greiner, Donald J. "Robert B. Parker and the Jock of the Mean Streets." *Critique* 26:1 (1984): 36-44.

Gross, Miriam, ed. *The World of Raymond Chandler.* London: Weidenfeld and Nicolson, 1977.

Guetti, James. "Aggressive Reading: Detective Fiction and Realistic Narrative." *Raritan* 2:1 (1982): 133-54.

Hamilton, Cynthia S. *Western and Hard-Boiled Detective Fiction in America.* London: Macmillan, 1987: 146-71.

Harp, Richard. "Tobacco and Raymond Chandler." *Clues* 9:2 (Fall/Winter 1988): 95-104.

Hart, Patricia. "Revisiting Chandler and Recreating Marlowe in Hiber Conteris's *El diez por ciento de vida.*" *Journal of the Midwest Modern Language Assoc.* 23:2 (1990): 1-16.

Highsmith, Patricia. "Introduction." In *The World of Raymond Chandler*. Miriam Gross, ed. London: Weidenfeld and Nicolson, 1977: 1-6.

Hoffman, Carl. "Spenser: The Illusion of Knighthood." *Armchair Detective* 16:2 (1983): 131-43.

Holden, Jonathan. "The Case for Raymond Chandler's Fiction as Romance." *Kansas Quarterly* 10:4 (1978): 41-47.

Homberger, Eric. "The Man of Letters (1908-12)." In *The World of Raymond Chandler*. Miriam Gross, ed. London: Weidenfeld and Nicolson, 1977: 7-18.

Houseman, John. "Lost Fortnight." *Harper's* August 1965: 55-61 (reprinted in *The World of Raymond Chandler*. Miriam Gross, ed. London: Weidenfeld and Nicolson, 1977: 53-66).

Howard, Leon. "Raymond Chandler's Not-So-Great Gatsby." In *Mystery and Detection Annual 1973*. Beverly Hills: Donald Adams, 1973: 1-15.

Humm, Peter. "Camera Eye, Private Eye." In *American Crime Fiction: Studies in the Genre*. Brian Docherty, ed. NY: St. Martin's, 1988: 23-38.

Isaac, Frederick. Laughing with the Corpses: Hard Boiled Humor." In *Comic Crime*. Earl Bargannier, ed. Bowling Green: Popular Culture Press, 1987.

Jacobs, David L. "Photo Detection: The Image as Evidence." *Clues* 1:2 (1980): 18-23.

James, Clive. "The Country Behind the Hill." In *The World of Raymond Chandler*. Miriam Gross, ed. London: Weidenfeld and Nicolson, 1977: 115-26.

Jameson, Frederic. "On Raymond Chandler." *Southern Review* 6:3 (1970): 624-50 (reprinted in *The Poetics of Murder*, Glenn W. Most and William W. Stowe, eds. NY: Harcourt, 1983: 122-48.

Jensen, Paul. "Raymond Chandler: The World You Live In." *Film Comment* Nov-Dec 1974: 18-26.

Johnston, Claire. "Double Indemnity." In *Women in Film Noir*. E. Ann Kaplan, ed. London: BFI, 1980: 100-111.

Kaye, Howard. "Raymond Chandler's Sentimental Novel." *Western American Literature* 10 (1975): 135-45.

Knight, Stephen. "'A Hard Cheerfulness': An Introduction to Raymond Chandler." In *American Crime Fiction: Studies in the Genre*. Brian Docherty, ed. NY: St. Martin's, 1988: 71-87.

_____. "'...a hard-boiled gentleman'--Raymond Chandler's Hero." In *Form and Ideology in Crime Fiction*. Bloomington: Indiana UP: 1980: 135-67.

_____. "Re-Formations of the Thriller: Raymond Chandler and John LeCarré." *Sydney Studies in English* 12 (1986-87): 78-91.

Kuhn, Annette. "*The Big Sleep* : A Disturbance in the Sphere of Sexuality." *Wide Angle* 4 (1982): 4-11.

Labianca, Dominick A. and William Reeves, Jr. "Dashiell Hammett and Raymond Chandler: Down on Drugs." *Clues* 5:2 (1984): 66-71.

Lachtman, Gavin. "The Legendary Sleuths of Pre-WW II Los Angeles." *San Francisco Chronicle Review* 1 Feb 1981: 10-11.

Lambert, Gavin. "A Private Eye: Raymond Chandler." In *The Dangerous Edge*. NY: Grossman, 1976.

Larsen, Michael J. "Miracles and Murder: Raymond Chandler's Fantastic Stories." In The Shape of the Fantastic. Olena H. Saciuk, ed. NY: Greenwood, 1990.

Lawson, Lewis. "'Spirituality in Los Angeles': California Noir in Lancelot." *The Southern Review* 24:4 (1988): 744-64.

Legman, Gershon. *Love & Death: A Study in Censorship*. NY: Hacker, 1963: 68-70.

Lev, Peter. "*The Big Sleep*: Production History and Authorship." *Canadian Review of American Studies* 19.1 (Spring 1988): 1-21.

Lid, R.W. "Philip Marlowe Speaking." *Kenyon Review* 31 (1969): 153-78.

Lott, Rick. "A Matter of Style." *Journal of Popular Culture* 23 (1989): 65-75.

Luhr, William. "Pre-, Prime-, and Post-Film Noir: Raymond Chandler's Farewell, My Lovely and Three Different Film Styles." *Michigan Academician* 15:1 (1982): 125-32.

_____. *Raymond Chandler and Film*. NY: Frederick Ungar, 1982.

MacDermott, K.A. "Ideology and Narrative Stereotyping: The Case of Raymond Chandler." *Clues* 2:1 (1981): 77-90.

Macdonald, Ross. "Farewell, Chandler." In *Inward Journey: Ross Macdonald*. Santa Barbara: Cordelia Editions, 1984: 37-42.

Maclaren-Ross, J. "Chandler and Hammett." *London Magazine* 3 (Mar 1964): 70-79.

MacShane, Frank. "Raymond Chandler and Hollywood." *American Film* April 1976: 62-69; May 1976: 54-60.

_____. "Writing Biographies." *Columbia Library Columns* 30:3 (1981): 17-27.

Mahan, Jeffrey II. "The Hard-Boiled Detective in the Fallen World." *Clues* 1:2 (1980): 90-99.

Marling, William. *Raymond Chandler*. Boston: Twayne, 1986.

Martin, Stoddard. *California Writers: Jack london, John Steinbeck, the Tough Guys*. NY: St. Martin's, 1983.

Mason, Michael. "Deadlier Than the Male." *TLS* 17 Sep 1976: 1147.

_____. "Marlowe, Men and Women." In *The World of Raymond Chandler*. Miriam Gross, ed. London: Weidenfeld and Nicolson, 1977: 89-101.

Maugham, W. Somerset. "The Decline and Fall of the Detective Story." In *The Vagrant Muse.* (London: Heinnemann, 1952: 91-122.

Mawer, Randall R. "Raymond Chandler's Self-Parody." *Armchair Detective* 14 (1981): 355-59.

Maxfield, James F. "Love in the Dark: Howard Hawk's Film Version of *The Big Sleep.*" *Clues* 14.1 (Spring-Summer 1993): 11-20.

Meador, Ray. "Chandler in the Thirties: Apprenticeship of an Angry Man." *Book Forum* 6:2 (1982): 143-53.

Michaels, Leonard. Review of *The Life of Raymond Chandler. NY Times Book Review* 16 May 1976: 1, 20, 22, 26.

Mills, Maldwyn. "Chandler's Cannibalism." In *Watching the Detectives.* Ian A. Bell and Graham Daldry, eds. London: Macmillan, 1990.

Milner, Jay G. "Morality and the Detective Hero: Raymond Chandler's Philip Marlowe." *Clues* 1:1 (1980): 116-18.

Moffat, Ivan. "On the Fourth Floor of Paramount: Interview with Billy Wilder." In *The World of Raymond Chandler.* Miriam Gross, ed. London: Weidenfeld and Nicolson, 1977: 43-51.

Moran, Carlos Alberto. "A Latin American Reading of Raymond Chandler." *Imagen* nos. 103/104 (1975); reprinted in *Review 76* (1976): 47-53 (trans. Paula Speck).

Monaco, James. "Notes on 'The Big Sleep' / Thirty Years After." *Sight and Sound Winter* 1974/75: 34-38.

Morgan, Neil. "The Long Goodbye." *California* June 1982: 81, 159, 161-2, 164.

Nelson, R. Faraday. "Raymond Chandler: Romantic Poet." *The Romantist* 6:8 (1982-84): 11.

Nickerson, Edward A. "'Realistic' Crime Fiction: An Anatomy of Evil People." *The Centennial Review* 25:2 (1981): 101-32.

Nolan, William F. "Chandler on Screen, TV and Radio--With a Look at the Many Mr. Marlowes." *Armchair Detective* 3 (1969/70): 23-26.

_____. "Portrait of a Tough Guy." In *Sinners and Supermen.* North Hollywood, CA: All Star Books, 1965; reprinted in *Xenophile* 38 (1976): 13-17.

Norman, Frank. "Friend and Mentor." In *The World of Raymond Chandler.* Miriam Gross, ed. London: Weidenfeld and Nicolson, 1977: 165-70.

Orel, Harold. "Raymond Chandler's Last Novel: Some Observations on the 'Private Eye' Tradition." *Journal of the Central Mississippi American Studies Association* 2:1 (1961): 59-63.

Orr, Christopher. "The Trouble with Harry: On the Hawks Version of the Big Sleep." *Wide Angle* 5:2 (1982): 66-71.

Palmer, Jerry. "The Negative Thriller." In *Thrillers.* NY: St Martins, 1979: 40-52.

Panek, Leroy Lad. *Probable Cause: Crime Fiction in America.* Bowling Green: Bowling Green U Popular P, 1990: 145-49.

Parsons, Luke. "On the Novels of Raymond Chandler." *The Fortnightly* 175 (1954): 346-51.

_____. "Simenon and Chandler." *The Contemporary Review* 197 (1960): 56-58.

Parker, Robert B. "Marlowe's Moral Code." *PCS* 1:1 (1977): 36-51.

Paul, Marcie. "Suspect Author: Hiber Conteris's Ten Percent of Life." *Latin American Literary Review* 18:35 (1990): 50-58.

Pendo, Stephen. *Raymond Chandler on Screen: His Novels into Film*. Metuchen, NJ: Scarecrow Press, 1976.

Pollock, Wilson. "Man With a Toy Gun." *New Republic* 7 May 1962: 21-22.

Ponder, Anne. "The Big Sleep: Romance Rather Than Detective Film." *Armchair Detective* 17:2 (Spring 1984): 171-74.

Powell, Dilys. "Ray and Cissy." In *The World of Raymond Chandler*. Miriam Gross, ed. London: Weidenfeld and Nicolson, 1977: 81-87.

Powell, Lawrence Clark. "'Farewell, My Lovely': Raymond Chandler." In *California Classics: The Creative Literature of the Golden State*. Los Angeles: Ward Ritchie, 1971: 371-81.

_____. Forward to The Raymond Chandler Omnibus. NY: Knopf, 1964: v-viii.

Priestly, J.B. "A Letter From Two Islands." *New Statesman and Nation* 9 April 1949: 349.

Rabinowitz, Peter J. "Rats Behind the Wainscoting: Politics, Convention, and Chandler's *The Big Sleep*." *Texas Studies in Language and Literature* 22 (1980): 224-45.

Reck, Tom S. "Raymond Chandler's Los Angeles." *Nation* 20 Dec 1975: 661-63.

Robson, W.W. "'A Home for the Truth': Literary Criticism in the Letters of Raymond Chandler." *Prose Studies: History, Theory, Criticism* 10:3 (1987): 259-69.

Ruehlmann, William. *Saint With a Gun*. NY: New York UP, 1974: 76-90.

Ruhm, Herbert. "Raymond Chandler: From Bloomsbury to the Jungle—and Beyond." In *Tough Guy Writers of the Thirties*. David Madden, ed. Carbondale: Illinois UP, 1968: 171-85.

Russell, D.C. "The Chandler Books." *Atlantic* 175 (Mar 1945): 123-24.

Schickel, Richard. "Raymond Chandler, Private Eye." *Commentary* 352 (Feb 1963): 158-61.

Schwoch, James. "The Influence of Local History on Popular Fiction: Gambling Ships in Los Angeles, 1933." *Journal of Popular Culture* 20:4 (1987): 103-11.

Sharratt, Bernard. "Question 6: Raymond Chandler, *The Big Sleep*." In *Reading Relations*. Brighton: Harvester, 1982: 205-17.

Shatzin, Roger. "Who Cares Who Killed Owen Taylor?" In *The Modern American Novel and the Movies*, Gerald Peary and Roger Shatzin, eds. NY: Ungar, 1978: 80-94.

Simpson, Hassell A. "'A Butcher's Thumb': Oral-Digital Consciousness in *The Big Sleep* and Other Novels of Raymond Chandler." *Journal of Popular Culture* 25.1 (Summer 1991): 83-92.

Sissman, L.E. "Raymond Chandler." *The New Yorker* 11 March 1972: 123-25.

Skenazy, Paul. "Behind the Territory Ahead." In *Los Angeles in Fiction*. David Fine, ed. Albuquerque: U New Mexico P, 1984.

_____. *The New Wild West: The Urban Mysteries of Dashiell Hammett and Raymond Chandler*. Western Writers Series no. 54. Boise, ID: Boise State UP, 1982: 28-44.

Smith, David. "The Public Eye of Raymond Chandler." *Journal of American Studies* 14 (1980): 423-41.

Smith, Johanna M. "Raymond Chandler and the Business of Literature." *Texas Studies in Language and Literature* 31 (1989): 592-610.

Spender, Natasha. "His Own Long Goodbye." The New Review 27 June 1976: 15-28; repr in *The World of Raymond Chandler*. Miriam Gross, ed. London: Weidenfeld and Nicolson, 1977: 127-58.

Spicer, Christopher III. "A Hard-Boiled Philosophy of Human Nature: Understanding People According to Spade, Marlowe, and Archer." *Clues* 4:1 (1983): 93-104.

Spiegel, Alan. "Seeing Triple: Cain, Chandler and Wilder on Double Indemnity." *Mosaic* 16:1-2 (1983): 83-101.

Spier, Jerry. *Raymond Chandler*. NY: Ungar, 1981.

Steele, Timothy. "The Structure of the Detective Story: Classical or Modern?" *Modern Fiction Studies* 27:4 (1981-82): 555-70.

Steiner, Thomas R. "The Mind of the Hardboiled: Ross Macdonald and the Roles of Criticism." *South Dakota Review* 24:1 (1986): 29-53.

Stowe, William. "From Semiotics to Hermeutics: Modes of Detection in Doyle and Chandler." In *The Poetics of Murder*, Glenn W. Most and William W. Stowe, eds. NY: Harcourt, 1983: 366-83.

Symons, Julian. "An Aesthete Discovers the Pulps." In *The World of Raymond Chandler*. Miriam Gross, ed. London: Weidenfeld and Nicolson, 1977: 156-65.

_____. "The Case of Raymond Chandler." *New York Times Magazine* 23 December 1973: 13, 22, 25, 27.

_____. "Marlowe's Victim." *TLS* 23 Mar1962: 200; repr. in *Critical Observations*. New Haven: Ticknor, 1981.

_____. "Tough Guy at the Typewriter." *TLS* 5 June 1981: 619-20.

Tanner, Stephen L. "The Function of Simile in Raymond Chandler's Novels." *Studies in American Humor* 3:4 (1984-5): 337-346.

Tarantino, Michael. "Movement as Metaphor: *The Long Goodbye*." *Sight and Sound* Spring 1975: 98-102.

Tate, T.O. "Double Talk, Double Play: Rewinding Raymond Chandler's *Playback*." Clues 14.1 (Spring-Summer 1993): 105-34.

_____. "The Longest Goodbye: Raymond Chandler and the Poetry of Alcohol." *Armchair Detective* 10:4 (1985): 392-400.

_____. "Raymond Chandler's Pearl." *Clues* 13.2 (Fall-Winter 1992): 177-95.

Tellotte, J.P. "Effacement and Subjectivity: Murder My Sweet's Problematic Vision." *Literature/Film Quarterly* 15:4 (1987): 227-36.

Thomson, James W. "Murder with Honor: Raymond Chandler." *New Republic* 22 July 1978: 28-31.

_____. "Raymond Chandler: Novelist." *Xenophile* 21 (1976): 52-53.

Thorpe, Edward. Chandlertown: *The Los Angeles of Philip Marlowe*. London: Hutchinson, 1983.

Warner, Nicholas O. "City of Illusion: The Role of Hollywood in California Detective Fiction." *Armchair Detective* 10:1 (1983): 22-5.

Wasserberg, Charles. "Raymond Chandler's Great Wrong Place." *Southwest Review* 74:4 (1989): 534-45.

Wells, Walter. "Grey Knight in the Great Wrong Place." In *Tycoons and Locusts: A Regional Look at Hollywood Fiction of the 1930s*. Carbondale: Southern Illinois UP, 1973: 71-86.

Wertheim, Mary. "Philip Marlowe, Knight in Blue Serge." *Columbia Library Columns* 37:2 (1988): 13-22.

Westlake, Donald F. "The Hardboiled Dicks." *Armchair Detective* 17:1 (Winter 1984): 4-13.

Wilson, Edmund. "Why Do People Read Detective Stories?" and "Who Cares Who Killed Roger Ackroyd?" in *Classics and Commercials*. NY: Farrar, Straus, & Giroux, 1950: 231-37; 257-65.

Winston, Robert P. and Nancy C. Mellerski. "The Detective in the Intertext: Freeling's Dialogue with Chandler." *Texas Studies in Language and Literature* 31 (1989): 611-33.

Wolfe, Peter. *Something More Than Night: The Case of Raymond Chandler*. Bowling Green: Popular Press, 1985.

Wyatt, David. "Chandler, marriage, and 'the Great Wrong Place.'" In *The Fall into Eden: Landscape and Imagination in California*. Cambridge: Cambridge UP, 1986: 158-73.

Zolotow, Maurice. "Through a Shot Glass Darkly: How Raymond Chandler Screwed Hollywood." *Action* Jan-Feb 1978: 52-57.

## D. Dissertations

Abraham, Etta Claire. *Visions and Values in the Action Detective Novel: A Study of the Works of Raymond Chandler, Kenneth Millar, and John D. MacDonald*. Michigan State U, 1973. DAI: 34/06A: 4833.

Anderson, David Louis. *The American Dream in Twentieth-Century California Fiction.* Carnegie Mellon, 1983. DAI 44/-4A: 1083.

Clancy, Thomas M. *The Tiresian Influence in Hemingway, Hard-boiled Fiction, and "Film Noir."* Oklahoma State U, 1988. DAI 49/10A: 3025.

Crider, Allen Billy. *The Private-Eye Hero: A Study of the Novels of Dashiell Hammett, Raymond Chandler, and Ross Macdonald.* U Texas at Austin, 1972. DAI 34/92: 722.

Dunkle, J. Robert. *The Long Goodbye: Raymond Chandler's Novel and Robert Altman's Film.* Florida State U, 1987. DAI 48/08A: 1559.

Feldman, Leonard Mark. *A Matter of Money: MOney and the World of the American Novel, 1893-1940.* U California, Los Angeles, 1981. DAI 42/08A: 3599.

Harred, Larry Dale. *The Artful Detectives of Dashiell Hammett, Raymond Chandler, and Ross Macdonald: The Uses of Literary Style.* Purdue, 1983. DAI 44/12A: 3684.

Nodine, Thad Randall. *Detecting Community: Joseph McCarthy, the Detective Form, and Recent American Fiction.* University of California, Santa Cruz, 1990. DAI 51/04A: 1230.

Parker, Robert B. *The Violent Hero, Wilderness Heritage and Urban Reality: A Study of the Private Eye in the Novels of Dashiell Hammett, Raymond Chandler, and Ross Macdonald.* Boston U, 1971. DAI 32/94A: 1965.

Sandgren, Peter Nelson. "Towards a Definition of Film Noir: Locating Two Chandler Films in the Noir Tradition. University of Connecticut, 1992. DAI 53/5: 1303.

Shatzin, Roger S. *Doubled Indemnity: Raymond Chandler, Popular Fiction and Film.* Rutgers, 1984. DAI 45/07A: 2105.

Thomson, James W. *The Slumming Angel: The Voice and Vision of Raymond Chandler.* U Pennsylvania, 1977. DAI 38/08A: 4833.

Ward, Kathryn Ann. *Clients, Colleagues, and Consorts: Roles of Women in American Hardboiled Detective Fiction and Film.* Ohio State U, 1988. DAI 49/08A: 2223.

Zinsser, David Lowe. *Watching the Detective: A Literary Analysis of the Works of Raymond Chandler.* New York U, 1982. DAI 43/02A: 443.

# Index

## About the Editor

J. K. VAN DOVER is Professor of English at Lincoln University in Pennsylvania. He has published on William Kennedy, Daniel Defoe, Erle Stanley Gardner, Ian Fleming, and others.